THE PHILADELPHIA
SHAKESPEARE STORY

Frontispiece : H. H. Furness and his grandson, Wirt
L. Thompson. (Courtesy of Furness Memorial Library,
Special Collections, Van Pelt Library, University of
Pennsylvania.)

THE PHILADELPHIA SHAKESPEARE STORY

HORACE HOWARD FURNESS AND THE NEW VARIORUM SHAKESPEARE

JAMES M. GIBSON

AMS Press
New York

Library of Congress Cataloging-in-Publication Data

Gibson, James M.
    The Philadelphia Shakespeare story : Horace Howard Furness and
the variorum Shakespeare / by James M. Gibson.
        p.   cm. — (AMS studies in the Renaissance ; 23)
    Bibliography: p.
    Includes index.
    ISBN 0-404-62293-3
    1. Furness, Horace Howard, 1833–1912. 2. Shakespeare, William,
1564–1616. Works. 1871. 3. Shakespeare, William, 1564–1616—
Editors. 4. Shakespeare, William, 1564–1616—Criticism and Interpretation—History—19th century. 5. Criticism, Textual—
History—19th century. 6. Editors—United States—
Biography. I. Title. II. Title: New variorum Shakespeare. III. Series: AMS studies in the Renaissance ; no. 23.
PR2972.F7G5   1990
822.3'3—dc20   87-45801
                                                                              CIP

All AMS books are printed on acid-free paper that meets the
guidelines for performance and durability of the Committee on
Production Guidelines for Book Longevity of the Council on Library Resources.

AMS PRESS
56 East 13th Street
New York, N.Y. 10003, U.S.A.

Manufactured in the United States of America

Contents

ACKNOWLEDGEMENTS

Permission to quote from the letters and papers of Horace Howard Furness has been granted by his literary heir Wirt Thompson, Jr. of Media, Pennsylvania, and by the following institutions and libraries having physical possession of letters of Horace Howard Furness and Horace Howard Furness, Jr.: The American Academy and Institute of Arts and Letters; the American Antiquarian Society; Mugar Memorial Library, Boston University; Bowdoin College Library; The British Library; Bryn Mawr College Library; University of California Library, Los Angeles; Columbia University Library; Cornell University Library; Dartmouth College Library; Dickinson College Library; Edinburgh University Library; The Folger Shakespeare Library; Houghton Library, Harvard University; The Historical Society of Pennsylvania; International Museum of Photography at George Eastman House; The Milton S. Eisenhower Library, The Johns Hopkins University; Department of Special Collections, Kenneth Spencer Research Library, University of Kansas; Brotherton Collection, University of Leeds; Manuscript Division, Library of Congress; Massachusetts Historical Society; Department of Rare Books and Special Collections, The University of Michigan Library; Special Collections Department, University Libraries, University of Nebraska-Lincoln; New York Historical Society; The New York Public Library; University of Notre Dame Memorial Library; Furness Memorial Library of Shakespeariana, University of Pennsylvania; Special Collections, The Charles Patterson Van Pelt Library, University of Pennsylvania; The University Archives, University of Pennsylvania; The Pierpont Morgan Library; The University of Rochester Library; the Shakspere Society of Philadelphia; The Shakespeare Birthplace Trust; Somerset Record Office; Friends Historical Library of Swarthmore College; Master and Fellows of Trinity College, Cambridge; The Watkinson Library, Trinity College, Hartford; Howard-Tilton Memorial Library, Tulane University; Vassar College Library; Walt Whitman Collection, Clifton Waller Barrett Library, University of Virginia Library; The Walter Hampden-Edwin Booth Theatre Collection and Library.

Permission has also been given by Iowas State University Press to quote from *The Letters of A. Bronson Alcott;* by Johnson Publishing Company (EBONY CLASSICS) to quote from William Still, *The Underground Railroad;* by New York University Press to quote from *Walt Whitman: The Correspondence;* and from the University of Pennsylvania Press to quote from Elizabeth Geffen, *Philadelphia Unitarianism 1796-1861* and George Stewart Stokes, *Agnes Repplier: Lady of Letters.*

Publication of this book has been made possible through the support of two research grants from the Penrose Fund of the American Philosophical Society and through grants toward the cost of publication from the Horace Howard Furness Memorial Library of Shakespeariana, The Charles Patterson Van Pelt Library of the University of Pennsylvania, and the generosity of the family and descendents of Horace Howard Furness.

Finally, my appreciation goes to Georgianna Ziegler, Curator of the Furness Memorial Library, and to the many other librarians who answered my queries about Furness letters; to Wirt Thompson, Jr., for the loan of Furness family papers; to James E. Barcus, former Chairman of the Department of English and Speech at Houghton College, for providing research assistance and to Cindy Quiter for typing many of the transcriptions; to Victor Carpenter, former Associate Professor of German at Houghton College, for translating the minutes of the Halle University faculty commendation of Furness; to Arthur Scouten and Roland Mushat Frye, former Professors of English at the University of Pennsylvania, for reading the text and offering many helpful suggestions; to my wife, who also read the text with a critical novelist's eye and without whose support the book could not have been written; and, finally, to William E. Miller, former Assistant Curator of the Furness Memorial Library, who encouraged, read, and criticized and whose idea this biography first was.

To

William E. Miller

Mentor, Friend, and long-time Assistant Curator of the
Horace Howard Furness Memorial Library of Shakespeariana

He was a scholar, and a ripe and good one,
Exceeding wise, fair-spoken, and persuading;
Henry VIII 4.2.51–52

SON OF NEW ENGLAND

Where were you bred?
And how achieved you these endowments?
—*Pericles* 5.1.116-17

Brooding over Philadelphia's Logan Circle, his head leaning against a knife, Hamlet contemplates the weary, stale, flat, and unprofitable uses of the world. At his feet the jester Touchstone, his head thrown back in laughter, watches children scramble for coins in the fountain, watches the high-heeled secretaries and the conservatively dressed businessmen, watches the street people and the lovers on the park benches and the traffic streaming down the Parkway, around the Circle to executive suites in Center City, and back again to fashionable homes in Chestnut Hill. "All the world's a stage / And all the men and women merely players" reads the inscription chiseled into the black marble base on which rest the bronze figures of tragedy and comedy cast by sculptor Alexander Sterling Calder and erected in 1928 by the Fairmount Park Art Association and the Shakspere Society of Philadelphia.

1

And should a curious passerby pause on his way past the statue to the Free Library, he would find recorded on the rear of the Shakespeare Memorial the history of Philadelphia's Shakespeare tradition. He would find there the names of actors contributed by Philadelphia to the stage: Thomas Wignell, William Wood, Joseph Jefferson, John Drew, Louisa Lane Drew, Charles Burke, James E. Murdock, E.L. Davenport, John Drew, Jr., and that prince of tragedy Edwin Forrest, whose portrayal of suffering humanity in *Othello* and *King Lear* remained for generations unsurpassed. He would find there also the names of Joseph Dennie, first American editor of Shakespeare; Asa Israel Fish, founder of the Shakspere Society of Philadelphia; Horace Howard Furness and Horace Howard Furness, Jr., editors of the New Variorum Edition of Shakespeare. How fitting that the city which gave America its premiere performances of *Macbeth* and *Hamlet*, its first edition of Shakespeare printed in 1795 by Bioren and Madan, and its first Shakespearian essay of American authorship penned by Philadelphia lawyer Joseph Hopkinson, should also have given to America its greatest Shakespearian scholar, Horace Howard Furness.

"It may be confidently affirmed that in the death of the editor of the New Variorum Shakespeare the world has suffered the loss of the most notable authority on the plays of Shakespeare of our time."[1] Those words of Felix Schelling, Professor of English at the University of Pennsylvania, echoed through the hall of the College of Physicians on January 17, 1913, as a distinguished assembly of Philadelphians gathered to honor the memory of Philadelphia's beloved Shakespearian scholar. Representatives from Harvard University, the American Philosophical Society, and the Shakspere Society of Philadelphia, seconded by letters from the New York Shakespeare Society, the Deutsche Shakespeare Gesellschaft, James Bryce, British Ambassador to the United States, and J.J. Jusserand, French Ambassador to the United States, all joined the University of Pennsylvania in praise of Furness the man, Furness the educator, Furness the Shakespearian reader, and Furness the scholar and editor of the New Variorum Edition of Shakespeare.

While the name Furness will forever remain a part of Philadelphia's Shakespeare tradition, the Furness story begins not in Philadelphia, but in Boston, where in the early eighteenth century the first American representative of the family arrived, possibly from

Scotland, since he used the Scottish spelling of the family name, Furnace. A baker by trade, Jonathan Furnace was married in 1731 to Elizabeth Milliken by Mr. Samuel Checkley, minister of the Presbyterian Church in Boston; and in 1740, he bought property on the corner of Cornhill and Water Streets, including a brick dwelling house, barn, stable, and bake house. Elizabeth bore him four children—Mary in 1732, who died before coming of age, John in 1733, Jemima in 1735, and Elizabeth in 1737. The family soon grew to include Jonathan's younger brother Benjamin and Elizabeth's sister Mary, both of whom were living in the household when Jonathan Furnace died in March 1745. Mary, who had apparently kept house since Elizabeth's death in 1743, and Benjamin then married in November 1745 and reared the children. Although the inventory of Jonathan's estate totaled some £4,000 in 1747, the expense of rearing four children apparently depleted their inheritance, and in 1755, no longer able to pay taxes and make repairs, the three surviving children sold the family property for less than half of its original value. In March 1762, John married Ann Hurd, daughter of Boston goldsmith Jacob Hurd.

John Furnass (or Furness as the family name now variously appears in the records) is listed in *The Boston Directory* first as a shopkeeper, then as a clerk in the loan office and, later with Thomas Walley, a merchant in the firm of Furness & Walley at No. 34, Long Wharf. During the Revolutionary War Sergeant John Furnass served for six months in Captain John Shapleigh's Company stationed on the seacoast at Kittery Point. By May 1784, he had amassed enough money to buy the property at 16 Federal Street, which became the family home for three generations, and moved there with his wife Ann and three sons John, Nathaniel, and William.

During his lifetime emerged two features which became characteristics of the later Furness family: their artistic talent and their Unitarian faith. Their first son, John, apparently inherited his artistic ability from the maternal side, as has been noted by Hollis French in *Jacob Hurd and his Sons Nathaniel & Benjamin, Silversmiths 1702-1781*: "John Mason Furnass, engraver and portrait painter, was the son of John Furnass and Anne Hurd Furnass, sister of Nathaniel Hurd, the engraver. Furnass was painting portraits in Boston in 1785. He was born November 11, 1762, and died of epilepsy at Dedham, Massachusetts, June 22, 1804. He made at least two portraits of John

Vinal, the old schoolmaster of Boston."[2] From this beginning apparently came the widespread family talent for drawing, the later portrait painting of William Henry Furness, Jr., and the architecture of Frank Furness.

In this generation the family also adopted the Unitarian faith, a commitment which flourished under the enlightened preaching of the Reverend John Clarke, minister of First Church, Boston, from 1778-1798 and of William Emerson, who succeeded him from 1798-1811. As early as 1792 John Furnass had some sympathy for the Unitarians, having sold at cost to the "Society of Christians called Universalists" a piece of land next to the Universal Meeting House on Bennet Street. By 1808, having deserted the the Presbyterian Church of his father, he was paying a weekly tax of thirty cents to rent a pew in First Church, and sometime between 1786 and 1814 Ann Furness signed an undated "declaration of faith subscribed by the members of the First Church of Christ in Boston."[3] At his death in 1810 the inventory of John Furnass's estate included "a Pew in the 1st Church" worth $380.[4]

The two younger sons of John and Ann Furnass, Nathaniel and William, also followed their parents to First Church. Nathaniel Hurd Furness, an accountant at Massachusetts Bank, had married Elizabeth Henchman in 1792 and was rearing a family of eight children when he made the change. On September 18, 1816, he signed "a declaration of faith subscribed by those who request baptism for their children,"[5] and a year later on August 24, 1817, six of his eight children, ranging in age from eight to twenty-five, were baptized in First Church. William Furness, who worked as an interest clerk in the United States Bank and then as a discount clerk at the Union Bank, married into a First Church family and evidently led the way for his brother. On June 22, 1797, William Furness, through whom the family line continued, and Rebecca Thwing were married by the Reverend John Clarke in First Church. The Thwings had long been prominent members of First Church. Rebecca, who signed the declaration of faith herself before her marriage, had been baptized as a child in First Church; and all five children of Rebecca and William were subsequently baptized into the Unitarian faith: John Clarke Furness in 1798 by the Reverend John Clarke; Ann Hurd Furness in 1799, William Henry Furness in 1802, and Joanna Tilden Furness in 1807 by William Emerson; and James Thwing Furness in 1812 by Dr.

Ware. After Rebecca's death in June 1814, William Furness purchased farm land near Medford and subsequently married Sarah Jenks of Salem in February 1817. The following June he paid $250 for "the Pew numbered twenty in the Reverend Doctor David Osgoods Meeting House in said Medford with all the privileges thereunto belonging."[6] Both children born to William and Sarah—Rebecca Thwing Furness in 1821 and George Washington Jenks Furness in 1824—were then baptized by David Osgood in the First Parish Unitarian Church in Medford.

William and Rebecca's second son, William Henry Furness, was twelve years of age when his mother died and the family moved from 16 Federal Street to Medford, but he had already formed in Boston his most important friendship: Ralph Waldo Emerson, son of the Unitarian minister William Emerson. Childhood companions and schoolmates, Emerson and Furness had entered Boston Public Latin School together in 1812 and the following year collaborated on Emerson's juvenile poem "The History of Fortus." Emerson supplied the poetry and Furness drew the illustrations. In 1816, at the age of fourteen, Furness entered Harvard College a year ahead of Emerson and pursued the classical curriculum of Latin, Greek, mathematics, moral philosophy, modern languages, and rhetoric; in 1820, he entered Harvard Divinity School where Andrews Norton held the Chair of Sacred Literature, Sidney Willard was Professor of Hebrew and Oriental Languages, and Edward Everett lectured on the Septuagint. In 1823, he was graduated from the Divinity School. At that time he had already fallen in love with a Salem girl, Annis Pulling Jenks, whom he frequently discussed with Ann Holmes, older sister of Oliver Wendell Holmes, another Boston friend he kept throughout his life.[7]

Furness preached his first sermon in Watertown in 1823 and continued to serve as candidate at churches in and around Boston although, as he confessed later in his *Fiftieth Anniversary Discourse*, he had "a hearty dread of being settled in Boston, whose church-goers had in those days the reputation of being terribly critical; and rhetoric then and there was almost a religion."[8] In May 1824 he received an invitation to spend three months in Baltimore as assistant to Mr. Greenwood, later the pastor of King's Chapel in Boston, and on his return home filled the pulpit of the small Unitarian society in Philadelphia during the month of August. The First

Society of Unitarian Christians, as the Philadelphia society called itself, a small congregation of persons of English blood, the first body in America to organize under the Unitarian name, had been founded in 1796 by Dr. Joseph Priestly. Though it had erected a brick church in 1813, the society had never had a settled pastor. Before Furness left Philadelphia in August 1824, however, he received a visit from a committee, which he later suspected "comprised nearly the whole meeting they professed to represent,"[9] asking him to become their pastor. He agreed, and on January 12, 1825 was ordained, beginning a ministry that would last for the next fifty years in Philadelphia.

In August 1825, he returned to Salem to marry Annis Pulling Jenks. Together they settled in Philadelphia, then a city of 140,000 people and sixty hours' journey from their families in Boston. In 1829 William's younger brother James joined the household, later purchasing his own house at 1420 Pine Street next door to his brother. From January 1825 to June 1826 the Furnesses boarded at 9 South Ninth Street; but expecting their first child, Mary Ann, who was born on September 24, 1826, they rented a house on the north side of Chestnut Street between Broad and Thirteenth Streets and acquired an Irish servant girl named Betsey. The following March they moved to Eleventh Street near Chestnut, and in August 1830 they moved again to Twelfth Street. Here in 1831 they had three Irish servants: a cook, a nurse, and a waitress. Mary Ann had died on June 30, 1828, but two other children arrived to fill her place—William Henry, Jr. on May 21, 1828, and in 1830, Annis Lee, named for her maternal grandmother Annis Lee Pulling. In April 1832, the family moved to the south side of Spruce Street below Broad, where they were living when Horace Howard, named after his maternal uncle, Horace Howard Jenks, was born on November 2, 1833. In August 1838, before the birth in 1839 of their final child, Frank Heyling, the family moved once again, buying for $7,000 the house at 1426 Pine Street where they remained for the rest of the pastor's active life.[10]

From the beginning Furness faced a cultured and cultivated congregation which set the intellectual tone for himself and his family. Most prominent was John Vaughan, one of the founders of the Philadelphia Unitarian Church, entertainer at the Wistar Association of every prominent visitor to Philadelphia, and member of every intellectual society in the city—serving as secretary, treasurer, and librarian of the American Philosophical Society; vice-president and director of the Athenaeum of Philadelphia; member of the executive council of the Historical Society of Pennsylvania; director of the Pennsylvania Academy of Fine Arts; and member of a score of other organizations.[11] On his first visit to Philadelphia, Furness had stayed for several weeks as Vaughan's guest in his rooms in the Philosophical Society's building at Fifth and Chestnut Streets, and later Vaughan became a frequent visitor in Furness's home. In 1908, in his *Historical Address delivered at the Installation of Charles E. St. John as Minister of the Unitarian Church*, Horace would recall the impression that Vaughan had made on the young Furness children.

> He used to take tea every Sunday evening at my father's, and then walk with him to the evening service. What remarkable stories he used to tell! We children listened with open eyes and ears. . . . He used to bring to us children oranges and bons-bons that he had received the evening before at the Wistar Parties. I have to this day a bon-bon which he gave me with a beautiful antelope on the embossed wrapper; its legs are thick and the color splotchy, but in my eyes the picture was too lovely to be destroyed in obtaining the sweet temptation within, so I feasted my eyes at the expense of my tongue and kept the treasure intact. No personage of note visited the city that was not entertained by Mr. Vaughan. It was said that if Charles the Tenth should be driven from France, he would be seen some day walking in Chestnut Street with John Vaughan.[12]

Among other prominent Philadelphians in the small Unitarian congregation sat Samuel Merrick, founder and president of the Franklin Institute; portrait artist Thomas Sully, who painted William Furness's portrait; and Shakespearian actress Fanny Kemble. Nor was such interest in the arts and sciences confined to a few parishioners. Between its founding and the Civil War, thirty-nine members of the Unitarian Church were shareholders in the Athenaeum of Philadelphia; eleven supported the Artists' Fund Society; twenty-three belonged to the Franklin Institute; forty were members of the Musical Fund Society; eight were elected to the American Philosophical Society; and seven Unitarians served as directors of the Pennsylvania Academy of the Fine Arts.

A lesser man might have been overshadowed by such a congregation, but in the rich cultural soil and refined atmosphere of his parish William Furness's own literary talents soon flourished. He himself joined the Athenian Institute, serving as a Counsellor from 1838 to 1844, was made an honorary amateur member of the Artists' Fund Society in 1842, and was elected to the American Philosophical Society in 1840. His contributions to general literature consisted chiefly of translations from German, a language he loved and taught his children to love. One of the earliest Americans to discover and appreciate German romantic literature, he collaborated with the Reverend Frederick H. Hedge, a Unitarian minister in Boston, on *Prose Writers of Germany* (1849), which was followed by his own translations of Shubert's *Mirror of Nature* (1849), *Gems of German Verse* (1851), *Julius, and other Tales* (1856), and his most important work—a translation of Daniel Schenkel's *Characterbild Jesu*, which appeared in 1866 with copious annotations of his own under the title *The Character of Jesus Portrayed*. His translation of Schiller's *Song of the Bell* (1850) was regarded by his contemporaries as the best ever made, and when the German population of Philadelphia celebrated the centennial of Schiller's birth in 1859, they chose Furness to deliver the oration, an essay on Schiller, at the Academy of Music.

While he loved German literature, he also promoted the work of his own countrymen. With publisher and bookseller Edward Carey, another Unitarian, he edited the literary annuals *The Gift* and *The Diadem* in 1844 and became chief editor from 1845 to 1847, soliciting contributions from Emerson, Longfellow, and Poe. This venture into publishing no doubt provided the impetus for the one surviving bit of juvenalia from his thirteen-year-old son, a newspaper called *The Tom-Tit*, "H.H. Furness, Editor, Proprietor, Printer and Publisher."

His chief literary inspiration, however, shone in his theological writing. In 1836, when his son Horace was just three years old, Furness's first book, *Remarks on the Four Gospels* appeared. He belonged to the extreme humanitarian school of Unitarian thinkers, who considered Christ an exalted form of humanity and either dismissed the miracles as legendary accretions to the essential historic truth of the scriptures or accounted for them by the intense moral and spiritual forces of Jesus.

"Quietly assuming the purely human origin and imperfect character
of the early Christian documents, freely indicating what he thought to
be crude or fabulous in their contents, and putting aside the traditional notion of the miraculous, he yet claimed for Jesus an extraordinary *degree* of those human powers which are always divine,
so that his 'wonderful words,' so far as they really happened, were
purely natural, yet in such exalted sense as to reveal to us the hidden
forces of the world and the indwelling fulness of its Author."

Thus wrote Charles Gordon Ames in reviewing Furness's theological
career for *The Harvard Graduates' Magazine*, and he continued, "In
his departure from traditional lines of apologetics and exegesis, and
in the free treatment of the Gospel narrative, he was a brave pioneer.
His 'Remarks' appeared two years before Emerson's 'Address,' five
years before Parker's 'Permanent and Transient,' twenty-seven years
before Renan's 'Vie de Jesus,' and but one year after Strauss had
startled the orthodoxy of Germany by his 'Leben Jesu.'"[13] Two years
later Furness expanded his *Remarks* into a larger volume entitled
Jesus and His Biographers. Aside from numerous sermons and articles printed in *The Christian Examiner* and other periodicals and
hymns collected in A.P. Putnam's *Singers and Songs of the Liberal
Faith* (1875), Furness devoted twenty additional books to refining
his understanding of the Gospels and the character of Jesus, the
most important being *A History of Jesus* (1850), *Thoughts on the Life
and Character of Jesus of Nazareth* (1859), and *The Veil Partly Lifted*
(1864). In recognition of his theological contributions, Harvard
called him back to Cambridge and conferred upon him in 1847 the
degree of Doctor of Divinity.

Theologically and philosophically, Furness's heart had always
remained in New England. He joined the Philadelphia Society of
Sons of New England and, carrying on Vaughan's tradition of hospitality, often entertained guests from Boston and Cambridge in his
home. In May 1828, for example, Furness met Bronson Alcott, who
was pursuing his educational reforms in Philadelphia. With the
encouragement of Furness and financial support from Quaker merchant Reuben Haines, Alcott opened a school for children in Germantown in February 1831, and two years later opened a similar
school in Philadelphia with fifteen pupils including William Henry,
Jr., then approaching his fifth birthday. Alcott's letter to Robert

Vaux, then President of the School Board in Philadelphia, reveals both Alcott's methods and Furness's high standards for the education of his children.

> It is my wish to operate chiefly on the characters of those committed to my care—to form and mature habits of accurate thought—pure feeling, and correct action—to fit the mind for the acquisition of knowledge, and inspire the heart with the love of virtue, and pursuit of excellence.—The results which I aim at producing, cannot, of course, be rendered immediately obvious, but will be, I trust, satisfactory and permanent in the end. If a few children, between the ages of four and ten years, could be collected from those parents who would enter with an intelligent interest into my purposes, and wait with the necessary patience for the production of results, I should highly prize the opportunity thus offered for making known my views on early education.[14]

When the school opened in April 1833, William Henry Jr.'s moral instruction began with *Pilgrim's Progress*, *The Fairie Queene*, *Paradise Lost*, the Bible, and the poetry of Coleridge and Wordsworth. When the school finally closed during the summer of 1834, Furness, together with Boston minister William Ellery Channing, secured for Alcott a school in Boston where he met for a time with greater success.

The Emersons, too, were frequent guests in the Furness home, as were the Furnesses in the Emerson home, and on several occasions Emerson preached for Furness at the Unitarian Church. The friendship, begun as children in First Church and the Boston Public Latin School, continued until Emerson's death when on April 27, 1882, Furness preached the funeral sermon at a private service at Emerson's house preceding the public ceremony at the Unitarian Church. *Records of A Lifelong Friendship 1807-1882: Ralph Waldo Emerson and William Henry Furness*, edited by Horace in 1910, captures the spirit of the long correspondence that linked Pine Street with Concord, a link philosophical as well as personal. When Emerson's philosophic essay *Nature* came out in 1836, Furness wrote to Alcott:

> I was longing for a vent for the feeling awakened by 'Nature,' which Mrs. Morrison left with me last evening, and which is ringing in my

soul like the voice of an angel. I feel I am poor, dumb, and blind; but my nature vibrates and quakes at the approach of I know not what. I seem to myself as a flower must look to a deaf and dumb child, seeing it through a closed window, in a rough wind, dipping up and down, but no hand moving it. It is a beautiful book. Except for the mention of Sham, and some other modern things, I should be sure it was written in Sir Thomas Browne's time. It is a poem. There is but little of it, I fear, into which I have fully entered. But I recognize a view I have had, originally suggested by your saying, as you used to do, 'That whether the facts of the New Testament were true or not,—were they pictures, they are still interesting and enlightening to you.' I never knew how to meet this observation of yours. I have since thought, and Emerson expresses the true idea, that facts are infinitely more valuable than pictures, because facts are God's fables, God's pictures . . .[15]

In a journal entry made in October 1838, Alcott linked the names of Furness and Emerson with members of the Transcendental Club— Frederick Hedge, Theodore Parker, George Ripley, William Ellery Channing, and a dozen others—as "living men." "These I deem the free men and the brave, by whom great principles are to be honoured amongst us."[16]

In this liberal and literary home, surrounded by books and the intellectual conversation of visitors, Horace began his education long before he was sent to dame's school to learn to read and write. By his own account he taught himself Latin, and in 1846, at the age of thirteen, he began German lessons with Mr. Knorr, no doubt accompanied by his sister Annis, who later made a career of translating contemporary German novels for publication by J.B. Lippincott Company. For mathematics and Greek he walked the two blocks from 1426 Pine Street to 15th and Spruce Streets to the home of Eugenius Nulty, self-styled professor of mathematics and languages. Nulty had held the position of Professor of Mathemtics at Dickinson College for two years and worked as an actuary for the Pennsylvania Life Insurance Company for twelve years before opening his own school in 1829. He had been elected to the American Philosophical Society, and received an honorary A.M. from the University of Pennsylvania, and was a member of the American Academy of Arts and Sciences. During the 1840s, when Horace sat in his classroom, Nulty read several mathematical papers before the American Philosophical Society and had others published in the

Society's *Transactions*. Despite his learning, or perhaps because of it, he seemed to have his own definite ideas about how Horace's education should proceed, ideas apparently not entirely viewed with favor by Harvard College. In 1850, the requisites for admission to Harvard College included an examination in Latin covering the whole of Virgil, Caesar's Commentaries, and Cicero's select orations and an examination in Greek composition. In September 1849, in reply to William Furness's evident concern, Jared Sparks, President of Harvard, wrote, "Our new catalogue will soon be out, & I will send you a copy, which will give the information you desire. If practicable, you had better let your son study the books we require, & that are studied here, rather than other books as substitutes. His progress in College will be facilitated by it."[17] When Horace was admitted to the freshman class on probation the following July, William Furness wrote to the Reverend Dr. Walker with some frustration, "My son Horace was very poorly fitted. His little Latin he got at home. His Greek from Mr. Nulty an eminent mathematician, who looks upon *all* the Colleges & upon every teacher but himself, with unmixed contempt."[18] Nevertheless, Horace had cleared the hurdle and prepared to take his place in the freshman class in September 1850.

Apart from the literary heritage gained from his father and the formal training received from Eugenius Nulty, the greatest literary influence on Horace in the years before Harvard College came from his father's friend and parishioner Fanny Kemble. When the English actress and her father Charles Kemble were playing in Philadelphia during the course of an American tour in 1832, Pierce Butler, wealthy Philadelphian and member of the Unitarian Church, had fallen in love with her, pursued her from city to city along the East Coast, and eventually married her in 1834. Butler brought her home to Philadephia where she attended with him the Unitarian Church and became a close friend of William Furness. Incompatibility between the imaginative and sensitive actress and the conventional, conservative plantation owner soon marred their marriage, and despite the mediation of William Furness, Fanny left Butler in September 1845, sailed for London, and, forced by financial difficulties, returned to the stage in the autumn of 1847. During the following spring she began a new career—Shakespearian reading—that she would pursue with great acclaim and financial success for the next twenty years.

Using a copy of Shakespeare marked by her father for readings he gave when deafness barred him from the stage, Fanny Kemble would read dramatically a two-hour, abridged version of each play, retaining the essential story and as much of the poetry as would fit into two hours' time. Having prepared twenty-four plays in such fashion, she read each in rotation, never repeating even the most popular until each had been read. She sat alone on stage behind a small reading table and used no dramatic costume other than a different dress for each play—white satin for *Romeo and Juliet*, soft green for *The Winter's Tale*, wine red for *Hamlet*. In a short time she had achieved great popularity as a Shakespearian reader in England and had booked engagements through June, when in late April she received a summons from the Court of Common Pleas in Philadelphia to face divorce proceedings filed by her husband Pierce Butler on March 29, 1848. Negotiations between their lawyers dragged on for the next eighteen months, Fanny insisting on a trial where she felt that she would be vindicated and secure some financial arrangement for her two daughters, Pierce trying desperately to avoid publicity and settle out of court.

Meanwhile, to maintain herself and pay her lawyers, Fanny continued her new career of Shakespearian reading. She may have read in Philadelphia during the autumn of 1848, although no newspapers carried an account and her application to use a lecture room at the University of Pennsylvania was "respectfully declined."[19] While conservative Philadelphia society remained closed to her during her divorce proceedings, she was welcomed by the more liberal literary hierarchy of Boston where she began a series of readings with *The Merchant of Venice* on January 26, 1849, Charles Sumner leading her to the platform and introducing her. Longfellow, after entertaining her one evening, read to her a sonnet written to commemorate her captivating interpretation of Shakespeare.[20]

> O precious evenings! all too swiftly sped!
>   Leaving us heirs to amplest heritages
>   Of all the best thoughts of the greatest sages
>   And giving tongues unto the silent dead!
> How our hearts glowed and trembled as she read,
>   Interpreting by tones the wondrous pages
>   Of the great poet who foreruns the ages,
>   Anticipating all that shall be said!
> O happy Reader! having for thy text

> The magic book, whose Sibylline leaves have caught
> The rarest essence of all human thought!
> O happy Poet! by no critic vext!
> How must thy listening spirit now rejoice
> To be interpreted by such a voice!

Fanny encountered similar acclaim in New York during March, and when she returned to Philadelphia to read in Sansom Street Hall on October 1, 1849, just ten days after she had reached a divorce settlement out of court, Philadelphia welcomed her with enthusiastic delight. "The simple announcement of these entertainments, so long and eagerly anticipated by our citizens, will more than fill the hall,"[21] predicted the *Evening Bulletin* on September 29; and after her opening performance of *As You Like It* the *Evening Bulletin* carried this review:

Mrs Frances Anne Kemble

A numerous and intelligent audience was assembled, last evening, at the Sansom Street Hall, to hear Mrs. Kemble read Shakespeare's "As You Like It." Many persons well remembered her inimitable personations of individual characters of the Bard, and some, perhaps, had attended her readings in the eastern cities, and others were strangers to her except by report; but we venture to say, none were disappointed last night. She went "from grave to gay, from lively to severe," with equal facility and success; and presented in turn, with singular force and fidelity, the true humor and peculiar characteristics of each personage—whether it was the sensible and dignified Duke Senior, the melancholy Jaques, or the "motley Fool" Touchstone. In each character she seemed perfect; and to us at least, though we had often and admiringly read the play, her manner of reading it, presented undiscovered beauties. We rejoice to hear that these entertainments are to be continued, and that the play of "King John" has been selected for to-morrow evening. We speak but the common sentiment in saying, that no more instructive or more interesting entertainment is now accessible to the intellectual portion of our community, and we anticipate a crowded house on every subsequent occasion.[22]

For five weeks of capacity crowds and prolonged applause Fanny Kemble read *King John*, *Richard II*, *I Henry IV*, *Henry VIII*,

Julius Caesar, Anthony and Cleopatra, Macbeth, Romeo and Juliet, Hamlet, Othello, (after which "the audience retired in a state of 'measureless content'")[23] *The Tempest, The Merry Wives of Windsor,* (during which "the audience were frequently convulsed with laughter")[24] *Measure for Measure, Much Ado About Nothing, Midsummer Night's Dream, The Winter's Tale, Twelfth Night, The Merchant of Venice,* and *King Lear.* This last play she read to a crowded audience at eleven o'clock on a Monday morning, and that afternoon the *Evening Bulletin* noted prophetically,

> "We venture to say that not one who heard her will ever forget the scene. In all but the scenery and dresses, this reading equalled, nay, surpassed the finest acting. What Mrs. Siddons must have been in Cordelia, or Booth when in his prime in Lear, that Mrs. Kemble was in both characters, while the fool, Kent, Goneril, Regan, Gloster, and other subordinates were rendered with the greatest naturalness and spirit. In the most pathetic parts of the drama Mrs. Kemble rose to the highest pitch of tragic power."[25]

One of those who listened to Fanny Kemble read that morning and at every other performance for the past month was the fifteen-year-old Horace Furness, who would later make his own mark as a Shakespearian reader. Furness never forgot the scene. Forty years later, when the question "How did you become a Shakespeare Student?" was posed to him, he replied,

> "I cannot but think that I have been peculiarly favored in my introduction to Shakespeare. When I was about fourteen or fifteen years old, during two winters between 1847 and 1849, Mrs. Kemble gave, here in Philadelphia, two series of Readings, and to both of them, with infinite kindness she sent me a card of admission. Thus to this gracious lady and venerated friend I owe the memory, vivid to this hour in many a scene and line, of her inimitable revelations of more than half of all of Shakespeare's plays."[26]

A second profound influence that he never forgot affected the impressionable adolescent Horace, an influence growing steadily as he grew during the 1840s into a black storm of controversy raging through the country and through his father's Unitarian Church: the abolition of slavery. The Unitarian Church had always stressed

humanitarian reform. Historian of Philadelphia Unitarianism Elizabeth Geffen has written:

> For the Unitarians, generally, universal perfection was to be obtained
> through humanitarian reform. They had cast off the Calvinistic tenet
> which held that all men were by nature sinners, eventually, if not
> immediately, to be punished by an angry God. Unitarians believed
> that all men were essentially good, created by a loving Father in His
> own image and therefore partaking of a measure of Divine goodness
> themselves. It was obvious that physical, economic, social, or politi-
> cal circumstances often made it impossible for men to realize their
> potentialities, but it was equally obvious that it was every man's duty
> to change such circumstances so that all men could live as their
> Heavenly Father had intended. . . . They attacked with concentration
> and thoroughness the problems of prisons, institutions for the insane,
> the deaf, the dumb, the blind, the issues of women's rights, peace,
> temperance, slavery. Always their aim was a moral and religious one.
> As all men were equal in the sight of God, so should they be given an
> opportunity to achieve equality on this earth. The levelling was to be
> upward, however. The ideal to be achieved was ultimate, individual
> perfection and there was to be no surrender to mass mediocrity.[27]

In Philadelphia Unitarians belonged to such organizations as
the Pennsylvania Institution for the Instruction of the Blind, the
Society for the Abolition of Capital Punishment, the Office of the
Guardians of the Poor, and the Philadelphia Society for the Information and Assistance of Persons Emigrating from Foreign Countries;
however, slavery remained a sensitive issue, and William Furness
avoided it as long as he could. Many Philadelphians had strong
family and business ties with the South, and Furness did not want to
risk offending influential members of his congregation like Pierce
Butler, who owned several hundred slaves on his Georgia planta-
tions. In 1830, William Lloyd Garrison had begun publishing his
abolitionist newspaper *The Liberator* in Boston, and in December
1833 he had organized the Amercan Anti-Slavery Society in Philadelphia just blocks from the Furness home; yet Furness did not even
meet Garrison until March 19, 1835 at the home of James and
Lucretia Mott. Furness disliked the strident tone and emotional
language of Garrison's crusade, although he confided afterwards to
a close friend, "I confess I like Garrison & always had a sneaking

feeling in his favour," but he added the pious hope that "His spirit I think will soften with success. Let us do him the utmost possible justice & that will soften his asperities."[28] Garrison, in turn, recorded his impressions of Furness in a letter to his wife: "I find he has an aversion to strong language and I think he is not yet prepared 'to go the whole.' Tomorrow we shall dine together." [29] In May 1837, however, Furness subscribed to *The Liberator*, and the following year when a mob burned down Pennsylvania Hall, meeting place for Philadelphia's antislavery societies, Furness delivered "A Sermon occasioned by the Destruction of Pennsylvania Hall," albeit an attack not on slavery but on mob violence and suppression of free speech.

Not until July 1839, on Independence Sunday, did Furness preach his first sermon against slavery, and heedless of opposition, now that his conscience had been aroused, he continued to preach abolition until the victory was won. "Ah, that dread subject of Abolition!" Horace later wrote in his *Historical Address*.

> It was the touchstone of this congregation! It was the fan which thoroughly purged the floor, scattering the chaff and gathering the wheat into a garner! How my poor father, with his intense love of gentle peace and confiding repose, agonized over it. How reluctantly he embraced it! How he strove to hide himself amid flowers from the voice of God calling him! But all in vain. Even though death for himself and starvation for his family were the penalty, he must scream out 'Lo! here am I!' His first 'Abolition' sermon (I have it so marked by him) was preached in 1839. He once told me with what quaking trepidation he ascended the pulpit that day, and the ineffable peace which stole over him when the service was over. Though he did not suggest it, it was clear that angels came and ministered unto him.[30]

Furness had good reason for trepidation, for Philadelphian pro-slavery sympathizers were becoming increasingly vocal and violent, and the church itself divided over the question of slavery. Some members, like Joseph Todhunter and Joseph Sill who belonged to the Pennsylvania Abolition Society, supported the pastor; others, including James Taylor, one of the founders of the church and a heavy financial supporter, withdrew their membership. In August 1842, when anti-Negro riots broke out among Philadelphia's Irish community, the mob set fire to the Negro Beneficial Hall and a Negro meeting house, while firemen refused to throw water on the flames. Furness, according to Garrison, was "the only Philadelphia clergyman who made the shocking outbreak the subject of a discourse."[31] Even as he preached that sermon, however, an opposition party had begun circulating a petition reading in part,

> we hereby declare it our conscientious conviction that in the occasional lectures by the Pastor on the subject of *Abolition of Slavery in the South* we perceive no good, present or remote, but on the contrary it sows the seeds of disunion and if continued, we earnestly believe it will greatly injure the Society as a body of Christians, creating hostile parties, where the holier bands of brotherhood should exist.[32]

The petition gained thirty-nine signatures, including some of the most influential and wealthy members of Furness's congregation; but a counter petition supporting Furness collected double that number, and, reassured, Furness redoubled his preaching of freedom and equality.

The news of street violence, angry voices in his father's study, and the disappearance of familiar faces from the congregation all made their impression on the young Horace during the decade. Even sixty-five years later he could vividly recall the tense Sunday mornings when his father spoke against slavery.

> When worldly-wise remonstrances and angry threats of breaking up the church proved of no avail,—then followed open demonstrations; when from the wording of the text the congregation became aware that in the sermon there would be impassioned pleadings for the slave and eloquent adjurations to guard liberty and the rights of man, then would fall a pin-drop silence, while the air was charged with a trembling apprehension of unknown consequences, broken suddenly, at the mention from the pulpit of 'African slavery,' by the opening and slamming of a pew door, and the furious stamping through the aisle to the exits, sometimes followed in a few minutes by a second and a third. On one occasion, a prominent member of the congregation after he had wrathfully risen from his seat and rushed forth, returned and commanded his trembling daughters to follow him to the door. Then my poor father's face would grow white to the lips, but still his

voice would continue to plead unfalteringly, imploring his hearers for the sake of the slaves, surely the least of all our brethren, in whom Christ commanded us to see himself, still more even for the sake of the masters, to heed his warning and the words of God.[33]

As the decade drew to a close, William Furness became even more vocal in his opposition to slavery, carrying the fight beyond his own pulpit. Although he never joined an antislavery society, he delivered his first speech before the Pennsylvania Anti-Slavery Society on December 19, 1849, and on May 7, 1850 at the annual meeting of the American Anti-Slavery Society in New York he shared the platform with Garrison, Wendell Phillips, Frederick Douglass, and other abolitionist leaders. All during the Spring the Senate and House had been debating the Compromise of 1850, including the Fugitive Slave Bill, and passions were running high throughout the country. For days before the meeting the *New York Herald* had vilified the speakers and inflamed the public. Unsurprisingly, after numerous interruptions, midway through Garrison's presentation of the resolutions, a gang of ruffians led by one-time Democratic patronage worker Isaiah Rynders rushed the platform in an attempt to break up the meeting. "The name of Zachary Taylor had scarcely passed Mr. Garrison's lips when Captain Rynders, with something like a howl, forsaking his strategic position on the borderline of the gallery and the platform, dashed headlong down towards the speaker's desk, followed, with shouting and imprecations and terrifying noise, by the mass of his backers. The audience, despite a natural agitation, gave way to no panic. The abolitionist leaders upon the platform remained imperturbable. 'I was not aware,' writes Dr. Furness, 'of being under any apprehension of personal violence. We were all like General Jackson's cotton-bales at New Orleans. Our demeanor made it impossible for the rioters to use any physical force against us.'"[34] Although Thomas Kane, son of Judge Kane of Philadelphia, leaped to the platform to protect Furness, almost provoking the fight that Rynders wanted, the calm composure of Garrison and "the genial manner, firm tones, and self possession, the refined discourse, of this Unitarian clergyman [Furness], was felt to have turned the current of the meeting"[35] and prevented the degeneration into violence. Four months after the incident of Rynders Mob, in September 1850, Millard Fillmore signed into law the Fugitive Slave Bill. Furness joined Henry Ward Beecher, Theodore Parker, and other prominent clergymen and laymen who publicly announced their readiness, in defiance of this law, to shelter fugitive slaves. As Horace prepared that autumn to enter the comparative calm of Harvard College, his father urged his congregation to defy the law and prepared to aid the Philadelphia Vigilance Committee of the Underground Railroad.

STUDENT OF THE WORLD

"O this learning, what a thing it is!"
—*The Taming of the Shrew* 1.2.156

"By your pardon, sir, I was then a young traveller."
—*Cymbeline* 1.4.39-40

In September 1850, with sixty-four other freshmen, Horace entered Harvard. Rarely did the subject of abolition intrude upon his weekly letters to his family, otherwise filled with news of classes and classmates and requests for new shirt collars or more letters from home. Only near the end of his senior year does his account of the celebrated Anthony Burns affair show that he had adopted for himself the convictions of his father. From January 1854 until its passage on May 22, 1854, Congress had debated the Kansas-Nebraska Act, which set aside the Missouri Compromise and permitted states west of the Mississippi to choose for themselves whether to enter the Union "slave or free." For five months the antislavery forces had worked to defeat its passage, and two days later on May 24, when Anthony Burns was arrested in Boston for theft and detained under the new Fugitive Slave Law, "the popular excitement at once rose to fever heat, during a week without a parallel since the days of the Revolution."[1] Wendell Phillips and Theodore Parker addressed a mass meeting in Faneuil Hall two days after the arrest, and an attack on the Court House in an attempt to rescue Burns resulted in the death of a deputy marshall. Although defended by Richard Henry Dana and other Boston abolitionist lawyers, Burns was sentenced to be returned to slavery, and on June 2, surrounded by armed troops to prevent his rescue, he was escorted through the streets of Boston to a revenue cutter ordered by President Pierce to take him back to Virginia. As he saw it from his vantage point at the third-floor window of the Commonwealth Building at the corner of State and Washington Streets, Furness described the scene in the Court Square on June 2:

> At about eleven the "Lancers" rode full gallop down the street, effectually breaking the crowd; as they passed, for the first time in my life I heard the howls of an enraged populace. It was horrible, and so loud were the groans & hisses & cries of "Shame!" & "Bloodhounds!" that the clattering of the horses' hoofs was almost inaudible. The instant that they had passed, some men, right underneath our window, lifted up a black coffin with "Liberty" on it. It was received with clapping of hands & cheers. Then it was that I thought I should see a man torn to pieces by the mob, for one bold Irishman rushed up to it & struck it a heavy blow with his fist; it toppled over, but was instantly raised again & the mob rushed at the man; the fellow ran for his life, the crowd after him plucking at him in the most bloodthirsty style; the police finally came to his rescue & protected him, but a man more thoroughly frightened I never saw, he was whiter than this paper. The coffin was subsequently suspended from a window in the very room where we were. The man who superintended this operation I afterwards observed very busy in one corner of the room, pouring some red stuff into little loose paper parcels. I went up to him & asked what that was for "Well," said he, "some folks are in favor of the Thompsonian practice and I want to see whether the soldiers down below belong to that class." The red stuff was Cayenne pepper. At about twelve o'clock the street beginning near Mr. Lothrop's house was cleared by the police; not a man was allowed to remain; a most singular effect; not a creature to be seen in the street at noonday.

From that time till near two they were occupied in stationing soldiers in every single street, alley, or court that led into State Street. In fact a rescue would have been *perfectly* impossible. At about two the procession came by, the "Lancers" first, then four or five hundred United States troops, & then a hollow square, of policemen three deep, with drawn swords, & poor Anthony Burns in the centre with four or five keepers around him. The hissings, hootings, & groanings were deafening. My friend of the Cayenne pepper threw his missiles many of which took effect on the heads, shoulders, & backs of the police; in spite of the horror of the scene I couldn't help laughing; handkerchiefs were instantly in demand & the police & deputy marshals were seized with irrepressible fits of sneezing The procession passed & I saw the last of poor Burns. The effect of the whole proceeding has been & will be productive of the very best consequences. Everybody is turning Abolitionist. The voice of the people on that day was unmistakable. This morning I heard Mr. Parker; the sermon as fine as the congregation, which was at least four thousand.[2]

Aside from this antislavery riot, which caused "the greatest excitement throughout College" and aroused even "sluggish student nature,"[3] Furness's four years at Harvard seemed to pass in a tranquil routine of lectures and recitations, essays and declamations. In fact, neither the schedule nor the curriculum left much extra time for a student, like Furness, striving to excel in his class. The school day began with mandatory Morning Prayers at seven o'clock during the first term and at six o'clock during the second, followed by breakfast and then the first recitation at eight o'clock. Classes continued until one o'clock, when dinner was served, and resumed from three until six. On Saturday morning classes met from eight until ten. During the Freshman and Sophomore years all students followed a set curriculum, consisting in the first year of Greek, Latin, mathematics, and history during the first term and Greek, Latin, mathematics, and chemistry during the second. To these subjects were added in the second year rhetoric, French, and natural history.

The freshman classes in Greek were conducted six days a week by the eccentric, but brilliant, Evangelinus Apostolides Sophocles. Eleven recitations were held each fortnight, and once a month the students wrote exercises in Greek composition. The dark eyes gleaming ferociously from under the shock of white hair and the brusque manner of the tutor intimidated many a student, but underneath the fierce exterior Sophocles reserved a tenderness for intimate friends, among whom Furness eventually won his way. Years later, when Furness wrote to his grandson Fairman Rogers Furness, then himself a student at Harvard, he recalled his favorite Greek professor.

> I hope also that you found some thing of value in the Hist. of the Greek Alphabet by my valued old friend and teacher, Sophocles, whose own history, by the way is not devoid of interest. He was born, as he once told me, on his 'paternal estate near Mt. Pelion,' and was educated in the Egyptian branch, I believe, of a Convent on Mt. Sion. He happened to be at sea on the Mediterranean, when the Greek Revolution broke out—in whose cause Byron sacrificed his life. 'We had a couple of Turks on board,' said Sophocles, 'and we cut off their heads & threw them over.' The Missionaries converted him from the Greek Church—sent him to this country where he drifted to Harvard College as tutor and died as Professor of Patristic Greek. He compiled a Byzantine Lexicon, one of the most scholarly and monumental works ever made in America—and, perhaps, in the world. I took great pains to learn Greek pronunciation from him, and once when one of the Greek Tutors asked him to give him a few lessons in it, he refused and told him to go to 'Furness, in the Junior Class,' which the tutor, Hooper by name, did & I drilled him in the art.[4]

In Latin the freshmen and sophomores read Horace, Cicero, and Livy and devoted one hour every fortnight to writing Latin. Recitations in geometry and trigonometry were held three times a week during the freshman year, and in the sophomore year instruction continued with algebra and analytical geometry. Twice a week in the afternoons the freshmen recited from Malkin's *History of Greece* and the sophomores from Tytler's *Universal History*. Chemistry required two recitations each week for freshmen and sophomores and attendance at a "course of Experimental Lectures parallel with the textbook."[5] During the second term sophomores replaced chemistry with biology, where they were instructed by Asa Gray, Fisher Professor of Natural History. All sophomores were required to study French, a language in which Furness excelled, for at the end of the year he was listed among seven others in a letter from the French tutor Emile Arnoult to President Sparks as one of the best French students in his class. For his classes in rhetoric, which included recitations, instruction in elocution once a week, and a theme every third week followed by criticism from the instructor, Furness was fortunate to sit under the renowned philologist Francis James Child, who had joined the Harvard faculty as Boylston Professor of Rhetoric and Oratory in 1851 and even then was working on his edition of *English and Scottish Ballads* (1857-1858).

After completing this rigorous course of general study, the upperclassmen were allowed some freedom of choice, although required courses still predominated. Every upperclassman studied four semesters of physics, four of philosophy, four of rhetoric—including declamations on such topics as "Whether it is just that a person be taxed by law for the support of religious forms & ordinances" or "Whether we should hesitate to publish the truth for fear that the world is not prepared for it"—two semesters of history, two of modern literature, and one each of Greek literature, Roman literature, and political science. Beyond these required subjects each upperclassman could choose two electives every term from the classical and modern languages or the sciences. For his electives Furness chose each semester additional courses in Latin and Greek, reading beyond his assignments "a great deal of both extra Latin and extra Greek, so much, that somehow Prof. Lane got to know of it & once flattered me immensely by asking me, before the class, to oblige him by looking out for a certain turn of expression in any of the authors that I might be reading."[6]

So well did Furness excel in his classical studies that at the beginning of his senior year Mr. Hooper, an instructor for freshmen, asked Furness to offer private tutoring in Greek to a freshman from Philadelphia named Starr. Furness's account of their first session suggests the serious attitude with which he approached his studies.

Starr came to me last evening for the first time. The experience of the past week had fully convinced him of the need he had of some such assistance if he had been at all doubtful on that point. Of the necessity there wasn't the slightest doubt. Tutor Hooper told him he would not admit him into College if he didn't come to me, so it was Hobson's Choice. I asked him one or two questions last evening of the simplest kind such as I had drilled him on in vacation & he answered them either very poorly or not at all. At one time he became groughty manifesting the disposition of anything rather than that of one desirous of learning. Determined to nip any such manifestations in the

bud, I gave a pretty sharp slap on the table, saying in the most severe
tones 'stop fooling this minute, Sir, sit up straight put your book in
front of you & attend!' He made considerably big eyes, but saw that it
was no joking matter & that it began to grow serious. I never saw him
better than he was after that in my life.[7]

Although Furness concentrated on classical studies, he responded with equal enthusiasm to his other classes. At the beginning of his last year, for example, he reported to his family:

The Senior Year thus far wags pleasantly enough. The numerous
lectures constitute a very delightful feature. Prof. Wyman [Jeffries
Wyman, Hersey Profesor of Anatomy] is excellent, on Comparative
Anatomy. He contrives to impart more information in an hour than
any one I have ever heard. Words are wanting to express the pleasure
I take in Prof. Longfellow's Readings of Faust [Henry Wadsworth
Longfellow, Smith Professor of the French and Spanish Languages
and Professor of the Belles-Lettres]. We all of us have copies of that
work & follow Mr. L. as he translates it into simple, literal language, &
now & then explains to us the connection, or gives us his ideas about
it. So you see that the hour spent with him must needs be very
delightful. And then his voice and manner, it would be a pleasure to
hear him read anything. Our readings of Chaucer with Prof. Child are
also very pleasant & on the same principle, only we do the reading. It
is needless to tell you how interesting Prof. Agassiz [Jean Louis
Agassiz, Professor of Natural History in the Lawrence Scientific
School] is on Geology. Yesterday had the weather been pleasant, he
was going to take us down to Nahant on a Geological Excursion, but it
was so cold & threatening that he went over to Somerville instead.[8]

Another expedition that fall with Professor Agassiz Furness described a few weeks later.

It was a splendid day and at ten o'clock we started with Prof Agassiz
to walk over to Roxbury to make geological examinations of the
Pudding Stone there. There were about forty of us, mostly Scientific
Students however, yet that was another cause of pleasure. For these
Scientifics are a most stupid set & there has been a great complaint,
on former occasions, that these sumphs have monopolised the Professor, asking him the most stupid questions, for instance one of them
yesterday asked him the difference between a boulder and a Pudding

Stone. I was accordingly determined that when I went, it should not so be. So soon after we started I ousted one of his Scientific body-guard & kept my position by his side during the rest of the walk & it was a walk of six miles. We reached Roxbury at about twelve o'clock, & examined the Pudding Stone to our satisfaction, while there one of the Scientifics clapped the climax of stupidity by bringing Prof. Agassiz a piece of an old clinker & wanted to know what singular mineral it was. When told that it was a piece of old coal he dropped it as though it had been a live one.[9]

Taking more than a passing interest in science, Furness joined the Natural History Society, serving as its vice-president and curator of entomology during his junior year and its president during his senior year. Under Furness's leadership the society began the custom of inviting various professors to attend the meetings. Although he was doubtful of its success, at the very next meeting on September 28, Furness succeeding in bringing Professor Agassiz.

I had invited Prof. Agassiz with hardly a hope that he would come, but to my great delight he made his appearance at the beginning of the meeting, accompanied by his son who is a member of the society. I did the honors of the occasion & conducted him to a seat. The order of performances in that Society is that members read papers on various subjects supplied to them by the President; and it very often happens that members neglect this duty, so that sometimes, when there ought to be four papers every meeting, there are only three, two & sometimes only one. This was unfortunately the case that evening. There was only one paper, but that was luckily on Geology, on the "Mauvaises Terres;" & after it was concluded I expressed my regret at there being so few performances, but said that the society would feel highly honored if Prof. Agassiz would favor it with any remarks on any subject that he might feel inclined; & he did feel inclined, for taking up the subject of "Mauvaises Terres" he told us all about them, drew diagrams on the blackboard, & spoke about twenty minutes in the most interesting style. After the meeting was over I showed him our collection & he expressed himself greatly pleased & said he should certainly come again & bring with him Dr. Leidy's report on these 'Bad Lands.' Not only was it exceedingly pleasant to have him there but it will prove the greatest benefit to the society.[10]

Among other clubs and organizations, Furness belonged to the Institute of 1770 and Alpha Delta Phi, the latter a society which "has to supply the Class with brains, other societies may provide the sinews & muscles, but the intellect comes from the Alpha Delta Phi."[11] On the humorous side Furness enthusiastically participated in the Hasty Pudding Club theatricals during his junior and senior years, doubling as chorister, actor, dancer, and designer of playbills even though he studiously tried to hide his artistic talent. "The other evening we had a regular meeting of the H.P.C., when my pictures figured conspicuously & were universally & copiously admired," he wrote on April 3, 1853. "It was asserted on all sides that it was by far the handsomest Bill ever gotten up. It has placed me at once to the rank of the first artist in the Class, as some maintain, I shall discountenance such an opinion as much as I possibly can. If allowed to prevail it would result in the most unconscionable demand on my time, for future Bills."[12] His acting debut came on April 1 that year, when he played Count Glorieux in *Sketches in India*, followed by the first intimations of stardom on April 29 in the part of Old Wiggins.

Last Friday we had a Hasty Pudding Meeting, when in a farce called 'Mrs. Wiggins,' I figured as a fat man. You can imagine how fat I was when I tell that by no possibility could I see my feet. My nearest and dearest friends could never have recognised me. I had on a bald wig with a few gray hairs on the back of my head. It was universally acknowledged to have been the best gotten up dress ever seen before the H.P.C. footlights."[13]

The peak of his stage career came on December 16, 1853, as he danced a stunning *pas seul* between the two farces *Who'll Lend Me a Wife?* and *Two Bonnycastles*.

"I anxiously expected the silk stockings till the last moment," he reported later, but as they didn't come I bought the longest pair of cotton that I could find, & made my debut in the dancing world as a Ballet girl last Friday night. For lack of anything better to tell you I will for your edification describe my dress. In the first place I purchased a pair of satin slippers, (perfect loves!) & sewed thereon two pink rosettes. I then bought eight yards of muslin & with the aid of Wadleigh in a very short time it was transformed into a pair of voluminous drawers & three very full skirts, reaching almost to my knees. This was all that I did in the making of my dress. The rest was gotten up by Miss Sallie Colburn & comprised a most charming pink bodice turretted thus [Here follows a sketch.] round the waist, in short its toute ensemble was somehow thus together with a very full skirt of white muslin trimmed with pink ribbons. On my head I had on a black wig with a double row of curls & on that a diminutive hat trimmed with black & artificial flowers, also the handiwork of Miss. C. When the curtain drew up, two fellows made their appearance at the back of the stage, with white waistcoats & cravats & walked solemnly down to the front with Jewsharps in their hands & seated on opposite sides of the stage after tuning their instruments struck up a popular air, by way of overture, & then at a preconcerted signal, as the bill announced, Signorita Phurnessi made her appearance & tripped down to the footlights amid peals upon peals of the most tremendous, deafening, & prolonged applause. Everything that she did, from her languishing & unvarying smile down to her walking on the points of her toes brought down the house & at the close she was vociferously encored. It was a great hit. It occurred to me that if you should desire it I would try to bring the dress home & would persuade the Signorita sometime or other to favor you with a Pas Seul. For mercy sake keep hush about this or my character for dignity & sedateness would be forever blasted. By the way will it be too much trouble to send on them stockings for my next appearance? It will greatly oblige me.[14]

Adds Lloyd Garrison in *An Illustrated History of The Hasty Pudding Club Theatricals*, "the first 'diva' of the Pudding ballet—'the unparalleled Signorina Furnessi'—was a 'vision' in 'tights and a thousand gauzy skirts in the highest professional style.'"[15]

Among his classmates Furness, by his own admission, was not a "popular fellow"; nevertheless, his circle of friends included many of the top scholars in his class—Charles Russell Lowell, John Chandler Bancroft, Edward Daves—and his long-time friend from Philadelphia, Atherton Blight.

The popularity that I possess is the kind I do care for," he wrote to his parents near the end of his junior year. To a large number of every class the epithet of 'dig' is a reproach, & I deservedly have that title, but I have been so consistent throughout in 'digging,' that my classmates cannot but feel a respect for me & think that I deserve every inch of the rank that I have acquired, & would feel quite sorry to see me seriously lose it. That I have lost some of it there is no doubt, I believe I am now the fourth. There is another thing that I might have done in order to gain so called 'popularity,' that is, visiting & associating more generally with my class. This I have never done, for I always have considered it & always shall, look upon it as a great waste of valuable time, if any desire my company they must seek it, and I assure you I have enough seekers, almost too many, for I am sometimes obliged to act quite rudely, such as keeping on studying with almost the same attention after the entrance of company as before. This however I do only to my most intimate friends, & they always understand it.[16]

This reputation for excessive studying or "digging," to use the college jargon of the 1850s, led to an amusing incident that term in Latin recitation. "I was scanning some Iambic Trimeters in Prof. Lane's room the other afternoon, the words were—Tu dignus qui sies (Plautinian Latin), I accordingly commenced 'tu dig-Iamb." (I am) & there was a general symptom of concealed laughter. I luckily kept my countenance and went on."[17]

Such serious attention to his studies, however, did not bar him from normal undergraduate social activities and occasional college pranks. The sitting room shared by Furness and Blight, furnished with desks, bookcases, tables, and easy chairs before the fireplace and decorated by Blight's generosity with red curtains, red cushions on the window seats, and twenty-four pictures on the walls, served as a natural meeting place for their friends; and, in spite of his disclaimer, Furness did his own share of visiting, as he recounted in January 1853.

Last Thursday, Twelfth Night, I was invited to a jollification in Putnams room, to meet some half a dozen fellows, all Alpha Delta Phi-men, and that one title implies every thing that's fine. We had a royal time. Steaming hot punch circulated freely, though not in my veins. I carried my baccy-box & smoked and sang for the benefit of the rest. About eleven o'clock there was an alarm of fire. The Omnibus Stable at the Port. An omnibus came up to spread the alarm. Instantly great coats and india rubbers were flung on, & we sallied forth. You know I have a penchant for improving my lungs,—there was a good deal of noise. I caught the omnibus just as it was returning, jumped on, several followed my example, & we rode every step of the way to the fire in great style. When there I excited great wrath from the firemen by repeating in a stentorian voice any orders which I might perchance hear, such as 'Play on. No. 3!' 'Stop playing No. 6!' & the like. To a disinterested Spectator I was the 'factotum' of the fire. Especially since as soon as I left the place it broke out with redoubled fury. I returned to the room after half an hours pleasing excitement. This I believe is the only incident of the week.[18]

Even with time out for fun and fires, Furness passed four years as an exceptional student and in the end carried away his just share of academic honors. In May 1853, he was elected, along with six of his classmates, to Phi Beta Kappa. The following year at the Class Exhibition on May 2, 1854, he was chosen to give an oration on "Emmanuel Swedenborg," and again at the Commencement Exercises on July 19, 1854, he delivered an oration entitled "Character of Christian Missionaries in the Middle Ages" and was awarded a detur, a handsomely bound edition of Milton's poetical works. When the final class rank was calculated, Furness ranked fifth, behind Charles Lowell, Edward Daves, William Potter, and James Kendall, out of a class of ninety-one. "While here," Sophocles later wrote to William Henry Furness, "he was regarded as one of the few *models*."[19]

Not yet twenty-one years old, Furness returned to Philadelphia with a good knowledge of Greek participles and the Latin subjunctive, but with little idea about a career and at loose ends in the relative quiet of 1426 Pine Street after the college camaraderie of 22 Holworthy Hall. Three weeks before commencement, on June 26, Annis had married Dr. Caspar Wister; Will was abroad, studying painting in Düsseldorf; and fourteen-year-old Frank was still too young to provide much companionship for his older brother. Inspired by Will's weekly letters from Düsseldorf, Horace, together with his close college friend Atherton Blight, began to plan the next stage of their education: a European tour.

Although Will had left home to study in Brooklyn in May 1849, he and Horace had become close companions during Horace's early college years. Will had moved on to Boston in November 1849, and by the time Horace arrived in Cambridge the following September, Will was settled in a studio, attending drawing classes, and busy with several commissioned portraits. For two years Horace had come into Boston from Cambridge on Saturdays, often bringing Blight with him, and the three of them had dined together at the Parker House. Will had played the part of the concerned older brother, at one point urging his father and mother to look after Horace's health.

He keeps studying hard, & sitting up late, worrying me, & losing color, flesh, & spirits. Don't let me worry you, but when he returns home I do not want him to look so pale as he has looked the other times that he has gone home to vacation. When I speak of his losing spirits I do not mean to say that he is low-spirited but that he has lost a great deal of that charming vivacity that he had when he returned home after vacation.[20]

As much as he enjoyed Boston, however, Will dreamed of studying abroad. He had admired the paintings at the Düsseldorf Exhibition in Brooklyn in 1849 and had received encouragement from historical painter Emanuel Leutze to study with him in Düsseldorf. Best known for his life size painting *Washington Crossing the Delaware*, Leutze had been reared in Philadelphia and then studied at the Royal Academy in Düsseldorf where he had remained until returning to the United States in 1859, when he was commissioned by the U.S. Congress to decorate a stairway in the Capitol with his painting *Westward the Course of Empire Takes Its Way*. "I can hardly tell you how much more anxious I am to go abroad since I have learned from your letter what Leutze says of my pictures," Will wrote to his parents in March 1852. "It seems to me it would improve me so much. . . . Why it really seems as if there were a sort of ethereal spiritual Essence of Raphael waiting at Düsseldorf only to be clapped into my brain & then made use of by me."[21] That autumn he reluctantly parted from Horace—"I cannot tell you how much Horace is to me & how very much I shall miss him if I have to leave him"[22]—and returned to Philadelphia to prepare for his voyage. In February 1853, armed with invitations from Leutze and letters of introduction from Thomas Sully, Will embarked on the steamer *City of Glasgow* bound for Liverpool. After studying with Leutze until August 1854, Will moved to Dresden for a month and then settled into an atelier in Munich that October.

When Horace and Atherton learned how cheaply Will was living in Düsseldorf—$7.00 a month for a room, including breakfast and a fire, on Jagerhof Strasse opposite the public gardens—they conceived their plan for continuing their own education abroad. They would spend two years in Europe, living for a year in Germany with Will and a year in France, spending the summer months traveling and the winter months living quietly, visiting the opera, studying, and mastering French and German. Furness would handle the money and make all the arrangements; Blight would provide the bankroll. The plan having been approved by their parents, Blight and Furness, accompanied by college classmate James Savage, left Philadelphia on October 11, 1854, on the steamer *America* bound for Liverpool. Arriving in England on October 24, they gradually made their way through London, Paris, and Strasbourg, reaching Munich and reunion with Will on November 8.

Furness and Blight were soon settled into two bedrooms and a parlor at 12 Theresien Strasse and had engaged a German teacher named Herr Wertheim, "a gentleman quite widely known in Munich & altogether a brick—For instance, he immediately introduced us into the Museum—a club where all the papers are to be seen, English & German & procured us tickets of invitation good for a month, after which we can become members."[23] Three days a week at nine o'clock in the morning Furness went to Herr Wertheim, reciting a lesson in grammar on the first day, translating from *Faust* on the second day, and from the second volume of Macauley's *England* on the third. On his own he read whatever other German he could lay his hands on. All that winter they kept resolutely to their schedule.

> I get up every morning at half past six & breakfast at half past seven, read all day long till I go round to Will's room at half past four or five, talk with him & see how he is getting along, or chat bad German with his little model if she's there. Then we go to dinner, and after dinner I prance about for an hour or so by way of a constitutional, & then Will usually spends his evening with us & we chat & read, while sometimes Jim plays on the piano, till we break up for the night. *'Und so fliessen meine Tage.'*[24]

Not every day, however, passed so studiously. In addition to their studies, Blight, Savage, and Furness sat in Will's studio for their portraits and varied their sedentary life with riding and dancing lessons as Furness wrote in December 1854:

> The dancing appears to promise the greatest fun. I have ached with laughter after each lesson. Our teacher is a Mad. Mayer, far uglier than Satan. to have to waltz with her myself puts me into fits of pain, & to see Blight waltz with her puts me into fits of laughter. For teaching us all the German dances & waltzes even if we have to take

a lesson every day for a year, her terms are 4 gulden & a half, in American money about $2.75!!"[25]

Before long they were introduced into one of the students' clubs and attended their first *Kneipe* or drinking party.

> The room was quite small with two tables round which were sitting about thirty fine looking fellows drinking beer & smoking, & shouting & talking at a most stunning rate. We were very kindly received & we immediately felt quite at our ease. Very soon after we entered the President called for a song & they instantly struck up 'Aus Noah aus dem Kasten war.' I never heard such magnificent singing in all my life. As soon as the song was finished everyone drank to his neighbors & the chatting continued until the next song was called for. I sat next to a capital fellow—the ideal German Student handsome, frank face, curly hair, with a long pipe & a little blue & white smoking cap. He was very much interested in hearing about American students, whether they had Kneip's & fought duels. On the subject of duels he was enthusiastic. He had already fought six & was to fight another the next day. He said it was 'gar lustig.' He had given four ugly wounds, he said, & had never received a single scratch. Some of the fellows there had frightful scars. Song followed song 'In einem Kuhlen Grunde,' 'Krambambuli,' & 'Es zogen drei Bursche,' besides others that I had never before heard.[26]

After six months of student life in Munich, Furness, Blight, and Savage had reached their goal of learning German and accordingly resolved to "come down like the Day of Judgment on the rest of Germany for the next three months."[27] While following their winter regimen, they had agreed not to speak English to one another, and before long Furness found himself speaking German so fluently that he felt "competent for almost any emergency whether it be for slanging a cabman or for turning a delicate compliment to a lady, the former accomplishment, by the way, I practise to B's infinite amusement, calling the cabmen all sorts of names, & expressing a wish that the D——l may catch them by the heels if there is the slightest show of imposition on their part."[28] On the first day's train ride from Munich to Nuremberg, relates Furness, "a gentleman got into the same car & entered into conversation with me & I was tickled by his asking me from what part of Germany I was from."[29]

For the next five months, then, the trio journeyed from Munich to Berlin, through Dresden and Prague across Austria to Vienna, up the Danube to Regensberg, across the Tyrol from Innsbruck to Zurich, and down the Rhine past Freiberg, Heidelberg, Frankfort, Wiesbaden, Coblenz, Bonn, Cologne, and Düsseldorf. Everywhere they went Furness collected relics—at Nuremberg a piece of mortar from the wall of Albert Dürer's atelier; at Weimar, a shred of Goethe's dressing gown and a piece of Martin Luther's robe; at Wartbourg Castle where Luther threw his inkpot at the devil, a chip from Luther's chest of drawers; at Prague, three hairs from the mane of General Ziska's horse; at the Council Hall in Constance, wadding from the Emperor Sigismund's chair. By his own admission he had "fairly enlisted in the regiment of relic hunters or as they are called in German 'Reliquienjager,'"[30] a propensity that would later cause him to decorate his library shelves with Shakespearian memorabilia. And everywhere they went Furness added to his collection of artists.

> Monday morning we paid our second visit to the Picture Gallery & again lost ourselves in admiration of Rembrandt, Paul Veronese, Van Dyck, & Rubens. You see the older & more experienced I grow I add more names to my lists of demigods. At first I had only Rembrandt & Van Dyck, & now I take Paul Veronese, unconditionally & Rubens 'cum grano.' Peter Paul is so fond of painting flabby, squelchy girls, only half concealing their nudity & indecency with flaming red mantels that you get perfectly wearied & disgusted with pink bulging knees & swelling elbows (Will calls them 'intense.') and I turn with relief & refreshment to the majestic, gentlemanlike portraits of Rembrandt & Van Dyck & to the deep colouring of Paul Veronese. Albrecht Dürer I haven't yet attained unto, his carvings in wood are miracles of minuteness & beauty but his paintings are altogether beyond my comprehension. Murillo I admire semi-occasionally but Carlo Dolce I detest & abominate. But bless me! what am I talking about? I determined never to talk Art with you, & here I am doing worse: writing myself an ass.[31]

The most picturesque entries in Furness's journal from the summer of 1855 record his walking tour of the Tyrol and Switzerland. After a description of the Hallstadter See and a dinner of lake trout at the tiny mountain village of Hallstadt, for example, appears this account of a peasant dance at the village inn.

On our way back we stopped at the house of a young peasant named 'Friedel,' who without any instruction has learned to carve little nicknacks very prettily out of the variegated stones found in the neighborhood; hearing that he played the Zither, I requested him to play a little for our benefit. We went up into his house which was an admirable specimen of the better class of peasants' dwellings. He played two or three tunes when I proposed that he should bring his Zither down to the Wirthshaus & see if he couldn't get up a dance & a song. This he consented to do, & after we had returned in a few minutes he made his appearance with half a dozen comrades, all peasants, some of them dressed in their picturesque costume, a green felt hat with feathers in it, black jackets, red waistcoats, leather breeches, bare knees, white stockings & shoes. I ordered beer for the crowd, & drank their healths, the music struck up, & two or three damsels making their appearance, the Hostess, the pretty Kellnerin, & one or two others, the men took their partners & commenced a Styerisch dance. There was nothing boisterous or rude about it; on the contrary everything was dignified in the extreme. The men put both their arms around the waists of the maidens, while the latter placed their hands on the shoulders of the former, then they commenced turning round not lifting the feet from the ground but sliding & keeping admirable time to the music. After walzing round the room two or three times the partners separated, the men going to the centre, &, clapping their hands to the music sang a verse of some song about 'a Bua und sein Deandel,' then joining their giggling partners, who had been walking around them in a circle, they twirled them round four or five times by holding the hand of the damsel above her head, & so making her perform the revolutions. After this the dance proceeded as before. After the dance the men refreshed themselves with beer, & lighting their pipes joined in song after song that young Friedel would strike up. Dance & song alternated & the men apeared to enjoy themselves highly. As for myself I have seldom passed an evening so entertaining & so altogether new and delicious. It was like the evenings that you read of in story books & see represented on the stage. At about twelve we left them over fresh mugs of beer to finish the evening as they chose.[32]

At Giesbach near Interlaken, Furness and Blight discovered two other Cambridge friends—Charlie Upham and Wilder Dwight—and after a quick trip by Furness to Paris and Havre to see Will off to Philadelphia, the expanded company continued down the Rhine together, reaching Paris in late October. Blight and Furness took rooms in the Cité d'Autin and quickly fell into their former routine, rising early, correcting excercises with a French teacher, reading and studying through the afternoon, and meeting their friends in the evening.

> In the course of the evening Dwight & Upham always drop in & we recount to each other the adventures of the day. We four fellows form what has long since been christened the 'Giessbach Club.' I don't think that four fellows ever got along more amicably than we do. There is just enough individuality in each to give a variety without discord. Upham full of simpleheartedness & puns, susceptibility & 'bon mots.' Dwight logical, precise & a vein of fun withal. Blight with a keen relish for humour, gentle conscientious, sits by quaking at times with laughter & at times deeply interested in discussions on European History, (which has been our standard topic of conversation for the last four or five months). 'Lastum sed non leastum,' as Binney used to say of himself, comes your humble servant, who sits blinking at the fire & smoking ferociously to give an air of sociability to the whole scene. Home news is always detailed, often extracts from home letters read. Sometimes all of us are seized with an attack of 'alloverness' & a little punch proves our panacea. The other night I brought before the notice of the club Haydens Life & read aloud in it for nigh three hours, to the interest of all. Such is the Giesbach Club, an excellent institution, as you can readily see, for four young men whose morals are forming, in this 'Vanity Fair.'[33]

Instead of spending the entire winter in Paris, however, Blight wished to see more of the Mediterranean. Accordingly after much discussion December and January saw Furness, Blight, Upham, and Dwight travelling by coach across Spain through Madrid, Toledo, Seville, Cadiz, and Granada. Crossing from Gibralter to Tangiers, they sailed east to Malta and Cairo, where after hiring a guide and inspecting the Pyramids, they continued their journey on horseback to Jerusalem and Damascus. From Beirut they sailed to Constantinople and across the Black Sea to the Crimea to retrace the charge of the light and heavy brigades while British and French troops still occupied the area. By June 1856, after viewing the monuments and ruins of Greece, Blight and Furness were again installed in their rooms in Paris. They visited the cathedrals at Chartres, Rouen, Beauvais, and Amiens, then crossed the Channel to England where they met Blight's family. While Blight traveled with them through the Rhine Valley and Switzerland, Furness returned to Paris again to work on his French during August, engaging two French teachers and voraciously reading Balzac, Dumas, Hugo, and Rabelais, before joining Blight again in Milan on September 14. "As for my knowledge of French," he later wrote, "I can by no means be called a master of the language. I can understand nearly everything that I hear, & can slowly reply, & the reply will generally speaking, be grammatical; but it will require long practice before I am perfectly fluent. I can speak French but can't talk it. I can read it with, I think, full as much ease as German."[34] By October 1856, Milan, Padua, and Florence behind them, Blight and Furness made their way once again from Paris to London to Liverpool and sailed for home just over two years after they had left Philadelphia.

Throughout the summer Furness's thoughts had turned and returned to what he would do when he arrived home. Having already determined somehow to study law, he had written during the spring to Professor Parsons to apply for the post of librarian at the Harvard Law School, hoping thereby to finance his return to Cambridge. When he discovered in July that the position had been filled for the next year, he wrote immediately to President Walker to inquire about any vacant proctorships in the college and to his father to inquire about "any young men who are in need of a highly moral & intellectual guide."[35] A proctorship was held open for him until September 1; however, the news did not reach Furness in Paris until September 4. Furness's father, however, met with greater success and arranged for Horace to tutor Edwin Farnham, son of one of his wealthy parishioners, and to prepare him for Harvard at a yearly salary of $600. Still with doubts about the arrangement, but for lack of a better course, Furness agreed and wrote from Paris on October 8, "Bring on your Ned Farnhams & your six hundreds a year! If conscientious devotion to his son is what Mr. F. desires, I trust he will never have reason to complain."[36] And so he arrived home on his twenty-third birthday, having forewarned his family of what to expect.

> You mustn't expect to see the *spiritual* young gentleman as delineated by Will's enthusiastic pencil, but a coarse, overgrown, freckled, small red haired fellow, with a brusque manner & bushy red

whiskers—hitching in his sentences & gait, & after the first burst of welcome taciturn, & if talkative inclined to snarl & to be peevish, intensely selfish & inordinately conceited. Such is the person whom you are to address as son & brother & try to love for the sake of old lang syne. Bear with me kindly at first & I will do my best to become more gentle & civilised.[37]

A PHILADELPHIA LAWYER

Shall Kate be my wife?—So please you—I am content.
—Henry V 5.2.351

We will have these things set down by lawful counsel.
—Cymbeline 1.4.178

Furness was still listed as a teacher in the 1859 *City Directory*, but how long he continued to tutor Edward Farnham, who was graduated from Harvard in 1866, and how many other pupils he had remain uncertain. During the winter of 1857 both Furness and Blight did give up the idea of returning to Cambridge and decided to study law together in Philadelphia. Attracted by the antislavery sentiments of prominent Philadelphia lawyer William Meredith, Furness arranged to read law in his office. A leader of the Philadelphia bar, Meredith had served as president of the select council of Philadelphia from 1834 to 1849 and secretary of the treasury under President Taylor in 1850, and was appointed Attorney General of Pennsylvania in 1861. The Philadelphia District Court Law Students'

40

Register bears the signature of Furness on June 15, 1857, followed by that of Blight on September 7. Two years later during October and November 1859 the *Legal Intelligencer* announced that they were ready to face the Board of Examiners. On 19 November, on motion of Meredith in District Court Furness was "admitted to practice of an attorney & Counsellor of this Court."[1] This action was followed two days later by his admission to the Court of Common Pleas. Furness opened his law office at 520 Walnut Street, where he was listed for the next sixteen years in the *City Directory* as an attorney and counsellor at law.

In May 1858, after his first year of study, Furness had become engaged to Helen Kate Rogers, daughter of Evans Rogers, a wealthy hardware merchant and long-time trustee of the Unitarian Church. After Furness's law practice had been established, the couple set their wedding date for June 12, 1860, with William Henry Furness conducting the service as he had for Evans Rogers thirty years before. After a honeymoon trip to New York, Horace and Kate settled into 222 West Washington Square with her father, her mother having been dead since 1852. For a brother-in-law Furness gained Fairman Rogers, Professor of Civil Engineering at the University of Pennsylvania and, since 1858, Dean of the Faculty of the Department of Mines, Arts, and Manufactures. For the first happy months life revolved peacefully around Washington Square, 1426 Pine Street, and Fairman and Rebecca's home on West Rittenhouse Square. Furness settled into the routine of drawing up wills and deeds, and at the Unitarian Church he became Superintendent of the Sunday School, a position he held for the next fifteen years. Neither legal profession nor marriage had fairly begun, however, before the rising turbulence of abolition and the election of Abraham Lincoln swept the nation and the Furness family into civil war.

During the early 1850s, while Horace studied in Cambridge and travelled in Europe, William Henry Furness had preached with increasing conviction against slavery. In 1852, with Lucretia Mott he travelled to Concord, attempting in vain to persuade Emerson to lecture in an antislavery course in Philadelphia, although by the end of that year Emerson did begin to speak out against slavery and on February 8, 1855, did lecture before the Philadelphia Antislavery Society.

Furness also took direct action, defying the Fugitive Slave Law and aiding runaway slaves on their escape northward to Canada. William Still, secretary of the General Vigilance Committee of the Pennsylvania Anti-Slavery Society, testified in 1872 to Furness's support of the underground railroad:

> Dr. Furness came into the cause when it was in its infancy, and had few adherents. From that time till the day of its triumph he was one with it, sharing in all its trials and vicissitudes. In the operations of the Vigilance Committee he took the liveliest interest. Though not in form a member he was one of its chief colaborers. He brought it material aid continually, and was one of its main reliances for outside support. His quick sympathies were easily touched and when touched were sure to prompt him to corresponding action. He would listen with moistened eyes to a tale of outrage, and go away saying never a word. But the story of wrong would work upon him; and through him upon others. His own feelings were communicated to his friends, and his friends would send gifts to the Committee's treasury. A wider spread sympathy would manifest itself in the community, and the general interests of the cause be visibly promoted. It was in the latter respect, that of moral cooperation, that Dr. Furness's services were most valuable. After hearing a harrowing recital, whether he would or not, it became the burden of his next Sunday's sermon.[2]

At the trials held when fugitive slaves were arrested or black citizens of Philadelphia kidnapped and abducted, Furness encountered such danger and threats that parishioners on several occasions came to church with loaded pistols ready to defend him. The fear was not altogether unfounded, for Horace later revealed that President Buchanan's Cabinet had discussed the possibilities of indicting his father for treason for counselling disobedience to the Fugitive Slave Law or, failing that, of inciting the increasingly violent proslavery mob to destroy the church. Only the strong disapproval of Judge Kane, United States District Judge of Pennsylvania, to whom the matter was referred, had quashed the case.[3]

Furness also formed during these years a close friendship with the abolitionist Senator from Massachusetts Charles Sumner. Furness had written to congratulate Sumner on his election in April 1850 and again in August 1851 after Sumner's eloquent oration attacking the constitutionality of the Fugitive Slave Law and moving its repeal, a motion that was voted down in the Senate forty-seven to three. On May 20, 1855, after condemning the violence in Kansas and attacking the Kansas-Nebraska Bill that would allow these states to choose for themselves whether to accept or abolish slavery, Sumner was assaulted on the Senate floor and caned into insensibility by Preston Brooks, House member from South Carolina. As soon as Sumner had recovered enough to travel, he sought refuge in the Furness home in Philadelphia and put himself under the medical care of Furness's son-in-law Dr. Caspar Wister. Although his flesh wounds had healed, he suffered from pressure on the brain, weakness in the spine, and great nervous sensibility. When he arrived in Philadelphia on 9 July, Dr. Wister described his affliction as follows:

> A condition of extreme nervous exhaustion, his circultion feeble, and in fact every vital power alarmingly sunken. At that time his steps were feeble and tottering, as in extreme old age; he complained of constant pain in the lower back and lower extremities,—in the latter it was a tired and weary sensation, and he had a sense of constriction and pressure about the head. At that time his pulse was quick and small, appetite languid, and his sleep broken, disturbed, and unrefreshing. All the above conditions were heightened by exertion either mental or physical.[4]

After trying the sea air of Cape May at the cottage of Furness's brother James and in August the more bracing climate of the Allegheny Mountains where he was visited by Furness, Sumner again returned to Philadelphia and remained there until late October, a guest of James Furness and a patient of Caspar Wister. Although reelected in March 1857, he left Washington in December, unable to serve because of his continuing disability. During the next two years of recuperation and for many years to follow, when Sumner passed through Philadelphia on his way to Washington or home to Boston, he frequently visited the Furness home.

In October 1859, John Brown's abortive attempt to spark a slave uprising and his raid on the government arsenal at Harper's Ferry, Virginia, provoked further antislavery activity from Furness. On Sunday morning, October 23, and again on Thanksgiving Day Furness preached about the affair and on Sunday, November 27, solicited contributions from his congregation to aid Brown's family. That evening he wrote to Will: "We had a fine church full on Thanksgiving Day & John Brown's wife was present, but I did not know it till I saw her after Service. I was glad I didn't, as I was under no manner of constraint. What the sermon was, you may learn from this week's Anti-Slavery Standard in which it will be printed."[5] On December 2, the day of Brown's execution, at a turbulent public prayer meeting held in Philadelphia's National Hall Furness gave the invocation and read a eulogy of Brown, interrupted by the hissing and hooting of Southern medical students who tried to break up the meeting. That night in his journal Horace wrote: "December 2nd, 1859. John Brown's last night alive. What a dreadful time. Nor can I analize my feelings. My reason is a hundred times convinced that he is really the man of all Americans to be more envied than commiserated. . . . Where will it end? I feel that with the twelfth stroke of tonight's bell this union or slavery ceases. Perhaps I may never live to trace the connected chain of events, but that some future Tacitus with keen-sighted vision will mark the second of December as the Era I have not the shadow of a doubt."[6]

After the execution Brown's body, accompanied by his wife and Hector Tyndale, was immediately hurried northward by train to Brown's home in North Elba, New York, to avoid the possiblity of mob violence. The body was to be removed from the train in Philadelphia, taken to an undertaker and prepared for burial, and then returned to the train to finish its journey. Long before the train arrived, however, a large, hostile crowd had gathered at the Broad and Prime Streets Station, necessitating a change in plans. Years later Horace related the scene in his *Historical Address*:

We were awaiting the train which was bearing northward the heroic martyr's body after it had been cut down from the gallows at Harper's Ferry. The Southern trains then entered the city at Broad and Prime Streets. Traffic and travel on that route from Virginia was suspended during some hours to give swift passage to a freight car bearing its tragic freight, with a single car attached bearing John Brown's widow and Hector Tyndale. A large and excited crowd, which the police had difficulty in controlling, gathered and jostled at every opening of the large station, into which there was no one admitted but Mr. Miller McKim [leader of the Philadelphia Anti-Slavery Society], my father, and myself,—these, with Mayor Henry and the Chief of Police were alone in that vast, cold, silent station (there may have been one or two others, but I do not remember them). The train was an hour late, and that weary, weary hour I walked with my poor father on my arm up and down that long, echoing platform I dared only now and then to look into his blanched face. Occasionally a few words were exchanged with Mr. McKim, whose face was as white as my father's. . . . At last in the far distance we discerned the train, and silently awaited its gradual drawing in to the station. As soon as it came to a stop, Hector Tyndale alighted. Never can I forget the excitement under which that brave, gallant fellow labored. He rushed to my father, exclaiming, and waving his arms, 'A miracle has happened! Dr Furness, a miracle has happened! The earth never opened to swallow up those fiends!' 'Control yourself, my boy. Calm yourself,' said my father, putting his hand gently on his shoulder. Then we entered the freight car, and there on the floor lay the long, rough box containing John Brown's body, just as it was when cut down from the gallows. A consultation was held and it was decided, in view of the intense excitement of the crowd on all sides of the station, not to take the body to an undertaker's, as had been at first arranged. The Mayor and Chief of Police dreaded an outbreak of the mob, which might prove to be with great difficulty controlled. Accordingly the crowd outside were deceived by a closely guarded, empty hearse which was rapidly driven away. And then, when all was quiet, the box was placed in a furniture car, and taken to Walnut Street wharf, on the way northward to its eternal rest at North Elba.[7]

As the South edged toward seccession and the nation toward civil war, both antislavery and proslavery demonstrations bordered on violence in Philadelphia. Five days after Brown's execution a "Great Union Meeting" was held on December 7, 1859, to counter the public demonstration for Brown. Attacking Furness and other Brown sympathzers, the organizers reminded the public that "Philadelphia has always been loyal to the Union. Her business relations with all sections of the country are such as to interweave her interests with those of the South as well as the North. Her prosperity is dependent upon domestic peace and harmony."[8] Two weeks after Brown's execution on December 16, when George William Curtis arrived at the Furness home to stay while speaking at National Hall on "The Present Aspect of the Slavery Question," Mayor Henry, fearing a riot, pleaded with Curtis in the interest of public safety not to speak.

Curtis consulted with Furness, who declared, 'If it costs the lives of all of us, we ought to go on.' The meeting proceeded as scheduled, but not before the police had arrested the ringleaders of the mob, including two Georgia medical students, both armed with loaded revolvers. All were placed in the cellar of the hall as a deterrent to the rioters' firing the building.[9]

That same morning, in a sermon subsequently printed in the *Evening Bulletin*, Furness had confronted the mob violence and urged his congregation to prepare to face death, if need be, for the sake of truth. "But the trouble cannot be escaped," reads the sermon in part.

It must come. But we can put it off. By annihilating free speech; by forbidding the utterance of a word in the pulpit and by the press, for the rights of man; by hurling back into the jaws of oppression, the fugitive gasping for his sacred liberty; by recognizing the right of one man to buy and sell other men; by spreading the blasting curse of despotism over the whole soil of the nation, you may allay the brutal frenzy of a handful of southern slave-masters; you may win back the cotton States to cease from threatening you with secession, and to plant their feet upon your necks, and so evade the trouble that now menaces us. Then you may live on the few years that are left you, and perhaps—it is not certain—we may be permitted to make a little more money and die in our beds. But no, friends, I am mistaken. We cannot put the trouble off. Or, we put in its present shape, only that it may take another and more terrible form. If, to get rid of the present alarm, we concede all that makes it worth while to live—and nothing less will avail—perhaps those who can deliberately make such a concession, will not feel the degredation, but, stripped of all honor and manhood, they may eat as heartily and sleep as soundly as ever. But the degradation is not the less, but the greater, for our un-consciousness of it. The trouble which we shall then bring upon ourselves, is a trouble in comparison with which the loss of all things but honor is a glorious gain, and a violent death for right's sake on the scaffold, or by the hands of a mob, peace and joy for victory. . . . Prepared to confront the crisis like men, let us with all possible calmness endeavor to take the measure of the calamity that we dread. God knows I have no desire to make light of it. But I affirm, that never since the world began, was there a grander cause for which to speak, to suffer and to die, than the cause of these free States, as against that of the States now rushing upon Secession.[10]

When South Carolina's troops fired on Fort Sumter in April 1861 and the long abolitionist struggle turned into Civil War, President

Lincoln immediately called for seventy-five thousand men to serve for three months. Philadelphia streets soon filled with the sounds of marching recruits learning to drill, and both Horace and his brother Frank joined the enlistment lines. Frank served in the Sixth Pennsylvania Cavalry, where he rose to the rank of captain and later received a Congressional Medal of Honor for rescuing a besieged outpost by dashing through enemy fire with a box of ammunition on his head. Horace, however, was rejected by every branch of the army because of incipient deafness caused by scarlet fever contracted shortly after his return from Europe.[11] Little did he know how that deafness would affect his later life; that April, though, it simply frustrated his aroused patriotism. Through the summer of 1861 he did serve as secretary to the Commission for Investigating the Alleged Army Frauds, appointed by Pennsylvania Governor Curtin to inquire into the mismanagement of food and clothing supplies, and eventually he found a permanent place of service in the United States Sanitary Commission.

At the outset of the war the army lacked sufficient surgeons; hospitals lacked blankets, clothing, and sufficient medical supplies. No efficient relief organization like the Red Cross existed to supply the lack, leaving exclusive and inefficient state organizations like the New York State Relief Association to care for its own soldiers. Thus in June 1861 President Lincoln appointed the Sanitary Commission, patterned after British medical relief efforts in the Crimean War, "to inquire into all the causes which might affect the health, and therefore the efficiency of the Army, and to advise the authorities in regard to the proper measures for the removal of such causes."[12] The Sanitary Commission supplied emergency food, clothing, and medical supplies on the battlefields, established a directory of all wounded soldiers recuperating in hospitals in and around Washington, and with a staff of ten or twelve physicians and surgeons supervised the inspection of the sanitary conditions in military camps, scrutinizing the water supply, drainage, ventilation, ambulance stores, surgeons' equipment—in short, everything from tasting the food to examining the privies and dumps—and completing for each camp a twenty-six-page Camp Inspection Return containing nearly two hundred questions. The Philadelphia Branch of the Sanitary Commission was formed on November 7, 1861, and in December opened a depository for supplies. Its relief work absorbed the energies of Horace and his friend Atherton Blight, who served throughout the war on the Commission's Protective War Claim and Pension Agency which sought to prevent fraud in the collection of remunerations.

After the battle of Antietam in September 1862, Furness hurried to the battlefield where he worked as a special relief agent and hospital inspector for the Sanitary Commission. "I broke off my letter yesterday in a great hurry owing to the ambulance having driven up to take me to a hospital some two miles off where the Commission want some investigations made," he wrote to his wife from Sharpsburg on September 25.

> The road lay directly in the path of the frightful battle of a week ago. The stand was made by the rebels first in a cornfield & then in a wood at the crest of a hill. I came to the wood first. It was ghastly and ghostly, although all the dead have been buried, yet every tree & branch proclaims deadly struggle; guns, bayonets, cartouche boxes, haversacks lay all around in frightful confusion, huge branches of trees were twisted off and hanging by splinters, while the trunks were everywhere scarred by minié balls. I must reserve description for word of mouth. I can only give you the barest skeleton of my day. I went to the hospital & reached there as it was coming on to rain, & had a furious fight with two rebel women & two men for not allowing us to bring the poor wounded into their house into rooms unoccupied. Whew! I emptied a whole hogshead of abuse & wrath on them & told them we'd take the lower stories & they might go up into the second story, & then if we wanted that we'd take it too & they might go up on to the roof, & we'd follow them there if need were & they might jump off & they actually cried & tears rolled down their cheeks at the thought of getting their bare floors dirty. I told them I had never seen such monsters, &c., &c. They said they were good Union until I so soundly berated them, when they showed their fangs & said they wished the Confederates had got us all.[13]

On October 3, Furness received permission from Dr. Lewis Steiner, Sanitary Inspector for Northern Maryland, to visit hospitals in and around Frederick, and for the next ten days busily distributed wagonloads of towels, coats, pantaloons, and barrels of porter to general hospitals and field hospitals overflowing with wounded Union soldiers and lacking both basic supplies and any efficient method of organizing and reporting the casualties. On October 10 he wrote,

Yesterday after dinner Charles, our driver, came in & said that there was a poor woman sitting on the front steps crying. I at once went out & found that it was a poor heart-broken German mother from New York who had come on in search of her wounded son; she had just reached here about an hour before & had instantly begun her weary, sad task. She had only asked timidly at the door of one or two hospitals, & receiving a careless negative from an indifferent sentry or nurse her desolation and woe seemed to overpower her, & she was crying in all the bitterness of a Mother's grief. I told her to cheer up & that if he was in Frederick we'd find him; so I started out with her, & around town we went, and after about two hours, out of the twenty-one hospitals we had visited twenty, & I had in my secret heart given up all hopes & was trying to persuade the poor worn Mother that her son had been transferred to Philadelphia, when we approached the last on the list. I generally made her wait outside while I went in & examined the register, & how her eyes hung upon my lips when I came out & even to the very last her face was full of hope until I said, 'no; no such name as Charles Metzger in this hospital,' & then she'd hurry away almost in advance of me in her impatience to reach the next hospital, without knowing where it was. I walked fast, not only to suit her eagerness, but the afternoon was waning, & once I said to her, 'Aren't you very tired?' She had travelled night & day from New York & had scarcely eaten since she left home. 'Oh, no,' said she, 'I shall not be tired when I see my son.' At the last hospital, the U.S. Barracks, on the list among the 'M's' there stood 'Metzger Charles 4th N.Y.' My heart really beat quickly at the sight of it, and after receiving the accurate descriptions of the tent & ward where he was to be found, I came out to meet this intense yearning Mother's face, which, although quite plain, had already begun to assume an expression that strikes feelings lying deep down in the heart; my face was as impassive as hitherto, for I was really afraid of the effect upon her. 'Mrs. Metzger,' I said, 'we have got to the end of our journey.' Quite Delphic, you perceive, in its ambiguous meaning, but my immobility of face was all lost upon her & she clutched at the true meaning & seizing me right by the arm ejaculated, 'Where is he? take me to him!' 'I shall not take you to your son until you grow calmer. He lies in one of those tents, & to see you so overcome as you are now might prove his death.' I kept the poor thing for at least three minutes waiting until I thought she'd rub her eyes out in trying to stop her tears & that I'd better take her in with her eyes in her head instead of in her pocket handkerchief. So I entered the tent & called out, 'Is Charles Metzger here?' No answer; I walked on a few steps & then repeated my question; then there came, 'Yes, I'm here.' I turned round for the

Mother; there she stood a few steps behind me, she'd caught sight of the handsome face & with arms outstretched, she cried, 'Mein sohn, mein sohn!' 'Why, mother!' was all the boy could say before his mother was covering his face with kisses.[14]

A few days after this incident Furness received notice that he had been elected an Associate Member of the Sanitary Commission, and Frederick Law Olmstead, Secretary and later Chief Executive of the Commission, called him to Washington to propose an expanded assignment: a speaking tour of New England to explain the Sanitary Commission and organize support in the smaller cities and towns for its relief work. Distasteful as such stumping of the countryside with posters and holding meetings in churches and schoolhouses seemed to Furness, he nevertheless found himself in New Haven, Connecticut, on October 28, beginning his canvas of New England with "full authority to organize related and contributing Branches and Relief Associations."[15] From November until June he worked his way through Connecticut, Massachusetts, New Hampshire, New York, and Pennsylvania organizing, smiling, pleading, and arguing until, as he complained to his wife in March, "I verily believe I could introduce myself & the purpose of my visit & a general sketch of the San. Com. in my sleep. It monopolises my thoughts & invades my dreams, damn it, when I want to dream of other things. And the devil of it all is that I know I do it all too well for me to drop it on the score of incompetence."[16] Competing state relief associations and suspicion in every state of a centralized organization based in Washington formed the enemies that Furness faced in town halls, mayors' offices, and parlors across cups of tea with ministers' wives and heads of ladies' societies. After making the rounds of town officials and clergy, securing a meeting place, and generating as much enthusiasm as he could during the day, in the evening Furness would give his speech long since memorized, collect donations and pledges, and organize the leaders of a new chapter of the Commission.

His account of his visit to Springfield in November describes a typical meeting:

It was a stormy night, or rather threatening, very wet & hugely muddy, so that the Church, the largest in Springfield, was not crowded as everyone said it otherwise would have been; the body of it was full the galleries were empty; there must have been betweeen four & five hundred present, full as many men as women. The meeting was opened by a hymn & a prayer,—the latter intensely orthodox in style imploring blessings on every human being absent & present, dead & living, beginning with Adam & ending with me in particular, 'whose wise counsels were to enlighten them this evening.' Then I unfolded San. Com. banner & spoke for an hour and a half. I didn't occupy the pulpit, but stood at the side of the Communion Table. I told them about Gilbert Cheney, the Connecticut brothers, the Mass. Rebel—I ended with Mrs. Metzger whom in public I call Brauner. A great many, in fact all the ladies, cried over the Connecticut brothers, but over Mrs. Metzger, all fell to work, the men as vigorously as the women—the weaker sniffings from the ladies & loud uncompromising blowings from the men almost drowned my voice for several minutes. But seriously, it is grand to see how one touch of nature makes the whole world kin & this story of Mrs Metzger which ends in purest joy always brings tears. I always seize this weak moment to implore them to strengthen the arm of the San. Com.[17]

By June he was tired. Aside from his hectic speaking schedule, he had accompanied Mr. Olmstead to the White House to see President Lincoln on behalf of the Sanitary Commission in November, and in December had rushed to Virginia to assist in removal of the wounded and to distribute emergency supplies, clothing, blankets, and food during the battle of Fredericksburg. With time out only for infrequent visits to Philadelphia, he had preached the cause of the Sanitary Commission with unflagging energy. During June and July 1863, however, the threat of invasion mobilized Philadelphia as Lee's army crossed the Potomac River and marched into southern Pennsylvania. Furness asked to be relieved of a proposed Sanitary Commission canvas of New Jersey and concentrated his subsequent work for the Commission in Philadelphia.

In November 1862, to combat the rising Copperhead sentiment in the city resulting from the succession of Northern reversals, patriotic Philadelphians organized the Union Club, soon changed to the Union League, whose purpose was, to use secretary George Boker's phrase, "to take treason by the throat."[18] Pennsylvania Attorney General William Meredith was elected president, and membership was open to all political parties, limited only by "unqualified loyalty to the Government of the United States, and unwavering support for the suppression of the Rebellion."[19] The clubhouse was established at 1118 Chestnut Street until after the war when the present clubhouse opened at Broad and Sansom. James T. Furness joined on 20 February 1863, followed by Horace on 23 March 1863, and Frank on 17 May 1865, after he returned from the war. In addition to raising and equipping nine regiments, finding employment for returned veterans, and helping to finance the war, the members carried on an effective propaganda campaign through their Civil War Board of Publication. Here Furness volunteered his editorial skills, editing among others one of the pamphlets of Robert Dale Owen, *The Future of the North West in connection with the scheme of Reconstruction without New England*, published in March 1863.

During the winter and spring 1863-1864, the Sanitary Commission sponsored Sanitary Fairs or Exhibitions in the principal cities of the North to raise additional money, beginning with Chicago and continuing with Boston, Cincinnati, Brooklyn, Albany, Buffalo, Cleveland, New York, Baltimore, St. Louis, Washington, and Pittsburgh. Preparation for the Great Central Fair in Philadelphia began in late February 1864, with John Welsh acting as chairman of the executive committee and Furness as recording secretary. Logan Square was chosen as the site for the Fair buildings, and beginning in April workmen erected large structures of wood and canvas covering over two hundred thousand square feet. Running across the square from Eighteenth Street to Logan Street was a great Gothic arch, 540 feet long and 64 feet wide, named Union Avenue. On either side stood large circular buildings, one housing the horticultural department with concentric rings of flowers encircling a lake and a fountain, the other housing a restaurant capable of seating one thousand guests. Extending outward from Union Avenue on either side ran four exhibit halls containing tables and counters for every imaginable exhibit from books and stationery, to clothing, hardware, farm equipment, jewelry, an art gallery, and displays from foreign countries. From the rafters and trees enclosed in the buildings hung banners, flags, and trophies, producing a festive and colorful display.

From February until the Fair opened in June Furness occupied himself with the details of some eighty to ninety committees organized to oversee everything from editing the Fair's newspaper *Our Daily Fare* to ensuring that three steam fire engines with hoses

connected and steam in their boilers stood ready around the clock
in case of fire. Even after the Fair closed, executive committee
meetings in Furness's law office dragged on through August and
September to mop up the details. Other members of the family
joined in the enterprise that absorbed the energies of hundreds of
people. Kate served on the Women's Post Office Committee; William
Henry Furness aided both the Committee on Fine Arts and Newspaper Editorial Corps; and his wife Annis headed the Committee of
Women and worked in the Children's Department. All the effort
came to a climax in the opening ceremonies on June 8, 1864. For the
next three weeks, until the Fair closed its doors on June 28 and the
last remaining goods were sold at auction, an average of 29,510
people streamed through the doors each day, with net proceeds of
$1,010,976.68 for the Sanitary Commission.[20] Even President Lincoln,
accompanied by his wife, visited the Fair on June 16, ironically his
last visit to Philadelphia until April 21, 1865, when Furness joined
other members of the Union League, dressed in dark clothing, white
gloves, and crepe upon the left arm to receive the body of Lincoln at
Independence Hall.

When the guns of the Civil War fell silent at last, a political era
ended for Furness. He had been born into the ranks of the bitter
opponents of slavery in the same year that the Philadelphia Anti-
slavery Society was founded. The battle for abolition had dominated
his earliest political awareness. No political issue in later years—
reconstruction, monopolies, tariffs, the gold standard, even the colonial expansion of the Spanish-American War—aroused or excited
him. Always he looked backward to the one great political issue of
his time, forever shrouded for him in idealism and principle. "When
you say that there is no romance in this side of the world, do you not
forget slavery?" he asked Charles Eliot Norton in July 1908, and
added, "The depths of that romance have hardly yet been
sounded."[21] Just months before his death in a letter to John Jay
Chapman, who was then contemplating a biography of William
Lloyd Garrison, Furness returned to the same idea.

Now is the time to discern the romance of it all. For blend it as you
may with religion, patriotism, or what you will, it remains thus far in
our history as our only true romance. The Revolution was tainted
with taxation, and touched the pocket—but the Abolition movement

from the scene of Garrison dragged through the streets of Boston by a mob of Boston 'gentlemen' to the twisting of our flag on the ruins of Sumter, including the John Brown episode,—here lies our great Romance.[22]

And at the end of that romantic quest Furness saw liberty and freedom affirmed. In 1863, he wrote to Edmund Muspratt, "To me the struggle is unspeakably grand, it has given me a country. From the first uprising of the people after the attack on Fort Sumter I have been joyous, proud, happy & exhilarated."[23] Thirty years later, in spite of all the intervening imperfections and failures of Reconstruction, he still believed in the ideal.

Then too remember that I am an old Abolitionist, and that I have been humiliated by the sight of fugitive slaves sent back from freedom into slavery by our courts—when every sense of manliness, of justice, of liberty seemed utterly dead in the nation. I didn't know what it was to have a country, until the first gun of the Rebellion was fired at Sumter, and a whole nation to be proud of sprang into existence here at the North."[24]

Beside this no other political issue seemed significant. During the presidential campaign of 1892 that pitted Benjamin Harrison against Grover Cleveland, for example, Furness confided to Sir Edward Strachey:

"After the Abolition of Slavery, for which I worked all that I could, no deep, moral issues were left to us. Tariff or Free Trade touched only the pocket. Both Cleveland and Harrison are excellent men, and so evenly balanced that I am forced to find a preponderance for the former in the possession of a charming 'winsome lady.' However, I shall not cast any vote at all, having agreed to pair off with my father, who, sturdy, uncompromising Republican that he is, would of course vote for Harrison."[25]

Even in the midst of the stirring events of Abolition and Civil War, however, life for the Furness family continued. The nursery at 222 West Washington Square was busily occupied with Horace and Kate's first son, Walter Rogers, born on June 7, 1861, followed by Horace Howard, Jr., born on January 24, 1865, and William Henry III born on August 18, 1866. Meanwhile, Horace's brother William Henry, Jr. had married before the war on October 3, 1859, and with his wife Hannah had lived for four years in Germantown before moving in 1863 to Cambridge. There, after a short illness, he died unexpectedly on March 4, 1867 at the age of thirty-eight. From 1848 until he left Philadelphia in 1863, his pictures had appeared almost annually in exhibitions at the Pennsylvania Academy of the Fine Arts, and before his death he had achieved some distinction as a portrait artist, having painted such well-known personages as Charles Sumner, Lucretia Mott, Emerson, and his own father. An obituary appearing in *The Nation* for April 18, 1867, noted that "his pictures exhibited in the New York spring exhibitions since 1860 have all been worthy of study. The portrait of a lady in the exhibition of 1865 was perhaps the most noticed and most admired; but other portraits have shown as admirable qualities and as great technical skill. He was in many respects the best portrait painter we had."[26] After William's sudden death it was left to Frank Furness to develop the family's artistic talent. He had begun his training before the war in the office of Philadelphia architect John Frazer, and after being mustered out of the Pennsylvania Cavalry in 1865, had continued his study in the New York studio of Richard Morris Hunt. In 1866, he returned to Philadelphia, marrying Fanny Fassitt on March 8, 1866, and setting up his own studio at 428 Walnut Street. In 1868, he joined with John Frazer and George W. Hewitt to form the firm of Fraser, Furness & Hewitt beginning a long line of public buildings in Philadelphia that fused elements of the neoclassical and gothic revival.

As the Sanitary Commission business dwindled after the war, Furness's law practice, limited by his increasing deafness, did not exhaust his capacity for work, and in his free time he turned to editing. With his father he read proofsheets of *The Unconscious Truth of the Four Gospels* (1868), and with his sister Annis he read proofsheets of her translation of *The Countess Gisela* for J.B. Lippincott Company. More significantly for his later career he joined with Philadelphia lawyer A.I. Fish to prepare the fourth edition of *The Practice in Civil Actions and Proceedings in the Supreme Court of Pennsylvania, in the District Court and Court of Common Pleas for the City and County of Philadelphia, and in the Courts of the United States*, the standard Philadelphia legal reference work originally edited by Francis Troubat and William Haly. Fish had first intended to issue the fourth edition in 1861 but, prevented by the war, delayed publication until 1867-1868. For the first volume Furness read proof-sheets, and for the second volume he prepared and rewrote the chapters on "Ejectment," on "Actions by and against Particular Persons," on "Foreign Attachment," and on "Domestic Attachment." From January until April he read proofsheets, compiled the table of contents, and prepared the index, finishing with Kate the last proof-sheet on April 7. "The instant that it, the hard incessant day & night toil of six months, was finished," reads his journal entry for this day, "Katie & myself embraced & promised each other a lobster salad. Sleepless night, haunted by work."[27] Although Fish expressed his gratitude to Furness in the preface to the second volume, years later Furness recalled, "The second volume of Troubat and Haly was almost wholly my work although Fish in the Preface gave me credit for only two or three chapters. I always regretted that I did not insist on having my name on the title page or back."[28]

Furness had originally met Fish shortly after his admission to the Philadelphia bar. Twelve years his senior, Fish had acted as his mentor and introduced him to such Philadelphia lawyers as William Ingham and Judge Sharswood of the Philadelphia District Court. The two soon had associated socially as well as professionally. On March 15, 1864, they had joined with a dozen other graduates of Harvard living in Philadelphia to found the Harvard Club of Philadelphia. Designed to renew their college days and to keep in touch with the University, the club at first had its own rooms and frequent meetings but eventually became an annual dinner club. Much more significant than their shared love of Harvard, however, was their shared love of Shakespeare and the Shakspere Society of Philadelphia where Furness had first met Fish in November 1860.

MONTAGUES, CAPULETS, AND
A SHAKESPEARIAN FEUD

We few, we happy few, we band of brothers.
                                   —*Henry V* 4.3.60

In November 1860, when Furness was admitted to membership in the Shakspere Society of Philadelphia, the Society was in its ninth winter. The charter members of the society—Fish, Garrick Mallery, Jr., Furman Sheppard, and Samuel C. Perkins—had first begun meeting in October 1852 at Fish's law office, No. 6, Mercantile Library Building, where they escaped the technicalities of law study and practice by reading through a Shakespeare play every Thursday evening, topped off with crackers and cheese and washed down with a glass of ale. These Shakspere Brothers, or Shakspere Apostles as they first called themselves, also instituted in that first winter the Annual Commemoration, held not on the anniversary of Shakespeare's birth but during the last week of December "because of the

fact that terrapin, canvas-back ducks and venison then abound,
whereas there is no good thing edible to be found in April."[1] By 1858
the Shakspere Society included more than a dozen members, and
officers were elected: Fish as Dean, Garrick Mallery as Secretary,
Huizinga Messchert as Treasurer, and William Ingham as Chairman
of the Library Committee. Now meeting every alternate Tuesday in
the Dean's office, the Society had settled into a more systematic
study of the plays, reading only one act in an evening and aided by
some six hundred volumes and pamphlets belonging to the Dean.
During the next winter the Society also began the custom of preparing and reading papers on subjects connected with the season's
readings. Into this society of literary and convivial lawyers, Furness
was introduced by Garrick Mallery on 13 November 1860, and two
weeks later on 27 November was admitted to membership by unanimous consent.

Immediately proposing his brother Will and his friend Atherton
Blight for membership, Furness brought to the Shakspere Society
exuberance and enthusiasm. His first recorded motion instructed
the Library Committee to prepare the Bill of Fare and order the
annual dinner, which a month later on 27 December called forth this
comment from the secretary:

> The exercises, both convivial and literary, were more lively than at
> any previous Annual, and certainly were more protracted, as the
> adjournment was with difficulty resolved upon after the more
> scrupulous Benedicks among the brethren had become horrified at
> the flight of time. The exact hour arrived at without any 'secession'
> from the table may not be recorded, but a hint may be taken from the
> fact that after the sumptuous repast had been thoroughly appreci-
> ated, sufficient time elapsed for a certain nameless member to grow
> enhungered again, and to require additional viands in the shape of
> raw oysters to sustain life before he would retire to rest.[2]

Furness also enthusiastically entered into the literary work of the
Society. During January 1861 the reading of *King Lear* began. On
January 19, he was appointed to a committee with Mallery and
Ingham to report upon the four folios, and on March 26 he read two
papers on the German editions of *King Lear*. In April, when the
Society took up the Sonnets, Furness reported first on Charles
Armitage Brown's *Shakespeare's Autobiographical Poems* and then
on Chalmers and Boaden's theories respecting the Sonnets.

During the next season the Society read *Julius Caesar* and *Othello* and then spent two years on *Hamlet*. The Society had now entered upon serious study of Shakespeare. "Every member," recalled Furness some twenty-five years later,

> had a copy of the Variorum of 1821, which we fondly believed had gathered under each play all Shakespearian lore worth preserving down to that date. What had been added since that year was scattered in many different editions, and in numberless volumes dispersed over the whole domain of literature. To gather these stray items of criticism was real toil, real but necessary if we did not wish our labour over the text to be in vain. It constantly happened,— remember it was before the days of Booth's 'Reprint,' Staunton's 'Photolithograph,' Ashbee's Facsimiles of Quartos, or of the Cambridge Shakespeare,—it constantly happened that we spent a whole evening over a difficult passage (and as we were all members of the Bar they were battles royal) only to find that the whole question had been discussed and settled by learned men elsewhere. Hence it dawned on us that if we were to pursue our studies with any of the ardor of original research we should exactly know all that had been said or suggested by our predecessors.[3]

To this end the Dean assigned to each member responsibility for the various editions and critical works at the beginning of each season. During the reading of *Julius Caesar* Furness studied Warburton's edition, Johnson's edition of 1765, and Delius's German edition. In May 1862, the Society concluded the reading of *Othello*, and the Dean assigned the editions for the next season's reading of *Hamlet*. Furness again took Delius's edition and the 1604 Quarto.

That summer, as Furness and his wife spent their usual vacation in the country near Media, the idea of a new variorum edition of Shakespeare was born. Preparing for the coming study of *Hamlet*, Furness made during July a large workbook, some eight inches thick, consisting of the text and notes of Karl Elze's 1857 edition pasted on larger blank pages. To these he added in his own hand textual variants and comments on the notes. This bulging volume he seems to have abandoned for a second, more comprehensive experiment, recalled years later in a letter to William James Rolfe:

> As for the time when I began to work over Shakespeare and study him with zeal, it began in '62 or '63 when I made a mighty Variorum

Hamlet, cutting out the notes of five or six editions, besides the Variorum of 1821, and pasting them on a page with a little rivulet of text. 'Twas a ponderous book, of Quarto size and eight or nine inches thick—I took great delight in burning it some years ago. But the work revealed to me that it was high time to begin a new Variorum, that we might start afresh. We are constantly threshing old straw.[4]

The Shakspere Society resumed its meetings in October 1862 with increasing diligence and good fellowship. Furness had been elected secretary on April 22, 1862, and the pages of the Shakspere Society Minutes, now carefully written in his own bold handwriting, whenever he could escape from Sanitary Commission business long enough to return to Philadelphia, record lists of adopted readings as the Society worked through *Hamlet* scene by scene, sifting the evidence for each conjectural emendation and textual variant. In October 1864, when the Society took up the study of *The Tempest*, the members improved upon this method of study by printing the minutes in the intervals between each meeting so that the criticisms and proposed readings could be preserved in permanent form. These minutes, collected in November 1865, were then issued in 1866 as *Notes of Studies on The Tempest: Minutes of the Shakspere Society of Philadelphia for 1864-65*. Printed Privately for the Society, 1866, a volume which one Philadelphia reviewer enthusiastically called "A record . . . of studies and learning, and acumen and wit, and gentle fellowship as beautiful and curious perhaps as any which any country has produced."[5]

Gentle fellowship and wit did prevail. The meager crackers and cheese of the first winter had given way to superabundant oysters and profuse lobster salad, and the glass of ale taken at "a hostel unknown to fame, and since decayed" had been replaced by the Dean's friendly punch bowl "to restore the lost phosphates of the brain." Shakespeare evenings concluded with chairs drawn around the cozy fire, amid the haze of pipes and cigars, and the regular toast of the evening "William Shakspere, gentleman." Meeting now in its own rooms at 735 Walnut Street, the Society had been expanded to include George Allen, the new Professor of Greek and Latin languages at the University of Pennsylvania, Doctor Charles P. Krauth, Judge George Sharswood, as well as the following members of the bar: Richard Ashhurst, Samuel Dickson, Charles Hutchinson, Alexander Johnston, and James Parsons. In this group of cultivated gentlemen and amateur Shakespearians, Furness began work in earnest during the next season's study on the new variorum edition of Shakespeare.

On October 16, 1866 the Shakspere Society began *Romeo and Juliet*. After opening the winter's study with an account of the quartos and folios and a review of the sources of the plot, the Dean made the usual assignment of the editions and critical essays and announced the intention to study some two hundred lines each evening. Furness took responsibility for Mommsen's reprint of the 1599 Quarto, Booth's Reprint of the First Folio, and Delius's Essays, with the other editions apportioned among the remaining members. How long the Shakspere Brothers studied *Romeo and Juliet* cannot be known owing to a break in the Shakspere Society records. When the records do resume on April 23, 1869, the Society had gone on to read *King Lear*, while Furness's journal for August and September 1869 shows him hard at work on the variorum *Romeo and Juliet*.

In October 1869, J.B. Lippincott and Company began to print experimental proofs as Furness tried to decide among different shapes, sizes, and styles of type. "Eight times did I remodel the first twenty pages of that volume," he wrote two years later to C.M. Ingleby. "As it now stands, it seems a task of no special difficulty, but no one who has not tried it, can imagine what entanglements impeded me at every step, and how appalling the mass of my materials loomed up before me."[6] Furness finally settled on different sizes of type for the text, the textual variants, and the commentary. At the top of each page appeared a few lines of the play with each disputed reading resolved according to the majority of editors and Furness's best judgment. Beneath the text in small type came a list of textual variants including in chronological order the editors that had adopted each variant reading. The bottom half of the page was devoted to commentary and explanatory notes from previous editors and critics. This new variorum would supersede the first three variorum editions—Isaac Reed's editions of Johnson and Steevens in 1803 and 1813 and James Boswell the younger's edition of Malone's Shakespeare in 1821—and add to them all the critical commentary of the following fifty years. Before this plan was finally settled upon, however, the proposed new variorum had provoked a public quarrel with the prestigious English editor of the Cambridge Shakespeare, William Aldis Wright of Trinity College, Cambridge, a quarrel that fortunately ended amicably and resulted in Furness's friendship with Wright and with another eminent English Shakespearian, James Orchard Halliwell-Phillipps.

In January 1870, J.B. Lippincott and Company had announced that the first volume of the *New Variorum Edition of Shakespeare* was in press, and on January 22, 1870 a letter from Furness had appeared in *Notes and Queries* to acquaint the English public with his proposal. Using the Variorum of 1821 as a starting point, Furness had originally intended to print from it the explanatory notes that had been accepted by subsequent editors and add to them any original comments from the same editors. The text and textual variants among the quartos and folios Furness proposed to reprint from the nine-volume Cambridge Shakespeare, published just four years earlier by William George Clark and William Aldis Wright. To these he would add all textual variants of subsequent editors from Rowe's 1709 edition to the present and indicate which editors had adopted or rejected which variants. This use of the Cambridge Shakespeare, which Furness admired so much that he tried to make his own volumes resemble in size and typography those of the Cambridge edition, was clearly intended as a compliment to the clear and precise editing of Clark and Wright.

Wright, however, did not see the compliment, and in the next issue of *The Athenaeum* appeared the following letter charging Furness and Lippincott with literary piracy.

Trinity College,
Cambridge,
Jan. 20, 1870.

I have just received from Messrs. J.B. Lippincott & Co., Philadelphia, a prospectus of a new edition of Shakespeare, of which they announce that the first volume, containing 'Romeo and Juliet,' is in the press. It is to be edited by Mr. Horace Howard Furness, but I hope it is the publishers who are responsible for the prospectus, and not the editor.

The prospectus states: 'The text will be that of the Cambridge editors, and to the textual notes of that edition will be added the various readings of the following editors: Singer (edd. 1 and 2), Knight (edd. 1 and 2), Campbell, Cornwall, Collier (edd. 1 and 2), Verplanck, Hazlitt, Hudson, Ulrici, Delius, Staunton, Dyce (edd. 1 and 2), White, Chambers, Halliwell, Clark, and Keightley. . . . To the literary public we beg leave to state that in this work there will be found not only the textual variations of the quartos and folios as given in the Cambridge edition of Messrs. Clarke (*sic*) and Wright, but also various readings of the different editions since 1821.'

In this statement there is a misrepresentation so gross that, whether intentional or not, I feel bound to protest against it. To have the whole of our hard work thus deliberately appropriated is of itself sufficiently aggravating, but not more than might have been reasonably expected. What I complain of is that Messrs. Lippincott & Co., by their prospectus convey the impression that the Cambridge edition contains only the various readings of the quartos and folios, and does not contain the conjectural emendations of the different editors since 1821, whereas it is impossible to open the book at any page without seeing that our plan includes all these. If they choose to print our notes in full, we are powerless to prevent them, but it would be better that they should say so plainly.

William Aldis Wright [7]

Like other authors in the days before international copyright laws, Wright was anxious to protect the Cambridge Shakespeare from alleged misrepresentation and potential piracy, but he had not reckoned with the Philadelphia lawyers of the Shakspere Society. When *The Athenaeum* with Wright's letter reached Philadelphia two weeks later, Furness and Furman Sheppard, a fellow lawyer and Shakspere Brother, examined the latest English cases of copyright law down to *Cox vs. Land and Water Co.* reported in *The Law Times* of 1 January 1870. Although convinced that the New Variorum as originally conceived could be published in London as lawfully as in Philadelphia, Furness, stung by the insinuation of piracy, resolved to renounce all use of the text of the Cambridge edition, to make his own collation of the quartos and folios, and to answer Wright's charges in *The Athenaeum*.

As the first order of business, Furness drafted a reply to Wright. Speaking as a member of the bar, he set forth in detail the differences between the proposed New Variorum and the Cambridge Edition and argued that the former constituted "(Legally speaking) an entirely new and original work, which is not intended to be, and never can be, a rival or substitute of either the Cambridge edition, or of any other since 1821."[8] Furness then announced his intention to give up the proposed use of the Cambridge editors' notes and text and finished the letter with a long discussion of errors, omissions, and shortcomings that he had discovered in the textual notes of the Cambridge edition. Not expecting the letter to be published in *The Athenaeum* because of its length, Furness asked Lippincott to incorporate the letter in a new publisher's circular, which he then sent to Wright on March 25.

Meanwhile, waiting for Wright's response, Furness began making his own collation of the quartos and folios, keeping a list of discrepancies in the Cambridge edition, in case Wright further attacked him in public. Furness had his own copy of the fourth folio, copies of the second and third folios borrowed from Edwin Forrest, and Staunton's photolithograph of the first folio. For the five quartos of *Romeo and Juliet* Furness relied on Halliwell-Phillipps's facsimiles of the quartos owned by the Shakspere Society. By the middle of March, Furness had compiled a list of some twenty to thirty discrepancies between the textual notes of the Cambridge edition and the facsimiles of the quartos, in addition to other discrepancies between the former and the eighteenth-century editons. Before Furness could be absolutely sure of his ground, however, he had to check the accuracy of his quartos as he was working not from the originals, as Wright had done, but from the facsimiles. As he was to do often in the first years of the New Variorum, Furness turned for help to Fish, who as early as 1865 had been in correspondence with Halliwell-Phillipps concerning purchases for the Shakspere Society library. Presuming upon this acquaintance with a mutual friend, Furness wrote to Halliwell-Phillipps on March 8 and again on March 15, asking him to verify the readings in the original quartos. Thus gathering evidence in his own defense and continuing in his revised plan to provide an original collation of folios, quartos, and early editions, Furness spent the month of March waiting for Wright's reply.

On April 4, 1870 Furness received letters from both Halliwell-Phillipps and Wright. After a hasty check of the original quartos in his possession, Halliwell-Phillipps verfied Furness's readings and assured him that he would be happy to offer any further information necessary, but then cautioned him against attacking Wright's collation of the quartos and folios.

You must bear in mind that hardly any two copies of the same edition are precisely similar, our old printers being constantly in the habit of correcting the forms after small impressions of plays had been issued, keeping the whole play in type. It is quite unsafe, therefore, to conclude that because one original copy varies from the readings given by Mr. Aldis Wright, that the latter is wrong (can Wright ever be wrong?) Thus for example, the reading given in III.iii.160 *learaing*, is almost certainly in the copy used by Mr. Wright, for it is difficult to conceive otherwise such an odd mistake.[9]

From Wright's letter Furness learned that *The Athenaeum* had printed his reply on March 19. Wright explained that Furness's letter had resolved the inference in the publisher's circular that the Cambridge edition contained no record of conjectural emendations since 1821, and he expressed his desire to keep the peace.

To your letter in the Athenaeum of Saturday I have written a reply, of the tone of which I trust you will have no reason to complain. There have been too many quarrels between Shakespearian editors for me to wish to add to the number. Indeed with yourself I have no quarrel at all. Your intentions with regard to us as expressed in your letter were as satisfactory as could be desired. . . . Let me express my hearty wishes for the success of your great undertaking. If there is anything I can do to further it, I shall be glad to do so. Should you have any misgivings about the accuracy of your readings from the quartos and folios I will clarify any that are doubtful.[10]

With astonishment that *The Athenaeum* had printed his letter and with relief to find a friend where he had expected a foe, Furness immediately wrote to Wright:

Philadelphia.
April 4, 1870

Mr. W. Aldis Wright
Trin. Coll. Cam.

My dear Mr. Wright,
Your very kind note of the 21st ult. I received only a few minutes ago, and from it I learn that my letter has appeared in "The Athenaeum" (Whereof I had not the faintest expectation on many accounts).

It would be difficult for me, were I to attempt it, to express to you the pleasure with which I read your note. All literary quarrels (and especially Shakespearian) are to me most odious, and although my daily profession forces me to live in the 'rank infection' of an atmosphere of antagonism yet I expect a purer air in the modern world of Shakespearian literature.

Of your very kind offer to verify any doubtful readings of the collation of the Qq & Ff I will gladly avail myself. I have carefully collated your textual notes with the original Folios, and with Mr. Halliwells Facsimiles of the Quartos, and have found some twenty or thirty noteworthy discrepancies. The majority of these I sent to Mr. Halliwell, fearing lest instead of finding errors in your notes I might be detecting mistakes in his Facsimiles, of which it was but right that he should receive the first notice. The same mail which brought me your note brought one also from Mr. Halliwell, in which he says that while the originals in his possession confirm his Facsimiles in all points (save one) yet undoubtedly the originals collated by you contained the readings that you record.

Argal, the replication which, lawyerlike, I was preparing in case you should attack me, falls to the ground—and to my great relief.

With your permission, I will, in my first leisure moment send you this list which, on your verification will be simply curious as illustrating the variations in copies of the same editions.

With assurances of my great respect, I remain my dear Sir, in very great haste

Yours sincerely
Horace Howard Furness.[11]

Expressing the same relief at the resolution of the quarrel, Furness wrote to Halliwell-Phillipps, confiding his intention to destroy the long list of some eighty or ninety errors, omissions, and misprints in Wright's collation of the eighteenth-century editors. Peace reigned in the Shakespearian world, that is until *The Athenaeum* for April 2, 1870 reached Philadelphia.

Although Wright had written a conciliatory personal letter to Furness on March 21, on the same day he wrote a public reply to *The Athenaeum*, the tone of which was anything but conciliatory. Dismissing Furness's reply as nine-tenths irrelevant and assuring him that he would "never make merry with his legal knowledge," Wright withdrew his charge of piracy only to attack Furness's editorial honesty and ability.

> Mr. Furness is compelled to take our work, for the simple reason that he cannot do without it, and it would be much more to the purpose to say so at once than to vapour about repudiating the obligation. We have no wish to disparage the severity of the task to which Mr. Furness has set himself, because we know by experience what it is; but when he talks lightly of the labour involved in collating twenty or thirty editions, we strongly suspect he does not know what collating means.[12]

Stung for the second time by Wright's imputations and perplexed by the unexpected biting tone of the printed letter, Furness again wrote to Halliwell-Phillipps on April 16:

> *Are* you personally acquainted with Mr. W. Aldis Wright? I cannot understand the quality of that gentleman. As I said to you in my last letter, he wrote me a most courteous & friendly letter, saying that the reply to me which he had sent to 'the Athenaeum' was such that I would 'have no reason to complain of its tone'—wishing me every success and offering to assist me in any way in his power. What was my surprise therefore to find in his printed reply the most unexpected imputation on my editorial honesty, coupled with doubts as to whether I knew what collating was etc ect. . . . I hate literary quarrels & will none of them. To my exceeding regret Mr. Wright has forced me to offer to the public the list of Errata in the Cambridge edition. I had a letter written but not posted offering this list to Mr. W. to be used for his next edition or to be destroyed, as he pleased. His attack on me was premature and ill advised to say the least.[13]

Two days later Furness posted his letter to *The Athenaeum*, offering Wright the list of some forty errors in the Cambridge editors's collation of the folios and quartos and double that number in the collation of the eighteenth-century editors of *Romeo and Juliet*.

Before the letter was printed in *The Athenaeum* on May 14, however, Furness and Wright had made their peace, and the quarrel had ended in friendship. On April 30, Furness again wrote to Wright:

> To your letter in 'The Athenaeum' of April 2nd I have sent a short reply wherein I have very carefully avoided any expression that could

wound or annoy the most sensitive. I cannot, however, refrain from expressing to you my sincere regret at the turn the discussion has taken, and at the position into which your letter as I think you will acknowledge, has forced me. You have compelled me to show my hand, which for the sake of the Cambridge edition I would gladly have kept for your private observation. The list of errors, omissions and misprints in the collation of modern readings, in the textual notes of the Cam. Ed., is, I must honestly confess, rather black and long, perhaps not as black and not as long as that which you may hereafter gather from my edition, more especially as the latter offers so many more sources of error. I heartily echo your aversion to Shakespearian quarrels and will none of them. You can readily understand that my time is far too much occupied to be trifled away in any such indecorous performances."[14]

As a token of his intention to keep the peace, Furness enclosed a Bill of Fare for the Shakspere Society Annual Dinner just past. Apologetic and equally determined to end the quarrel, Wright wrote to Furness on April 19 from the Isle of Wight, where he had just received Furness's letter of April 4. "Your letter of the 4th instant which was forwarded to me here this morning has given me sincere pleasure because it convinces me that in spite of a little sparring we shall be good friends after all. We have really the same end in view and it will be hard if we cannot agree upon it. I beg that, if in the warmth of controversy I have said anything which may be disagreeable to you, you will have the kindness to forgive it."[15] Having received Wright's renewed promise of support for the *New Variorum*, Furness resolved to let the public controversy take care of itself. With assurances of help and good will from the two most highly respected Victorian Shakespearians, Furness now settled down to read proof for *Romeo and Juliet* whose printing had begun on April 18.

As *Romeo and Juliet* edged toward its publication date, Shakespearian scholars on both sides of the Atlantic wrote to Furness with words of encouragement and offers to help. With his fellow American editors of Shakespeare, Henry Norman Hudson of Boston and Richard Grant White of New York, Furness had been in correspondence for some time concerning their textual changes in the play. Both proved extremely cooperative. Hudson wrote often to suggest emendations, assuring Furness "I take much interest in the work you are prosecuting."[16] Wrote White, "If I can ever serve you in any way in your great undertaking, by way of hunt or verification, pray command me."[17] About this time Furness also began corresponding with Samuel Timmins of the Shakespeare Memorial Library in Birmingham, having sent him a set of the bills of fare from the Shakspere Society and a copy of *Notes on the Tempest*. Timmins replied in August 1870, "I shall be very glad to see the first volume & will give it all the help I can by my own or my friends' pens."[18]

With George Allen of the Shakspere Society helping to read proof, Furness passed the summer at Lindenshade amid proofsheets and lists of corrections. After a week's vacation at Cape May in August, Furness again returned to the tedium of reading proof. "My 'Romeo & Juliet' will be through the press, in a few weeks," he wrote to Halliwell-Phillipps on September 15, "and I hope it will meet your approval. I myself am upperly sick of it, and disheartened, & cannot persuade myself that any one will care a fig for it."[19] At last the long job ended. On October 14, he again wrote to Halliwell-Phillipps, "Before this reaches you I shall have finished the last proof sheet, and am prepared to dismiss the work to the public with Dr. Johnson's 'frigid tranquillity'."[20] In December J.B. Lippincott and Company announced in a new publisher's circular that the first volume of the *New Variorum* was ready, and on December 6, Furness confided to Halliwell-Phillipps, "I am ever so much obliged to you for your words of cheer about the Romeo & Juliet. It ought to appear now any day. I look forward with much pleasure to sending you one of the earliest copies."[21]

The first copy reached Furness in January 1871: over three hundred pages of text, textual notes, and commentary plus appendices on the source of the plot, the date of the play, the text, the costuming, and excerpts from foreign criticism by the likes of Philarete Chasles, Albert Cohn, Lessing, Goethe, and Ulrici, criticism too general to be placed elsewhere in the volume. Forty-four editions of the play—four folios, five quartos, and thirty-five editions from Rowe (1709) to Keightly and the Cambridge Edition (1865)—were collated and all textual variants were noted. Following each textual variant appeared a list of which editors had adopted or rejected the various readings and who was the first to adopt each reading. One hundred and fourteen critical and exegetical works—seventy-five English, thirteen French, and twenty-six German—in addition to the above editions were scoured for commentary and explanatory notes. All this, plus a full reprint of the Danter Quarto, or bad quarto of 1597 that varied too greatly from the other early editions to be placed in the collation, took exactly 480 pages, in the publisher's words "a library of the costliest Shakespearian literature."

Soon gift copies were on their way to new and old Shakespearian friends: to Wright, Halliwell-Phillipps, Howard Staunton, Blanchard Jerrold, and John Payne Collier among his English friends, and on his own side of the Atlantic to White, Hudson, Hiram Corson, Bayard Taylor, and the members of the Shakspere Society of Philadelphia to whom the volume was affectionately dedicated. Two members of the Shakspere Society Furness singled out in the preface for special commendation: Professor George Allen "whose mature judgment, and ripe and accurate scholarship, have frequently afforded me, while the work was going through the press, that aid and comfort, which only those can appreciate who have entered upon the thorny, perilous, and bewildering path of an editor" and A.I. Fish "whose name has been so long associated in this city with the study of Shakespeare, and who has for many years been the Dean and the moving spirit of 'The Shakspere Society of Philadelphia,' [to whom] I owe my warm acknowledgments for his friendly interest and unfailing sympathy, as well as for the unrestricted use of his library where my own was deficient."[22] When the Shakspere Society next convened on February 7, 1871, with A.I. Fish in the chair, the following resolutions were offered by Samuel Dickson and unanimously adopted:

Resolved that the thanks of the Society are due to Messrs. J.B Lippincott & Co. for the admirable manner in which the volume of The New Variorum Shakespeare just issued has been prepared and brought out.

Resolved that in the opinion of this Society no single volume yet published in America is at all equal to this in value as a contribution to Shakespearian literature.[23]

Warm letters of congratulations soon poured into 222 West Washington Square from White, Ingleby, Jerrold, Keightly, Charles Knight, and others. One of the first letters came from Furman Sheppard, who almost a year earlier had helped Furness examine English copyright law when Wright had first attacked the Variorum in *The Athenaeum.* "My first feeling is one of wonderment at the industry, labor, tact, good sense and discrimination which it displays." Then expressing a wish that many other Shakespearians would heartily echo, Sheppard continued, "I do not see how you could render a greater service to the taste and scholarship of this generation than by completing your proposed work. I most sincerely hope that your life and strength may be spared to enable you to do so and to live long thereafter in the enjoyment of the well earned renown which it will justly secure for you."[24] Wrote Hudson, "I am fairly amazed at the diligence, the wide sweep of investigation, and so far as I can judge, the accuracy of your workmanship. Should you go through the whole series of plays in the same manner, I am sure your work will mark an important era, in Shakespearian literature."[25] Hiram Corson praised *Romeo and Juliet* as "an honour to American Shakespearian scholarship,"[26] and Bayard Taylor, having just finished reading proofs for his edition of *Faust* wrote, "Your first 'Variorum' is here, and is a noble volume. But what a labor! I have read enough to make me feel that my own completed task is a smaller matter than I had supposed. You are really piling up a pyramid 'with newer might.'"[27] Praise came too from the English editors of Shakespeare. Halliwell-Phillipps noted its "superiority over all the other variorums,"[28] and Howard Staunton, having received the volume while recovering from a severe illness, promised, "My first leisure hours shall be devoted to your charming book."[29] Collier wrote, "I admire your 'Romeo and Juliet,' as kindly sent to me, extremely. It is a grand result of a noble study of the greatest poet the world has ever produced."[30] Gratifying as these private expressions of praise might be, the proof of the Variorum came in the public pages of *The Athenaeum, The Nation,* and *The New York Times.*

Local reviewers took great, and perhaps not unjustifiable, civic pride that the *New Variorum* was prepared, printed, and published all in Philadelphia. The *Legal Intelligencer,* departing momentarily from legal notices and court calendars, welcomed the volume produced by a Philadelphia lawyer. "Had this volume of a new *Variorum* Shakespeare been published anywhere in America, it would have been an event, calling for mention even in these columns; but 'edited' by a Philadelphia lawyer, and issued by a Philadelphia publisher, it would be unpardonable if the *Intelligencer* did not extend to it a few words of greeting. Since the admirable Essays of Horace Binney Wallace, we recall no purely literary venture by a member of this bar."[31] The *Evening Bulletin* predicted that the work "when completed, will stand in the libraries of educated men throughout this country and in foreign lands, as one of the most distinguished monuments to the literary acquirements of Philadelphia's publishers," and A.I. Fish, reviewing the volume for the *American Literary Gazette and Publishers' Circular*, could not refrain from praising the Shakspere Society that had inspired and nurtured the volume. "And what wonder, then, that a *new* Variorum is demanded? And who so proper to supply this want as a mature member of a long-established Shakespeare Society, with the aid of a finished scholarship, and the study of a lifetime by himself and kindred spirits. And let us rejoice that in our own city, by a scholar of our own, from a printing press and publishing house of our own, in a mechanical garb that must command admiration, this great step towards a just text and a sound interpretation has been taken."[32]

Other reviewers echoed that note, expressing national pride in the accomplishments of American scholarship at a time when the ability of American scholars, and particularly American Shakespearian scholars, was not rated very highly. Puffing its own publication, *Lippincott's Magazine of Popular Literature and Science* boasted, "In point of typographical execution, in beauty of paper and in all mechanical details, it is as handsome a volume, perhaps, as any American bookseller has yet published."[33] Wrote James T. Fields in the *Boston Transcript*,

> Horace Howard Furness . . . is entitled to the thanks of all who feel an interest in American scholarship by his Shakespearian studies as exemplified in his 'New Variorum edition' of 'Romeo and Juliet.' It is an honor conferred on his country as well as on himself when a man is able to accomplish with perfect success such a task as Mr. Furness has chosen for a life labor of love. We congratulate Philadelphia that one of her sons has thus set about a work which America will be proud of in all time to come."[34]

Such self-conscious competition of budding American scholarship with established English and Continental academic tradition is succinctly summed up in an apocryphal conversation quoted by a later reviewer of the tenth volume of the Variorum:

> *The German student to his American friend*: But you cannot have Universities in America, for you have no scholars.
> (*American friend says, feebly, that we have scholars.*)
> *G.S.*: But if you have scholars, where are their books?
> Produce the books, I beg of you, produce the books.

And in defense of the apocryphal American, the reviewer goes on to note, "Dr. Furness's 'Variorum Shakespeare' is one of the works to be produced upon such an occasion."[35]

English reviewers, though somewhat more restrained, generally agreed. After subjecting the textual notes of the Variorum to close scrutiny at all points in which they differed from those in the Cambridge Shakespeare, the reviewer in *The Athenaeum* reported, "Misprints may, we believe, be found in both, but are extremely rare, and only to be discovered after a very microscopic search." Then almost grudgingly he concluded his list of errors with the faint praise, "The edition claims to be a critical one, and we are glad to find that the claim may fairly and fully be allowed."[36] By the end of the long review, however, having warmed to his subject, the writer expressed his admiration for American scholarship.

> It is a source of much satisfaction to find that this, the most exhaustive work on any one of the Shakspeare's plays, comes from America. That the scholars of England and America may always be ready to afford each other mutual aid in illustrating the sources of their common language (as, indeed, has often happened already) must always be the desire of all who have the interests of both countries at heart.[37]

More enthusiastically, the reviewer in *The Spectator* placed Furness in "the foremost rank of Shakespearian scholars" and added his own praise for American Shakespearian scholarship.

> The title-page bearing the imprint of Philadelphia is an irrefragable and, in a manner, monumental testimony to the fact that the fealty of the citizens of the United States to our great poet is as true and

unswerving as our own, bearing, moreover the promise that when England as a nation shall cease to be, the words of Shakespeare will be the objects of fond and fervent study among the inhabitants of the mighty Western Continent.[38]

The Stratford-on-Avon Herald simply called it a "Shakespearian Wonder" from America, [39] and Samuel Timmins in the *Birmingham Daily Post* firmly set aside any national rivalry with his dictum, that to Furness "all true Shakespereans will owe their very hearty thanks; and all will hope that life and health may be long continued, till so great a work is complete and America has the honouor of producing the best and completest edition of Shakespeare's immortal plays."[40]

Reviewers could find only one fault in the Variorum: the inclusion of too many varying opinions of the commentators—comments often erroneous or not to the point—and not enough of Furness's own opinions. Richard Ashhurst, familiar with Furness's critical acumen from Shakspere Society discussions, wrote in *The Penn Monthly*,

There is, perhaps, one thing we could desire; that is, that Mr. Furness had given us a little more of his own views, and not confined himself to setting before us the views of each contending editor so fully and so strongly that we are left at a loss to make up our minds between then, and vainly wish he would come down from the calm impartiality with which, like Jove, he marshals the contending hosts, and take a part, and tell us which side we should espouse.[41]

Observing that sometimes the correct explanation does not even appear at all, *The Athenaeum* critic added, "With respect to the notes, we think that Mr. Furness has erred on the side of fulness: some of those retained are but poor, and we think he might very safely have exercised his own judgment and spared himself some labour by boldly and decidedly rejecting them; and by replacing them, in at least some cases, by more valuable remarks of his own."[42] Although praising Furness for his wide reading and good judgment, R.G. White in *The New York Times* called him "the very Autolycus of his tribe—a snapper-up of unconsidered trifles" and argued that he could have safely omitted the "unimportant" conjectural emendations of critics like Howard Staunton, Mrs. Cowden Clarke, or Coleridge and much of the French and German criticism in the appendix. On the latter he waxed both chauvinistic and eloquent.

> Some of us seem to think that it is the correct thing to be very much impressed with the profundity of German 'philosophical' criticism, and to be very thankful for it, when, in very deed, the liking for it is not spontaneous and hearty, but the most factitious, artificial fashion in the world. In all that we have read of German criticism, we do not remember one illumination of a dark passage, one straightening of a crooked one, one happy conjectural emendation of the text, one needed and successful illustration of language from contemporary writers, one analysis of character which seemed the result of a simple receptive condition of mind capable of action and feeling sympathetic with the poet in his creation, united with a capacity of intuition and reflection upon the problems of psychology. And all that German effort at profound analysis of Shakespeare's philosophy, and his dramatic system, and his moral purpose, and the inner life, is sheer maundering and moonshine.[43]

To this opinion Furness would eventually come himself, but in *Romeo and Juliet* he strove for impartiality. Years later Furness wrote to Rolfe, "To avoid the imputation that I was self-seeking in attaching my puny name to 'the greatest in all literature,' I resolved that I would be the merest drudge, simply arranging and codifying the notes of others and would utter no faintest chirp of my own. But, as you know my resolution did not hold out, and now, ever since I edited *Othello* I gabble like a tinker."[44] And to White, whose opinion in Shakespearian matters he valued above all others in America, he replied:

> You are perfectly right. There are many comments retained which might have been judiciously omitted but I was so anxious to do impartial justice to all, and to make myself as impersonal as possible that I preferred to err on the side of liberality—and if our acquaintance were only a little riper & I were a little more sure of my man, I might perhaps confess to you that you had some little share in making me retain a little twaddle here & there from dear Mrs. C[owden Clarke] & others. Do you remember your dreadful words: 'Publishers & politicians may disregard the rights of an author but by men of letters they should be loyally respected.' And I didn't want to be classed among the Publishers & Politicians. But in all serious-

ness—I have struggled hard to give every one his due, & to let every
one have a fair chance to say his word—of its value let others judge.[45]

So hard did Furness struggle to give every one his say that the
commentary on just one word in Act III, scene 1, line 6 spilled over
into twenty-eight pages of the appendix. While impatiently waiting
for nightfall and Romeo, Juliet gives the following monologue:

> Gallop apace, you fiery-footed steeds,
> Towards Phoebus' lodging: such a waggoner
> As Phaethon would whip you to the west,
> And bring in cloudy night immediately.
> Spread thy close curtain, love-performing night,
> That runaway's eyes may wink, and Romeo
> Leap to these arms, untalked of and unseen.

The problem here comes in line six from the word "runaway's." The
word appears in all the early editions except the bad quarto of 1597,
and although most modern editors retain it, few can agree on its
meaning. Warburton, the first to comment in 1747, thought that it
referred to the sun, here named "runaway" because of the swiftness
of its ride with Phaeton—a meaning followed by Theobald and
Johnson. Steevens, followed by Rann and Cornwall, argued that it
renamed "night" from the previous line since Juliet wished to retard
the flight of night and prolong Romeo's stay. Lunt suggested
"Phaeton" whose steeds "ran away" with the sun. To Douce and
Massey it meant "Juliet" about to "run away" from marriage to Paris,
and to Seymour it meant "Romeo" about to "run away" with Juliet.
Other critics emended the word to solve the dilemma. Heath in 1765
changed "runaway's" to "rumour's," a reading followed by both
Hudson and Grant White in his 1854 edition, then rejected by White
in favor of Warburton's explanation in his 1861 edition. More suggestions follow, limited only by the ingenuity of the arguments:
unawares, unwary, rude day's, soon day's, roving, runagate, runaway
spies, and a dozen others. Such a record of divergent opinion
formed the purpose of the *New Variorum*, and in Furness's defense
The Nation reviewer argued its value:

In deciding what to admit, the editor has exercised a liberal judgment.
He has preferred, with reason, to err on the side of fulness rather than

of defect. Perhaps he feared that by a stricter method he should exclude much that to some readers would seem interesting and useful. One aim of his work was to present a history of Shakespearian interpretation; and for this it was necessary that imperfect or erroneous views should appear in it as well as the correct. Often, indeed, the correct view is seen in a clearer light, and with greater force of evidence, when placed in contrast with the imperfect or erroneous.[46]

Before the reviewers of *Romeo and Juliet* stopped applauding, Furness had already turned to *Macbeth*, the second volume of the *New Variorum*. When beginning the variorum in 1866, he would recall years later, "I chose *Rom. and Jul.* as the first, merely because I was enamoured with the play and I thought 'twas probable that I should never edit a second."[47] Even in June 1871, he confided to Ingleby, "I hope to go to press with 'Macbeth' in November, but how many of the plays I shall edit, I cannot tell. It's purely a labour of love on my part and although the labour we delight in physics pain, yet the labour is terribly severe & verges close upon overtaxing the strength of any one man."[48] Yet during the summer of 1871, verifying variants with White, borrowing early editions of *Macbeth* from Timmins, and dispatching bibliographical queries to Halliwell-Phillipps, Furness had firmly embarked on the variorum voyage that would carry him through fifteen Shakespeare plays and a lifetime of Shakespearian study. The *New Variorum* had been launched.

THE EARLY VARIORUMS
1871-1880

One touch of "Shakespeare" makes the whole world kin.
—*Troilus and Cressida* 3.3.175

Three months before the first copy of *Romeo and Juliet* reached Furness, Providence intervened to insure the future of the *New Variorum Edition of Shakespeare*. On October 6, 1870, Evans Rogers died, leaving to his son-in-law a bequest of $10,000 and to his daughter, Helen Kate Furness, a trust fund valued at more than $750,000. Judged to be one of seven millionaires in the city of Philadelphia in 1845, Evans Rogers at his death left an estate worth close to $1,700,000 to be divided, after special bequests had been paid, between his son Fairman and his daughter Kate. Included in the bequest were the Rogers house at 222 West Washington Square, the adjacent house at the corner of 8th and Locust, and three houses on the north side of the street at 711 Locust, 719 Locust and 723

Locust, as well as properties in St. Louis and New Orleans. With income from the trust fund Furness purchased between 1872 and 1878 the remaining five houses on the north side of Locust Street between 7th and 8th Streets to complete his ownership of the entire block. The most important investment, however, was books.

Hoping to purchase a complete Shakespeare library in one stroke, Furness offered $15,000 for the Shakespearian portion of the library of Thomas Pennant Barton who had died in 1869. This Shakespeare collection, with its 1,442 critical works and 959 editions including twenty-two Shakespearian quartos, all four folios, and such scarce copies as the first American edition published in Philadelphia and the first Boston edition, comprised the finest Shakespearian library outside of the Shakespearian departments of the British Museum, the Bodleian, or Trinity College, Cambridge. Unfortunately, Barton's widow would not separate the Shakespeare books from the larger collection and attached conditions that precluded a private buyer. Although Furness intimated that he would go much higher in his bid, the widow would not budge. The Barton Collection went to the Boston Public Library, and Furness went to his booksellers to begin collecting his own working library.

Again Furness turned to Halliwell-Phillipps, from whom he purchased a rare complete set of Ashbee's facsimiles of the quartos (of the fifty copies printed only thirty-one had been preserved, and only twenty complete sets were then still in existence). From Halliwell-Phillipps's generosity also came Furness's first two Shakespearian quartos: an imperfect copy of the 1608 *Henry V* inscribed "with the kind regards of J. O. Halliwell, 2 January 1871" and in March the 1630 *Pericles*, a fine copy that prompted Furness to reply, "Do you live in Shakespearean Quartos knee-deep, that you can be so lavish of them? Or, which I strongly suspect to be the case, is it solely your own generous heartsome nature which prompts you to impoverish your own shelves in order to enrich others & make them overjoyed?"[1] From Halliwell-Phillipps too came the advice to commission Alfred Russell Smith, the London bookseller, to purchase the necessary rare books at English auctions. During 1870 Furness had already purchased from A. R. Smith the Second Folio (1632) for £37, Rowe's first edition (1709) for £1.12s, and Johnson's first edition (1765) for £2.2s. Now Furness instructed A. R. Smith to secure everything as it became available, and on February 13, 1871, at the dispersal of the Corser Library, Smith bought the First, Third, and Fourth Folios.

> The first Folio (1623) was a very fair copy, almost entirely perfect, with its defects supplied by facsimiles, and possessing, what is one of the greatest rarities of a perfect copy, the Original Verses opposite the title. It was cheaply sold for £160. . . . The third Folio (1664) a fine copy, in old morocco, was proportionately the dearest of the set, bringing £77. The fourth, of common occurrence, brought £12.[2]

In rapid succession during 1871 came Pope's nine-volume Shakespeare (1728) for £1.7s, Hanmer's six volumes (1744) for £2.2s, Rowe's nine volumes (1714) for 18s, Theobald's seven volumes (1733) for £1.1s, Malone's ten volumes (1790) for £1.15s, and, from Bernard Quaritch, Johnson and Steevens's ten-volume edition (1773) for £3.10s. Other notable purchases included the 1542 Chaucer Folio for £8.10s, the undated *Hamlet* with Shakespeare's signature forged by William Henry Ireland on the title page for £28, the 1611 *Hamlet* for £33, and three Pavier Quartos (printed with false imprints in 1619 by William Jaggard) which had belonged to the Shakespearian editor Edward Capell—the 1600 *Merchant of Venice* for £100, the 1608 *King Lear* for £20, and the 1608 *Henry V* for £25.

Over the next decade Furness spent some £1,600 (over $8,500 at the prevailing exchange rate of twenty-seven cents to the shilling) with Alfred Russell Smith alone, to mention nothing of his regular purchases from Albert Cohn, bookseller and bibliographer for the *Shakespeare Jahrbuch*, in Berlin and from his French bookseller in Paris. By 1873 Furness estimated that he had over two thousand Shakespeare books; and before J. Parker Norris described Furness's library in his "Shakespearian Gossip" column of *The American Bibliopolist* in 1875, Furness had added the good 1608 quarto of *King Lear* with manuscript notes by Capell, the 1612 *Richard III*, the 1619 *Pericles*, the 1631 *Taming of the Shrew*, the 1635 *Pericles*, with manuscript notes by Theobald, and the 1639 *I Henry IV*. His collection of German and French editions of Shakespeare Norris judged to be the most complete in the United States. Virtually every source of Shakespeare, edition of Shakespeare and his contemporary dramatists, and every modern critical work Furness purchased for his editing of the Variorum.

Furness housed his books on the second floor of 222 West

Washington Square. One room held the general dramatic works including study books and annotated acting copies of the great Shakespearian actors, such as John Philip Kemble's stage copy of *Taming of the Shrew* and Edwin Booth's copy of *The Merchant of Venice*. In the hallway stood bookcases containing the editions of the Elizabethan dramatists. The rare books and relics Furness kept in the front room of the second floor, a room not merely a library but, as George Dawson, member of the Birmingham Shakespeare Society described it to Samuel Timmins, "an English news room & a Shakespearean shrine."[3] Massive black walnut bookcases, appropriately carved, covered one side and one end of the room. Overlooking Washington Square, three spacious windows draped with dark red material admitted a soft light; and the remaining end was filled with a large fireplace, above which hung a full length portrait of Helen Kate Furness. The ceiling was decorated with a fresco of Shakespeare's coat of arms. Near the ceiling in the center of the Locust Street side hung a framed rubbing of the famed curse on Shakespeare's grave. Below the rubbing and between two of the large bookcases stood a plaster copy of the Stratford Bust, framed in a deep circular panel of black walnut, a gift from J. Parker Norris. In front of the bust stood a small case holding the Shakespeare relics: an iron gauntlet taken from the grave of Edward Heldon, supposed pallbearer of Shakespeare now lying buried in Frederick, Virginia; the piece of Shakespeare's mulberry tree and the sliver of oak cut from a beam in Shakespeare's Birthplace, both given to Furness by Ingleby; and the skull that was used for many years at the Walnut Street Theatre in *Hamlet*. Given to Furness by S. Weir Mitchell, the skull bore the names of Kean, Macready, Kemble, Booth, Forrest, Cushman, Davenport, Murdock, and Brooks, all of whom had addressed it as poor Yorick's last remains.

The most precious relic lay in a glass case of its own—the Shakespeare gloves given to Furness on January 17, 1874, by Fanny Kemble to show her appreciation for the Variorum *Romeo and Juliet* and *Macbeth*. These gray buckskin gauntlets with gold thread embroidery and a gold fringe sewn onto an edging of pale pink silk had surfaced at Stratford in 1769 at the time of Garrick's Shakespeare Jubilee. Given to Garrick by the actor John Ward, the gloves had originally belonged to one William Shakespeare Hart, a glazier by trade, who lived in Bridge Street in Stratford-upon-Avon. According to Hart, who gave the gloves to Ward in 1746, family tradition regarded them as heirlooms, "the only property that remains to our famous relation."[4] At Garrick's death the gloves passed to his widow who bequeathed them in 1822 back to Ward's granddaughter, the actress Mrs. Sarah Siddons, sister of the two Kemble brothers John Philip and Charles. Mrs. Siddons bequeathed them to her daughter, Mrs. George Combe, by whom they were given to her cousin Fanny Kemble and then to Furness. That Shakespeare ever touched these buckskin gauntlets remains uncertain, given the sudden boom in the relics trade during the Stratford Jubilee, but their certain association with Garrick, Siddons, and Kemble makes them more interesting than most alleged relics. Wrote Furness, "That they are veritably Shakespeare's Gloves, I hope; that they belonged to Garrick, Mrs. Siddons & Mrs. Kemble I know, and with that I am satisfied."[5] Quipped Furness's father, while showing visitors around the library, "Without the shadow of a doubt those were the very gloves which Shakespeare *did not* wear when he handled human nature."[6]

Everywhere around the room hung framed photographs of Furness's Shakespearian friends: Clark, Wright, Halliwell-Phillipps, Ingleby, Timmins, Collier, Norris, Hudson, Cohn, Keightly, Corson, Hart, Ulrici, Kemble. An irrepressible collector of photographs, Furness confessed to Ingleby, "I have a foolish weakness of seeing the faces of those with whom I am brought into daily contact in my studies."[7] In the middle of the room stood a large desk of black walnut, carved to match the bookcases. Here day after day and night after night, surrounded by the faces of his Shakespearian friends, his Shakespearian treasures, and his Shakespearian books, Furness worked on *Macbeth*, *Hamlet*, and *King Lear*.

Furness had begun gathering the books for *Macbeth* almost before *Romeo and Juliet* had issued from the press, and by November 1871 the first scenes were ready for the printers. Days devoted to law practice, social engagements, and business pushed Shakespeare into the evening hours. "My days are filled with a round of trivial duties," Furness confided to Rolfe, "and when night comes I have to peg away at Shakespeare, for these Phlistines of printers are upon me."[8] And to Ingleby he wrote, "The overseeing of these books through the press is the most exhaustive part of the work. Four pages a day is as much as the printers can set up or I correct. I never look at my MS but verify every reading & quotation afresh. And as

proofsheets come at night & have to be returned in the morning—
the East is glimmering with some streaks of day when I creep up to
bed, jaded to rags."[9] Thus pegging away at Shakespeare, Furness
passed the winter of 1872, and by May, when the literary lawyer
became gentleman farmer and thoughts of textual variants and
conjectural emendations turned to top-dressings and underdrain-
ings, the printers had set some sixty pages. During the summer at
Lindenshade Furness and his father translated German and French
criticism. Refreshed by an August vacation in Niagara, Saratoga, and
Boston, Furness wrote to Halliwell-Phillipps from Niagara Falls that
he hoped to finish the printing by Christmas.

As the printing resumed in October, Furness struggled to resolve the textual difficulties and yet stay ahead of the printers, often
debating a textual crux until the last possible minute. To Hiram
Corson, Professor of English at Cornell University, he wrote, for
example, in October:

> My dear Professor,
>
> In Macbeth I, vii, 66 'That memory the wonder of the brain, Shall be *a*
> *fume*' can this be parallel to *a flame, afire*? And ought it not to be
> printed as one word? Do you know of any parallel instances of its
> use? I write in hot haste, for though I noted the point long ago, & have
> kept it constantly in view in my various readings I have not been
> successful, and now the printers are upon me. I *ought* to send them
> the copy containing these lines tomorrow but I shan't until I hear
> from you.
>
> Yours faithfully
> Horace Howard Furness
>
> Prof. Corson
> Ithaca
> 21 Oct. 1872.[10]

Many such letters discussing textual difficulties and proposing new
readings passed back and forth between Cornell and Philadelphia,
and on more than one occasion Furness begged for offprints of
Corson's interpretations to send to Collier, Staunton, Ingleby, Halliwell-Phillipps, Elze, Ulrici, and his other English and German
Shakespearian friends. Corson's argument for "an Anthony it was"
(*Antony and Cleopatra* 5.2.86-88) so charmed Furness that he exclaimed, "If Shakespeare didn't mean that he ought to be ashamed of

himself & I hope the Devil will give him a deep prod with his fork for the oversight."[11]

Similar exchanges occurred between Furness and Ingleby, whose books *Shakespeare Hermeneutics* and *Centurie of Prayse* had given him great familiarity with Elizabethan literature. The debate over the possible double entendre in Davenant's spelling of "bone-fire" in the drunken porter's speech, "I had thought to have let in some of all Professions, that goe the Primrose way to th' everlasting Bonfire" continued even after the Variorum *Macbeth* had been printed. Did "th' everlasting bonfire," originally spelled "bone-fire" from the custom of burning old bones but altered to "bonfire" under the influence of the French *bon*, refer simply to the fires of hell, or did Shakespeare indend a pun for syphilis, "the French disease" as it was known in the sixteenth century. Here and elsewhere Victorian sensibility clashed with Elizabethan frankness. In spite of Ingleby's arguments for the former, Furness consistently upheld the latter. "Unquestionably," he wrote to Ingleby after one such exchange, "it is nicer to adopt the cleanlier meaning. But where are your parallels? or your authority?"[12]

As the printing of *Macbeth* continued, Furness found himself at the hub of an international network of Shakespearian commentators all eager to collaborate on the Variorum. From Joseph Crosby in Cincinnati to Ingleby in Ilford, Essex, from William James Rolfe's column in *The Literary World* to Howard Staunton in the pages of *The Athenaeum*, from Hiram Corson at Cornell to Wright at Trinity College, Cambridge, stretched the debate over Shakespeare's text. Nor was the desire for Variorum fame confined to Shakespeare's editors. Everyone with a favorite interpretation or emendation sent it to Furness for inclusion in the Variorum. People plied him with questions about the first American edition of Shakespeare or the best edition to purchase, asked for a convenient list of books on *Hamlet* or Shakespeare's references to dogs, and solicited his opinion on disputed points for their local Shakespearian club. Even after his conclusions had appeared in the Variorum editions, Furness received letters from readers eager to continue the discussion. After finishing *Othello*, for example, Furness wrote to Ingleby,

I don't care a tinker's cuss or a dram of eale whether Cassio was damned in a fair wife or a fair life or even whether he were damned at all. And yet I get letters every week from all over the Union anxious to discuss the whole question over again with me in correspondence. I think seriously of having a blank form printed, urging the fact that as we have not days & nights of Arctic length I must beg to be excused from reentering into a disucssion what I have settled for my own satisfaction in my published notes."[13]

Nevertheless, sifting each interpretation and emendation, no matter how unlikely, and searching for contemporary examples to corroborate it, Furness worked to construct once and for all the best text of Shakespeare based on the opinions of the majority of the ablest commentators.

Great labor for small reward! *Romeo and Juliet* had not been a financial success. J.B. Lippincott had agreed to take on the Variorum *Romeo and Juliet* at no cost to Furness above his literary labor because he wanted to enter the International Industrial Exhibition in Vienna during 1873, and an edition of Shakespeare seemed to be a suitable entry. J.B. Lippincott Company did win an honorable mention in the Division of Publishers of Educational Books, but at the high price necessary to cover the costs, the first volume of the Variorum was a commercial failure. Disappointed with the public reception of *Romeo and Juliet* and complaining to Halliwell-Phillipps about "Lippincott's exorbitant price,"[14] Furness negotiated in November a new contract that guaranteed the future of the Variorum. Lippincott would furnish the press work, the paper, the binding, and the publishing; Furness would furnish the stereotype plates, paid for out of his own pocket, and that cost would be deducted from the price of the book. With Furness subsidizing the Variorum up to $2,000 per volume, Lippincott lowered the price to $3.00 per copy, and in early December Furness signed the publishing contract for *Macbeth*, privately complaining to Ingleby, "I have the grim satisfaction of feeling that if the Public blackguard my performance they don't have to pay anything for it."[15] Not until two years later did *Macbeth* sell enough copies to produce a small royalty check of $139.73; even after forty years Furness had received only $28,574.63 in royalties, a sum far below his own investment.

Outwardly, then, Furness offered his books to the public to help the cause of Shakespearian scholarship, never receiving during the long history of the Variorum a penny of profit; inwardly he chafed against publishers in general and his in particular. After the new contract for *Macbeth* had been signed, he wrote to Rolfe, offering commiseration for the slow sales of Rolfe's school Shakespeare:

> The publishers are your true scapegoats; it's all along of Harpers and Lippincott. They ought to drop every other venture & throw everything into Shakespeare. Who cares for their twaddling Magazines? The only special comfort I can give you is that in your marrowbones you should be grateful that you don't live within earshot of your publisher. A man's tongue is more rasping than his pen—a pen sticks deep & ink festers, but the tongue lays bare whole handbreadths of quivering nerves. 'Mr. Lippincott, you put the price of the book too high.' 'Too high!! the price has nothing to do with it; your book wouldn't sell if I put the price at seventy-five cents.' As I think I once said to you, how I revere the memory of Campbell who gave as a toast 'Napoleon Bonaparte, because he once shot a publisher.'[16]

And to Corson, who had complained to Furness about his own publisher, Furness wrote:

> You must bear in mind that if Holt is a sharper, Lippincott is a dullard. I doubt if it be possible to have a more irritating man to deal with. We both of us hate each other poisonously. His soul is as impervious as adamant to everything but gain & men who can't write books that will sell like Ouida's novels, are the scum of the earth. This is entre nous, for outwardly we are closer than the Siamese twins.[17]

The occasional outburst notwithstanding, Furness and Lippincott had struck a bargain that would continue for more than fifty years of the Variorum venture; and with the publishing future now secure, Furness turned once again to reading proofsheets.

The pace quickened as winter merged into early spring and *Macbeth* edged toward publication. With the text and notes behind him, Furness labored in the appendix, selecting, condensing, rearranging, and, conscious always of the book's length, cutting the general criticism of the play. Norris faithfully copied out extracts from the critics only to have Furness cut and chop as the printers neared the appropriate spot. In its final form the appendix retained a full reprint of Davenant's 1674 adaptation of *Macbeth*, extracts from Holinshed and the *Wintownis Cronykil* for the source of the plot, essays on the date of the play, the character of Macbeth (did

Macbeth really see Banquo's ghost?), extracts from Thomas Middleton's *The Witch* (probable source of the witches' scene in the fourth act), excerpts from foreign criticism, and an essay on the difficulty of German translations of *Macbeth*, highlighted by some twenty different German versions of "Double, double, toil and trouble; / Fire burn and cauldron bubble."

Fish had proposed a full bibliography of *Macbeth*, but Furness decided in favor of a list of over two hundred and fifty books cited and consulted, a list proofread and corrected by Norris. On March 16, Furness wrote to Halliwell-Phillipps, "This week finished my 'Macbeth,' and within three weeks thereafter I hope to have a copy from the press. You may be sure one of the very earliest copies I shall send to you."[18] And on March 20, Furness wrote in his journal, "This evening I wrote D.D. (Dead and Done for) on the last proofs of Macbeth—the Preface and the Bibliography."[19]

The first copy reached Furness on April 9, and soon gift copies were on their way to new and old Shakespearian friends. Both the gift list for *Macbeth* and Furness's correspondence during these years reveal the extensive, yet personal, ties that he had established in the Shakespearian world. Fellow editors of Shakespeare received fraternal support and encouragement. Out of gratitude for Staunton's 1866 photolithographic facsimile of the first folio, Furness supported the series of less than happy textual emendations proposed by Staunton during his declining years and published in *The Athenaeum* between 1872 and 1874, urged that Staunton be placed on the civil pension list, and contributed to the support of his widow after his death in 1874. With Hudson he discussed difficult passages and exchanged articles as Hudson prepared his school edition of Shakespeare. So interested did he become in helping Hudson solve the debate over "young Abraham Cupid" (was it Abraham, Abram, Auburn, or Adam?) for Hudson's school edition of *Romeo and Juliet* in 1873, that Furness wrote one of his few critical articles for *The Penn Monthly* in July to settle the current newspaper dispute. For Wright and his Clarendon Edition, Furness had only generous praise, as he had for Rolfe and his school series of English Classics in spite of the painstaking scrutiny for misprints and errors that Rolfe gave to each Variorum volume as it arrived. "Oh, my! I should think you'd be ashamed!" Rolfe would prod after detecting a small error in *Macbeth*. "If I set up to be a Variorum, I'd *be* one . . . the Camb. ed.

makes the same lapse—which accounts for *your* making it, I spose; but I thought you bragged that you looked up these things for yourself. Got you now—haven't I, you miserable humbug?"[20] Meekly accepting the rod, Furness carefully filed such corrections for change in future editions. So generous was Furness's nature that even Collier, whose infamous forgery of the second Folio had been a matter of public record since 1859, received only kind words and sympathy for his rejection by the literary public. Wrote Furness to Ingleby, whose books *The Shakspeare Fabrication* (1859) and *A Complete View of the Shakspere Controversy* (1861) had helped to expose Collier,

> For myself, I have never taken any very great interest in the Collier controversy. It is a little world of itself; it only impinges on mine, does not include it, and so I have let it alone preferring to think well rather than ill of a man. . . . Is there no imaginable excuse for such curious literary freaks? There was for Collier so very, very, little to gain and such a huge amount to lose that the attempt seems madness. Poor old Man! He has my profound commiseration under either alternative, of guilt or innocence; if innocent, he deserves everyman's sympathy; if guilty, how frightfully keen must be his remorse."[21]

Refusing to judge, Furness continued to befriend Collier and consult him on questions of word usage and disputed readings long after he had been abandoned by other Shakespearians.

Nor were his friendships confined to literary discussions. Before Fanny Kemble left Philadelphia in 1874, Furness and his wife had regularly visited her at 1812 Rittenhouse Square, bringing fresh asparagus and lettuce and mushrooms from their greenhouses at Lindenshade. Their kindness, plus the excellence of *Romeo and Juliet* and *Macbeth*, prompted Fanny's gift of the Shakespeare Gloves in January 1874; in return Furness and his wife had made for her a bracelet engraved with lines from Marlowe "A belt of straw with ivy buds / And coral clasps and amber studs," a gift which, in spite of her close acquaintance with the Furness family since the 1840s, she refused. The English Shakespearians Furness continually plied with gifts distinctly American. To Halliwell-Phillipps he sent maple sugar from New England, Indian moccasins from Niagara Falls, and reed birds—that annual autumn Philadelphia delicacy that reached Halliwell-Phillipps in an indelicate condition of decay. To Ingleby he sent clay figurines representing scenes from Irving's "Legend of Sleepy Hollow" and cuttings of American flowers from the gardens of Lindenshade, and to Furnivall he sent samples of hominy, grits, and Indian corn. For Christmas gifts in 1874 Furness sent buffalo and in 1875 antelope. Commissioned during the summer from hunters in Omaha, the buffalo haunches received an enthusiastic reception.

> Dear old Collier's servants regarded it with awe and superstition as the *'Devil's hind leg.'* Halliwell escorted his friends to the larder to examine it, & is to have the skin tanned for a carriage rug etc., & Timmins (heaven's sunshine on his generous heart!) sent steaks all over the United Kingdom, etc. etc. & you [Ingleby] too praised it beyond my highest hopes. I was awfully put out that I couldn't get a fifth haunch for Furnivall. But another year I may have better success. We must gather these buffaloes while we may. They are fast becoming extinct.[22]

Praise for *Macbeth* and encouragement to continue the Variorum came from unexpected sources. The Birmingham Shakespeare Society signalled its solidarity with the Shakspere Society of Philadelphia in a privately printed flier praising the first two volumes of the Variorum "as emphatically the best edition of Shakespeare's works." Signed by Samuel Timmins, C. M. Ingleby, and George Dawson, among others, the flier praised Furness for his "untiring industry" and his "labour of love" and expressed the desire "in the interests of international literature, that an edition of Shakespeare edited and printed in America, so well worthy of support, should be more widely known."[23] American scholars recognized Furness by electing him to memberhsip in the American Philological Association in 1873 and inviting him to address their annual meeting that July at Lafayette College. Wrote the then president Francis March, "You must have many dishes ready for the feast of languages, and even fragments from Shakespearian baskets are good anytime."[24] The most gratifying response for Furness, however, came from the farthest distance: from the prestigious Deutsche Shakespeare Gesellschaft of Weimar. Even while Furness was busily translating and condensing German criticism on *Macbeth*, the Deutsche Shakespeare Gesellschaft met for its annual meeting on May 25, 1872, and elected him an honorary member. Joining Halliwell-Phillipps and Charles Knight, two members of the old Shakespeare Society and the only other foreign honorary members, Furness entered a select society of international scholars. Over the years other English honorary members would include Furnivall, Timmins, Wright, Clark, Adolphus Ward of Cambridge, and C.E. Flower of the Shakespeare Birthplace Trust; the only other American elected during Furness's lifetime would be Theodore Roosevelt in 1911.

Furness acknowledged the honor with gift copies of *Macbeth* to Hermann Ulrici, president of the society; to Karl Elze, editor of the *Shakespeare Jahrbuch*; and to the society's patron King Johann of Saxony. After receiving a diploma in 1874, he wrote with pride to Ingleby:

> The German Shakspere Society have made me an Honorary Member & sent me quite a gorgeous diploma. I know not whether in their Honorary Memberships they are most select or most generous; at any rate I value it highly, and am inclined to put it after my name on the title page of Hamlet (if that ever sees the light.) Don't you think I ought to do so? I remember long ago that I denounced to you the custom so prevalent here in America of putting 'degrees' after names. But there are degrees and degrees. And with any foreign recognition like this, coming unsought, I confess I am gratified."[25]

Although his taste for much of German scholarship had soured (in the same letter to Ingleby he criticized Schmidt's *Shakspeare-Lexicon* and the translation of Maetzner's *Grammar* for inaccuracy and incompleteness), he still savored the sweet recognition from German scholars; and despite the prevailing notion in Germany that the Germans had discovered Shakespeare and understood him better than did his own nation, the magic of Shakespeare formed a common bond, and Furness's list of correspondents grew to include Ulrici and Elze, both professors at Halle; Nikolaus Delius, editor of Shakespeare and professor at Bonn; Reinhold Köhler, librarian in Weimar; and F.A. Leo, professor in Berlin. "One touch of Shakespeare makes the whole world kin," Furness often wrote in his letters, adapting Ulysses' speech in *Troilus and Cressida*; and the seed of friendships planted by *Romeo and Juliet* and watered by *Macbeth* flourished in the cultivated correspondence and scholarship produced by this group of international Shakespearians.

Even before many of the gift copies of *Macbeth* had arrived in

England and Germany, Lippincott announced that the first edition had sold out, and on June 13 Furness authorized a second edition. "I think it will please you to learn," he wrote jubilantly to Halliwell-Phillipps, "that Lippincott pronounces 'Macbeth' a great success, commercially. Judging from 'Romeo & Juliet' it was thought that five hundred copies would supply the demand for this second volume. But that number was exhausted in six weeks, and Lippincott is now going on with the second edition."[26] Throughout the summer and fall reviewers praised the second volume of the Variorum, again faulting only the overwhelming fullness of the notes, the uselessness of much of the German criticism, and the lack of editorial comment; but Furness had already turned to *Hamlet*. As early as March, while waiting for the printers to finish *Macbeth*, Furness had discussed with Ingleby his choice for volume three; and by June, even though Karl Elze urged him to take up next *The Merchant of Venice*, he had already began work on *Hamlet*.

While Furness held center stage with *Romeo and Juliet* and *Macbeth*, Mrs. Furness had been quietly perfecting her own Shakespearian part. Her first scholarly work, the *Index of the Pages in the Volumes of Wm. Sidney Walker on Which Occur Citations from the Plays of Shakespeare* (1870), had been originally compiled to aid her husband in his work on *Romeo and Juliet*. Superseding a similar index by F.A. Leo to Walker's three-volume *A Critical Examination of the Text of Shakespeare* (1860), the small book proved so useful to Furness and other members of the Shakspere Society that fifty copies were printed privately by the Society's printers and distributed to Staunton, Wright, Brae, Elze, Cohn, White, and other members of the growing Shakespeare fraternity. Later that same year she began work on *A Concordance to Shakespeare's Poems: an Index to Every Word Therein Contained* (1874), designed to supply the omission of the poems in Mary Cowden-Clarke's *The Complete Concordance to Shakspere: Being a Verbal Index to All the Passages in the Dramatic Works of the Poet* (1845). Having received warm encouragement from Mrs. Clarke, she worked steadily alongside her husband until a trial volume, the concordance to *Venus and Adonis*, was published by Lippincott in May 1872 and circulated for suggestions. Wright suggested the distinction between verbal and substantive uses of the same word; Furnivall wanted "that" divided under five subheadings. Ingleby and Wright argued for the omission of particles and prepositions; Corson wanted the particles retained. And thanks to Corson, American scholarship prevailed. "Such a doughty lance in favor of the poor little despised particles, we had never before had tilted, in our presence," wrote Furness to Corson. "We mistrusted ourselves for a moment when such a scholar as W. Aldis Wright reasoned their need. But now, brandishing your letter we'll smiling mock at Satan's rage, and face a frowning world."[27]

Slow going at best in the days before computer compilation, the concordance crept with petty pace towards completion. The poems contain over six thousand lines and nearly fifty thousand words, and the concordance—ranging from one use of "witty" to 363 of "love" to 1413 of "and" and 1456 of "the"—duly recorded each word, each instance of its use, and the line in which it appeared. *Macbeth* came and went. In April 1873, when sending a copy of *Macbeth* to Halliwell-Phillipps, Furness wrote, "Mrs. Furness has completed the Concordance to the Poems, and is now at the final revision of the mass of MS before sending it to press. I hope it will be published next autumn."[28] By late June, however, with completion no closer and the birth of their daughter Caroline looming larger, Furness wrote again to Halliwell-Phillipps to announce the delay in the concordance and the postponement of their proposed English vacation. "After finishing 'Macbeth' I have continually said that I would take a vacation and Mrs. Furness and my boys under my arm and spend a summer in England. But then I always calculated upon Mrs. Furness's having finished her 'Concordance' at the same time; in this she has been delayed, or rather, it has taken her longer than she thought, and so while waiting for her to finish I have plunged into 'Hamlet,' and so now, that must be completed before I can take mine ease in mine English inn."[29] The English vacation postponed until 1880 and *Hamlet* begun, Mrs. Furness worked at the concordance until the first copy came off the press on May 5, 1874.

Response, both public and private, was enthusiastic. *The North American and United States Gazette* called the concordance a "fine evidence of womanly culture and scholarship in this country" and boasted that "with this and the Variorum it is difficult to see how Shakspearian scholars can hereafter do more than ruminate what has been completed in every phase and stage."[30] In *The Penn Monthly* Fish called it "the foundation for a convenient critical and linguistic study of the Poems, which has been denied to all preceding scholars";[31] and in a letter to Furness Wright added, "most of all I have to thank Mrs. Furness through you for laying all students of Shakespeare under a lasting debt of gratitude. I cannot tell you what a comfort it is to have her Concordance to the Poems. It marks a new era in Shakespeare Literature. Before, there was always a degree of uncertainty as to whether a word or phrase or a construction was or was not Shakespearian: now all such doubts are laid to rest forever."[32] The *North American Review* urged her to begin a variorum edition of Shakespeare's Poems, and Halliwell-Phillips urged her to undertake a concordance to the entire works of Shakespeare.

Time and expense, however, precluded such elaborate projects for Kate Furness. By her own calculation it would have taken fifty-four years at her rate of work to complete a concordance to the entire works, and the cost prohibited even the contemplation of the task. The stereotyped plates for *A Concordance to Shakespeare's Poems* had cost Furness almost $4,000, and, as Mrs. Furness wrote to Halliwell-Phillipps, "We are not people of expensive tastes except in the matter of books and are quite willing to spend a good deal of money in getting out books which but a handful of people want to buy, but there must be some limit to even such dissipations."[33] Even a concordance for *Hamlet*, to accompany the next volume of the Variorum, was abandoned due to the increased expense and bulk of the volume. In the end she settled for an index to some of the more important notes in the first volume of the Variorum *Hamlet*. At her own desk not far from his in the Shakespearian library, going through commentaries and noting references, Kate kept pace with her husband as he charted the wilderness of *Hamlet* criticism. When no visitors or social engagements interfered, the two spent their evenings over Shakespeare, working together until about eleven when she retired to bed, leaving him alone with his books and his pipe until two o'clock in the morning. "It is a delightful thing," wrote Norris in his "Shakespearian Gossip" column, "to see husband and wife so thoroughly in unity as Mr. and Mrs. Furness. They are to the United States what Mr. and Mrs. Charles Cowden Clarke are to England; though Mr. Furness is far ahead of Mr. Clarke as a Shakespearian."[34]

In spite of Kate's help, discouragement and delay dogged his progress through *Hamlet*. On April 30, 1875, after almost two years in Elsinore, Furness complained to Corson, "I am going at the veriest snail's pace in Hamlet. A million cares infest my days and my nights; and days, weeks, and months rush by and leave nothing but wrack behind."[35] And a month later on May 30, five days before leaving his winter work behind for the flowers and farmer's life at Lindenshade, he confided to Ingleby,

> I get terribly low in mind about it sometimes. I am so now. I don't believe that there are more than six people in this huge world that care a rap about it, and probably five of them care for it only because they love me. What the sixth one cares for it for, God only knows. . . . One thing that conduces more especially to my gloom this evening is that the conviction has been forced slowly on me that I cannot finish Hamlet in time to go to press next November—and as that month is the only one in the year in which I can go to press, it means that I must postpone the issue until 1877 (Great Heavens!) If I press on I know I shall break down, perhaps utterly.[36]

The sheer size of *Hamlet*, the mass of Germain criticism to be translated, to say nothing of the English criticism to be read, and the shuttling of the Furness family between Washington Square in the winter and Lindenshade in the summer all contributed to his depression. After two years of work, Furness had finished only the first three acts of *Hamlet*, together containing five hundred lines more than in all of *Macbeth*, but not enough to go to press in November 1875. He could not begin printing in any other month since it took four or five months to finish the book during which time he needed his library in the city to verify the collation and quotations. By working through the summer in the country, he could have finished Acts IV and V by November, but the library could not be moved to Lindenshade, and the appendix with its translations of German commentry still needed to be written.

Ingleby, seconded by Corson, attempted to solve the dilemma by suggesting that Furness hire a copyist for the commentary, but Furness dismissed that suggestion as impractical. "As for any clerical help," he explained,

> I'd have a private secretary in a minute if it would be the least use. I have all possible help in this Appendix—but it is impossible to use an amanuensis for the commentary. I've tried it. Parker Norris most kindly copied out for me all of Joseph Hunter's notes on Hamlet (no

small task). I've finished three Acts and have used his copy but once, I think . . . You see, I never can tell beforehand what I shall want or how much. Hunter may have pages of comment, and I may want but a sentence of it all. So it's quicker for me to write that sentence than to hunt it out in Norris's MS., cut it out, and insert. And then I modify, transpose, etc etc. I'm sadly afraid it's not possible to abridge the labour, *and* I do get tired of it.[37]

Furness also rejected Ingleby's second suggestion, that he finish the text and go to press with volume one in November while leisurely working on the appendix for volume two the following year, in order to avoid a four-year gap between *Macbeth* and *Hamlet*.

Your suggestion about printing Hamlet in two volumes had already occurred to me, but I abandoned the idea because I found it impracticable. In reading up for my Appendix I came across many notes that are too brief and disjointed to appear by themselves, separated from the context, and which must therefore fall into file in the commentary. Now if the first volume were printed & I found half a dozen such morceaux I should tear out the few remaining locks which Nature has left on my head—and the whole thing would be a failure in my eyes ever after. No, no, when I prepare the last page of copy the door must be open for changes in the first. And the terror that now seizes me at times is lest I fail in carrying in my head the whole mass of material, bearing in mind what I have rejected and what adopted.[38]

Resolving finally to spend the summer of 1875 on the appendix, to begin Act IV in the fall, and to delay publication until 1877, Furness took arms against the sea of German criticism and, with the aid of his father, worked through the summer translating and selecting extracts from German commentary.

"Did ever a man have such a Father as I?" exclaimed Furness to Ingleby at the end of that summer. "What do you think the dear blessed saint has been doing for me all summer? Translating the German criticisms on Hamlet! I have done nothing but read and mark & he has translated. That whole department is practically finished, comprising extracts from over twenty different authors. I am now at the French."[39]

Refreshed by a September vacation in Boston, Newport, and New York, Furness returned to his winter's work, and by the end of

November 1875, he had begun collating the texts for the last scene of the last act. Although he estimated that three months more would finish the play, distractions continued to delay his progress. "My time seems to be wasted from morning till night," he complained to Ingleby in January.

> The days fly past swifter than thought, and I accomplish nothing I have no sooner dressed myself in the morning than I have to undress to go to bed, and sometimes I think it isn't worth the trouble but I'll just stay in bed, and at intervals thrust my head out and shout Monday, Tuesday, Wednesday & so on till the week be done. When I was a boy we used to have such things as days and weeks—now years and decades have taken their places And I have done nothing. Mrs. Furness won't listen to my proposal to go and live in Upernavik—in the Arctic Circle—there with a day six months long one might accomplish something in a month of thirty days. I have entreated and pleaded with her, but budge she will not. So here I have to stay wasting my time till the sexton's spade knocks me o' the mazzard.[40]

By April 1876, however, the text and commentary, now almost three times the bulk of *Macbeth*, were virtually complete. Still Furness delayed, trying to include extracts from the most recent *Hamlet* criticism before sending the manuscript to the printers, until Ingleby accused him of "not only editing but acting Hamlet, forever postponing and procrastinating all action."[41] Furness promptly bundled the first act off to the printers, and by the end of April the proofreading had begun.

> "My proofs come in at night," he explained to Furnivall, "and I feel bound to return them in the morning—no small task. I verify every textual note in the four Folios, the four Quartos and about thirty modern editions, in certain tough passages I examine over fifty modern editions. Six and sometimes eight pages of that kind of work (not to mention the Commentary) will be apt to keep you up till nigh, if not past, dawn."[42]

By June the first act, comprising over 120 pages, had been cast, and Furness suspended printing until October while he devoted the summer to finishing the appendix at Lindenshade.

Again he struggled with the German commentary. "I have never before in my life been harder pushed," he wrote in September to Ingleby.

> At times I must have averaged thirteen or fourteen hours a day, 'pegging' away at the German critics on Hamlet. I have read and digested (Heaven help me!) at least four thousand pages of German ponderosity. My Father, blessed Father that he is! has busily & steadily translated the passages that I have marked. He translated a great quantity for me last summer, but I found when I came to revise it for the printer, that a large quantity was useless repetition. So I began de novo & went through the whole job again, and I have simmered the great mass down to about a hundred printed pages in the Appendix, at which the printers are now busy: I don't think there is any repetition in any of the extracts that I have given from about fifty different German commentators, and I have tried to get what was best & most creditable in each one—and really I must confess that the result as I read the printed proofs is something extraordinary— the keeness, the shrewdness brought to bear on every sentence of the tragedy is fairly, when one sees it in the whole mass, astonishing.[43]

After such Herculean labor in sifting, sorting, extracting, and translating, Furness had nothing but praise for German criticism of *Hamlet*.

> It is too late a week with SCHMIDT's *Lexicon* and a dozen *Shakespeare Yearbooks* on our shelves to cast any slurs on German Shakespeare criticism," he wrote in the preface to *Hamlet*. "Were such the intention, German criticism could well endure them with equanimity. For the indefatigable labour, the keen analysis, the sympathetic and loving appreciation with characterise the treatment of SHAKESPEARE by German men of letters, comand the warmest admiration."[44]

Partly because of their particular devotion to *Hamlet* and also because of his genuine pleasure over his honorary membership in the Deutsche Shakespeare Gesellschaft, Furness decided to dedicate the variorum *Hamlet* to the Deutsche Shakespeare Gesellschaft of Weimar.

Mutual admmiration abounded. Thanking him for the gift of champagne and the compliment to the Society, Hermann Ulrici, president of the society, responded, "With joyful anticipation I look forward to your 'Hamlet' . . . the German Shakespeare Society will consider the dedication of the work a mark of high honor."[45] Baron von Loën, vice-president of the society, wrote, "I am indeed proud of the honour you bestow upon our society and myself; we shall do our best in Shakespearean study to answer your kind and honourable acknowledgments. We shake most heartily the hand you stretch out over the ocean to your german [sic] congenial thinkers."[46] Later, after receiving the finished volume, Karle Elze added, "Your edition of Hamlet has won the hearts of all German Shakespeareans and will secure for you a lasting place in the field of Shakespearean literature."[47]

With the appendix then behind him, Furness began the push to finish the printing and proofreading, which had resumed in October. By early December the printers had reached act three, scene two, and on January 11, 1877, the publication contract was signed. As January merged into February and February merged into March, virtually all correspondence ceased except the hastily scrawled notes to Norris asking to borrow books or soliciting his help to hunt for references or to verify citations. With Fish preparing the bibliography of *Hamlet* and with Norris helping wherever possible in the proofreading, Furness pushed on through the whirlwind of proofsheets, turning night into day and then working through the day as well. Catching an hour's nap before dinner from five to six in the evening and then reading proof until four or five in the morning, he worked frantically through March, sometimes for fifteen hours a day. In mid-March a query from Corson about the publication date provoked a humorous, yet weary, reply:

> I've almost a mind never to forgive you. Ya had '*heard*' forsooth that Hamlet was out, & rested in the supposition that I hadn't sent you a Copy!! Fie on't! From among the very earliest copies that come to my hand, one goes travelling Cornellward. No, Hamlet is not out & will not before a month yet. Ugh! I'm near dead with fatigue and disgust. The book is the failure of my old age. It's too big a job for any one man to undertake.[48]

Finally on April 1, the last proofsheet returned to the printer. "Not two hours ago, I finished Hamlet," he wrote to Ingleby. "Great heavens! what a relief. Good, bad, or indifferent, I don't care; the work is done, and it is the best I can do."[49] After clearing up the library, rearranging the books, and reopening his correspondence with Collier, Halliwell-Phillipps, and Fleay, Furness, half delirious with his newly acquired freedom, set off to Maryland with his oldest son Walter for a week of snipe shooting.

The first copy of *Hamlet*, which had been published first in England to avoid an unauthorized reprint, reached Furness on April 26. Despite his valiant effort to compress the book into one volume to avoid the tiresome tirades against Shakespearian commentators, the finished work exceeded 900 printed pages, and Lippincott insisted that it be divided into two volumes. The text, textual notes, and commentary alone in volume one stretched on for 479 pages. Six times the commentary on just one line pushed the text completely off the page. The "dram of eale"(1.4.36) required seven pages of commentary, and the word "eisel" in Hamlet's questions to the Queen at Ophelia's grave "Woo't weep? woo't fight? woo't fast? woo't tear thyself? / Woo't drink up eisel? eat a crocodile?"(5.1.262-63) received five pages of explanation. In this crux, after duly recording explanations ranging from the Yssel River in Denmark to the Nile River in Egypt, Furness bravely downed his cup of "eysell," the archaic word for vinegar. Here, as elsewhere, Furness exercised editorial caution. Although he announced in the preface to *Hamlet* his intention to form his own text, in practice he rarely departed from the received text if an ounce of meaning or allusion could be twisted from it. "In one qualification for an editor I know I am lacking parlously," he remarked to Ingleby.

> I haven't courage enough. When I began Hamlet I vowed to myself that I would be as liberal as the air. I would make what text I pleased. I give every other text on the same page & why shall I not please myself. So I go valiantly on over all the smooth places but when a tough passage confronts me, my courage oozes out & I hug the shore mapped out by Dyce & Staunton & the Cambridge Editors. I remember I once wrote to Corson, whose opinion I hold in high esteem, that I had decided upon a certain reading & he replied that if I so printed it; he should be *sick* for two days![50]

The second volume of *Hamlet*, containing the appendix, had 429 pages. Beginning with an essay on the date and text, Furness discussed the evidence for the lost play of Hamlet, known as the Ur-Hamlet, and then reprinted in full the corrupt 1603 quarto, probably a memorial construction of the full text. Following this came

The Hystorie of Hamblet, an English translation in 1608 of Bellefor-
est's French version in *Histoires Tragiques* (1576) of the *Historia
Danica* of Saxo Grammaticus, and also a new translation by Furness
from the German of *Fratricide Punished* or *Prince Hamlet of Denmark*, a memorial reconstruction of Shakespeare's play performed
by English actor John Green and his company in Dresden in 1626. In
addition to extracts from the English, German, and French critics,
the appendix also contained essays on the characters, the duration
of the action, and interpretations of various actors gathered
together by Norris. Drawing the most fire from reviewers was Furness's assertion, given without explanation after forty pages of English criticism on Hamlet's insanity, that Hamlet was neither mad nor
pretended to be so. "Critics are falling foul of me in all directions,"
he wrote to Francis J. Child, "for saying in my Preface to Hamlet that
the Danish Prince was neither mad nor pretended to be so. Though I
have reasons as thick as blackberries for my opinion, I think I shall
take warning by the Indian judge Macaulay refers to, whose de-
cisions were received with applause until on an unlucky day he gave
his reasons for them, and I shall maintain a discreet and masterly
silence."[51] In spite of volleys of protest from reviewers in *The Nation*
and *The Athenaeum*, no one took up Furness's challenge to "account
for Hamlet's being able, in the flash of time between the vanishing of
the Ghost and the coming of Horatio and Marcellus, to form, horror-
struck as he was, a plan for the whole conduct of his future life."[52]
Years later, however, when a Miss Margaret Jackson, on behalf of her
women's Shakspeare class in Wallingford, Connecticut, asked Furness to explain his opinion, he replied,

> Never make any apologies for writing to me on any Shakespearean
> subject. I'm frightfully busy, so that my answers must be of the
> briefest, yet I'll try to make them really answers. In using the word
> 'mad' I have a right to maintain that it shall mean uncompromisingly
> crazy—not eccentric, nor odd, but a downright unsettled intellect.
> Such a case of Madness Shakespeare has given us in Ophelia. Does
> Hamlet ever act or speak like Ophelia? A case of pretended madness
> Shakespeare has given us in Edgar's 'Mad tom' in Lear. Does Hamlet
> ever act or speak like 'Mad Tom'? Hamlet may be beside himself with
> grief for a time, but many a man is likewise so, whom no one would
> think of calling 'mad.' Of course Hamlet's apology to Laertes is a mere
> quibble—not worth considering. He never acted towards Laertes as

he says he did, and his actions at Ophelia's grave was mere rant as he himself calls it—but not one trace of madness in it, nor pretended madness. 'Are you answered?' as Shylock says. Think of Ophelia and Mad Tom, and you'll not accuse Hamlet of either madness or pretended madness.[53]

Praise for the Variorum *Hamlet* poured in from Wright, Longfellow, Child, Delius, Hudson, White, and others, but the most gratifying encouragement came from Harvard University. At its graduation exercises in Sanders Theatre on June 27, 1877, Harvard conferred upon him an honorary Master of Arts degree in recognition of the "extraordinary merit and value of his Shaksperian work." Wrote former classmate and then president of Harvard Charles W. Eliot, "The University is proud of your achievements, and looks forward with keen interest to the forthcoming fruits of your continued labors."[54]

Hoping to capitalize on the success of *Hamlet* by going to press with the next volume of the variorum in November 1878, Furness turned almost immediately to *King Lear*. From Lindenshade he wrote to Child in August, "I have begun to work on 'Lear' and am reading endless wearisome German stuff on the violation of the family relations as the basis of the tragedy. And with the thermometer at 90 degrees. Ora pro nobis."[55] By January 1878 he was collating the quartos and folios, and in February he enlisted Norris's help in collating the eighteenth-century editions.

The pace of work and circumstances, however, conspired against him. Even in January, as he grappled with the bibliographical puzzle of the quartos and folios, his resolve began to fade. "I had hoped to go to press with Lear next November," he confessed to Ingleby, "but Hamlet has aged me. I can't work as hard as I could last winter. 'What I am pleased to term my mind' gets very weary."[56] By March he had stopped working altogether. "I've had a touch of Halliwell's ailment: an utter aversion to work," he wrote in April. "For the last few weeks I have loathed the sight of my library table, and the thought of touching Shakespeare in the way of work has filled me with unutterable disgust. I have given way to it & am beginning to feel better, but it has been a dreary winter."[57] Death, illness, and financial failure in the family deepened his despondency. On February 21, after a short illness, Hodge, the tutor to the

Furness boys, had died abruptly, and Furness had assumed responsibility for the boys' lessons until a new tutor could be engaged.
Grammar lessons by day and *King Lear* by night soon led to exhaus-
tion. Early March found him sick with cold in bed where he received
news of the death of a kinsman James Castle and, three days later on
March 15, news of his uncle's failure in business. Even two weeks at
Atlantic City failed to lift his spirits, and on April 23, Furness missed
the annual Shakspere Society dinner, his first absence in eighteen
years. Unable to face Shakespeare and unsure that he would even
finish another play, Furness retired to Lindenshade for the summer,
leaving his Shakespeare books in town untouched.

Nevertheless, another unexpected encouragement revived the
Variorum. In June 1877, shortly after the Variorum *Hamlet* with its
dedication to the Deutsche Shakespeare Gesellschaft of Weimar has
reached Germany, Karl Elze and Hermann Ulrici, both officers of the
society and professors at the University of Halle, had moved that the
Halle faculty grant Furness an honorary Doctor of Philosophy degree. Their praise was both generous and genuine:

> Among contemporary Shakespearian scholars, Horace Howard Fur-
> ness of Philadelphia stands out as one of the finest; he can be called
> without exaggeration the leading Shakespeare scholar in America
> The New Variorum Edition (vol. I: Romeo & Juliet, vol. II: Macbeth, III
> & IV: Hamlet) begun by him in 1871 and carried on with astonishing
> diligence, distinguishes itself not only by its exhaustive erudition and
> mastery of the material *in toto*, but also by a sensitive and well-
> thought out criticism resting on a solid foundation of classical learn-
> ing. This edition has won the unanimous acclaim of all the
> Shakespeare-connoisseurs in America, England, and Germany, the
> more so since it answers a real need. The New Variorum Edition by
> Furness possesses yet another merit, which is to be found in only one
> other cast among English-speaking Shakespearian scholars; with the
> sole exception of Prof Ward of Manchester (author of the excellent
> *History of English Dramatic Literature*, London, 1875, 2 vols.), the
> English-speaking Shakespearian scholars either cannot handle Ger-
> man at all or do it very poorly. Prof. Furness has such a thorough
> knowledge of German Shakespearian criticism that not even the most
> trifling contribution to the literature escapes him. With his solid
> knowledge is associated a no less solid and benevolent judgment of
> German works, which are defended by Mr Furness against some
> limited English ill will in the foreword to the recent third volume

(Hamlet). In these circumstances we, the undersigned, believe that Mr Furness has earned the right to honorable recognition by the Germans, and it is hoped that this may have, moreover, an encouraging and positive effect on the continuation of his far-reaching and industrious undertaking. We therefore herewith move that the Philosophische Fakultät grant Horace Howard Furness, Esq., of Philadelphia, for the reasons herein given, the degree of Dr. der Philosophiae, honoris causa.

Halle, 14 June 1877   K. Elze
                                       H. Ulrici[58]

At the faculty meeting on June 20, 1877, one dissenting vote had made it impossible to grant the degree, but a year later on August 2, 1878, Ulrici and Elze again moved that the degree be granted, and this time the motion passed unanimously. "I hasten to inform you," wrote Elze to Furness after the faculty meeting,

that an hour ago you have been elected by our faculty a Ph. D. hon. causa. This well-earned recognition of your signal merits in the field of Shakespearean lore and criticism cannot give you more pleasure than it does to me. Indeed no German university had a stronger call to pass a vote of thanks to you than Halle where two Shakespeareans hold chairs. You have so essentially contributed to introduce German learning in America and England that Germany must be very ungrateful, if it did not acknowledge your merit.[59]

The diploma Furness passed on to Norris as "a sort of Shakespearian fragment"[60] to print in his "Shakespearian Gossip" column, but the honor and recognition he treasured. To A. F. Pott, Dean of the University of Halle, he wrote:

This most flattering acknowledgement of my humble labours is a reward higher than I had ever dreamed of, and I cannot exaggerate the pleasure that it gives me, nor the pride which I feel I can justly take in it. It is encouragement indeed to have a voice of approval reach me over so many thousand miles of land and sea, from a land too, whose supremacy in scholarship the world acknowledges, and from a university so renowned.[61]

And to Ingleby he exulted:

As for Lear, I haven't worked an hour on it this summer, and for the simple reason: I couldn't. I grew ineffably weary of all that kind of work and I am not at all sure that I should ever have touched another play again. But last week there came such a pleasant encouragement to me to go on, that my youth is renewed, & with it, zeal. The University of Halle sent me a Diploma, honoris causa of Ph.D. with such a flattering commendation of my edition that I am bound to finish another play if only to parade on the title page the honour I have received. Indeed, I am not ashamed to acknowledge the excessive pleasure that this most unexpected honor has given me.[62]

As if to feed his rekindled enthusiasm, a second honor reached Furness a few days later in the form of *The Family Library of British Poetry from Chaucer to the Present Time (1350-1878)*, edited by James T. Fields and Edwin Whipple and bearing the dedication "To Mr. and Mrs. Horace Howard Furness, whose help to the better understanding of Shakespeare has made debtors of all who study the greatest of English Poets, this volume is cordially inscribed by the editors."[63]

Encouraged by these unexpected honors and refreshed by vacation trips to Newport and Cape May, Furness moved back into town from Lindenshade on November 14, 1878, ready to resume his winter's work. With Norris's help in searching for stray comments on *Lear* and in collating the nineteenth-century texts, Furness worked steadily through the winter until by May *King Lear* was ready to go to press. Yet another unexpected honor had spurred him to complete the manuscript in time to go to press the following November. On March 14, 1879, at the 113th annual commencement of the Medical School, the University of Pennsylvania conferred upon Furness the honorary degree of Doctor of Laws. This third honorary degree since the publication of *Hamlet* apparently silenced all doubts about the continuation of the Variorum. After again that Spring hinting to Ingleby that *King Lear* might be his last play, Furness quickly admitted, "In point of fact I suppose I shall go on editing these plays until the curtain falls."[64]

With all the work completed for *King Lear*, except the bibliography which Norris had taken charge of, Furness devoted the summer months to preparing a second edition of *Hamlet*. From the early days of the Variorum, Furness had enlisted help from Norris and Rolfe in spotting errors and misprints for correction in future editions. William James Rolfe, who had formerly served as headmaster of the Cambridge High School and now devoted his time to editing a Shakespearian column in *The Literary World* and preparing a school edition of Shakespeare for Harper & Brothers, brought to this task his characteristic humor and enthusiasm. "Sometime at your convenience pray send me a list of such typographical errors as you may have found in Rom. & Juliet & Macbeth," Furness had written to Norris as *Hamlet* was going through the press. "Rolfe of Cambridgeport is after me with an awfully sharp stick & has found bushels!"[65] When Lippincott had proposed a new edition of *Hamlet* in May 1879, Furness again turned to Norris, Ingleby, and Rolfe for help.

While preparing his own school edition of *Hamlet* in 1878, Rolfe had combed the Variorum for misprints and kept up a running correspondence with Furness on the errors of *Hamlet*'s ways. "I've been looking over the first few pages of your *Hamlet* while a-fixin up my text," he wrote on March 17, "and I don't dislike it pretty bad in the main. You pick up some bad tricks of punctification from the Camb. editors, while you improve on 'em in spots. You evidently don't believe in the colon. . . ."[66] On March 24, he began,

> You dear old Variorum: Might a feller ask you a question or two—just for information? On p. 107 of your *Hamlet*, vol. I., wherefore 'unmixed' in line 104? You must have an ear for music, and a long one, to make melody out of with that scansion 'Unmix'd' suits my briefer ear, mi-boy. What a puncticous see-saw you keep up with your "ands" and your commas! . . . On page 167, you have " 'Faith," and on page 120 and several places "Faith." Didn't mean to—eh? But you aint to be trusted, you vacillating Variorum of a demd wiggling weathercock! I'd rather be a pagan heathen with no faith at all than to have two of 'em. A nice son of a Christian clergyman *you* are, with your brace of theologies—aint you? There's a nice bit of unrighteous indulgence in punctification on page 168: 'those, that would give,' etc. Only about three commas too many in one sentence. What do you expect to come to in your old age, if you sling commas round in that prodigal way in your youth?[67]

Finally after a dozen such letters had passed to Furness in three months without a reply, Rolfe concluded his scrutiny of *Hamlet* with an ultimatum:

> I should like to send you a list of *Hamlet* misprints and so forth before you depart to that warm climate where the eternal devil is even now

kindling a fire under one of his biggest cauldrons for you. But you don't want me to do it! You're afraid to look on the fearful catalogue! That's why you don't write to me! But how would you like to have me print the list in the *Literary World* or in Norris's "Shakespearian Gossip" or some such public place—eh? Bile me into applesauce if I don't do it soon if you don't write to me in a repentant frame![68]

The first to acknowledge the stubborn misprints that survived even the most careful proofreading, Furness confessed once to White, after failing to notice one of White's articles, "No Orestes was ever pursued by the Furies with more venom than a certain Percentage of Errors and Oversights follows up every man's most conscientious work."[69] Philosophically he accepted Rolfe's corrections and made the changes in each new edition. Norris's comment, while he proofread the bibliography for *King Lear*, "If any one has a good opinion of himself let him try to compile a Bibliography and it will take it out of him"[70] proved itself tenfold with the innumerable possibilities for misprints and errors in the Variorum textual notes and commentary.

In September Furness and family set off on a three-week vacation in Newport, Lenox, and Boston where they left Walter to begin his first year at Harvard. Arriving home in mid-October, Furness immediately applied the finishing touches to the commentary on *King Lear*, signed the publishing contract with Lippincott on November 11, and began the printing. To Ingleby he wrote in December,

If there be 'no word of Lear' in my letters, it is because I have too much of him in my daily (or rather nightly) life. I have been driving the printers at a desperate pace, & they in turn have driven me; it is now merely a question of time, which of us will kill the other; at present the odds are heavily in favour of the printers. When Lear is published the editor will be probably either dead or a slavering idiot, most likely the former, the latter would not be much of a change.[71]

Until the last possible minute before returning the proofsheets to the printers, Furness debated the textual enigmas with Norris, Hudson, Ingleby, Fleay, and Joseph Crosby, sometime Shakespearian critic from Zanesville, Ohio. Most puzzling to Furness in *King Lear* were the lines of Gloucester to Regan and Cornwall defending his aid to Lear in the storm:

> If wolves had at thy gate howl'd that stern time,
> Thou shouldst have said: 'Good porter, turn the key,
> All cruels else subscribe.' (3.7.62-64)

Wrote Furness to Ingleby in August, "I don't think I ever cudgelled my brains over a passage in Sh. more liberally than I have over 'All cruels else subscribed,' & I have become so bemazed and befogged that I don't know whether Shakespeare wrote Crosby or Crosby wrote Shakespeare. All I can remember of that note in the Epitome by Crosby is that was almost a waste of time to read or write it."[72] When the printers finally reached this scene, Furness had his answer ready. After duly recording the emendations and explanations of other commentators, he argued his own interpretation.

> This is to me the most puzzling phrase in this play, more puzzling even than 'runaways' eyes' or 'the dram of eale'; the multitude of emendations proposed for these latter show how easily the idea of the phrase is grasped: anybody, and everybody, is ready with an emendation there; here it is different. None of the interpretations are, to my mind, satisfactory . . . . In a case as puzzling as this, anything, as Dr. Johnson says elsewhere, may be tried; my attempt is seen in the text. Not unnaturally, I think it is the true reading; it adheres to the venerable authority of the First Folio, making 'subscribe' an imperative like 'turn.' The drift of the whole passage is the contrast between the treatment which Regan's father had received and that which would have been dealt, in that stern time, to wolves and other animals, howsoever cruel. "Thou shouldst have said: Good porter, open the gates, acknowledge the claims of all creatures, however cruel they may be at other times;' or perhaps: 'open the gates; give up all cruel things else,' i.e. forget that they are cruel."[73]

Time and again throughout the commentary on *King Lear*, Furness set forth his own opinions, corrected the mistakes of previous commentators, and added sarcastic quips to what he termed "sign post criticism" or labored explanations of obvious points. "Can anything be more irritating," he complained to Fanny Kemble,

> than a sententious explanation of a line whose meaning is as clear as the sun at high noon? No one knows, how often at such notes I grind my teeth in impotent rage—and yet having assumed the position of an impartial judge for the benefit of the public I must sum up the

evidence on both sides, indifferent whether the matter in dispute be a potato or a diamond. Then too pray remember, in mitigation of my monstrous volume, that as Shakespeare is 'myriad-minded,' to that extent are the phases under which he is viewed by his innumberable admirers—one critic is daft over the metre; another, over his contemporary allusions; another, over the order of his plays; another, over the legal, medical, botanical and religious allusions etc. etc. The sum of all these represents the Shakespeare-world; and a microcosm of that world I try to give, retaining as decent a respect for the dead as though I were in the personal presence of the living.[74]

Irritation often overruled such resolutions, however, and his impatience showed as he increasingly stepped out of his variorum objectivity to settle editorial disputes to his own liking. "What once made me laugh in foolish criticism," Furness confided to Fleay, "now makes me surly."[75] And the critics applauded. "I was glad to see more bits of your own criticism than before,"[76] wrote Furnivall when the volume appeared; and Norris, Crosby, and White, who in his *New York Times* review strongly objected to the inclusion of much nonsensical commentary, all agreed.

With increased editorial expression in the Variorum comentary came increased comment at least privately to his friends on the meaning of the play. To Ingleby he confided:

Lear interests me far more than any tragedy I have yet studied. I wouldn't exchange it for two Hamlets. I don't think Shakespeare himself knew what Hamlet meant, but he knew and we all know, very well what Lear means. And then the infinite pathos! Where is the pathos, that stirs the depths, in Hamlet? certainly nowhere until the final blow is struck & Hamlet dies. To me the only defect that there is in Lear, is ineradicable, & that is the character of Cordelia. Unless she had acted as she did in the first scene there would have been no tragedy, but she is none the less disagreeable on that acc't. She loved herself far more than she loved her Father, & she cared more to spite her sisters than to gratify him. Of the prime virtue of renunciation she hadnt a jot. Either this, or she was a stupid girl & hadn't quickness enough to parry her doting old Fathers question with some playful extravagence (Ask Rose how she manages you). There are the horns of the dilemma, choose ye. In the Fifth Act, I grant you, she is divinely lovely. But she *ought* to have come to the rescue of her Father; she was the cause of all his misfortunes, & she rightly pays what our friends the Germans call the tragische Schuld with her life. But, Oh! the poetry throughout the play! that is ineffable. [77]

And he later added to White, "As for Cordelia (will you swear by Acheron not to betray me?)—as for Cordelia (you swear not to blab don't you?) as for Cordelia—I strongly suspect she was—a minx! After the line 'With washed eyes Cordelia leaves ye!' how I did long to insert the stage direction (Exit—with a flirt of her petticoats)."[78]

The fool he discussed with Edwin Booth:

What you say about the Fool is perfectly true. His rasping of Lear's quivering nerves is well nigh incomprehensible, unless we suppose one of two things (I don't want to be bumptiously dogmatic & restrict the solution to two and only two methods, I mean that there are only two ways in which 'what I am pleased to term my mind' has solved the puzzle for me). First: although the Fool is one of Shakespeare's most marvellous creations yet to a large extent he is the typical Fool of the age. Now, you know as well as I, that those fools were nothing if not rude and insolent to the very last degree. A tender gentle fool would be almost as false as a dandified Caliban. Therefore Shakespeare had to make the Fool cruel in his gibes, or give him no gibes at all, which would have been absurd. This is one of my solutions and I think a poor one. The other is, that the Fool is one of those gentle transparent simple hearted people who weep with those that weep and laugh with those that laugh and yet out of the very simplicity of their nature, will utter the most cruel home truths. Saturated with his own grief for the King he really doesn't see how his words pierce and goad. They are so much less than he feels that he doesn't see how sharp they are. (D—n quill pens!) This solution I like better. I think Macready went far astray when he gave the part to a young girl. Ah no, the Fool is an older man than Lear in worldly wisdom. Grizzling hair has cleared his brain. Luckily for you, my dear fellow I was interrupted here, and amidst the hurtling engagements of the next few days I don't know when I shall be able to excruciate you further— Therefore, ever so many happy New Years to you! (Tucket sounded) and to Mrs. Booth, whose Hand I reverently kiss.[79]

On February 14, 1880, Furness returned the last proofsheet to the printers, and less than a month later on March 11, the first copy was in his hands. Following the tradition begun with the dedication of *Romeo and Juliet* to the Philadelphia Shakspere Society and continued with the dedication of *Hamlet* to the German Shakespeare Society, he had dedicated *King Lear* to the New Shakespeare Society of London. In addition to text, textual notes, and commentary, the Variorum *Lear* contained extracts from Nahum Tate's eighteenth-century adaptation of the play and essays on the text, the date of composition, the source of the plot, the duration of the action, Lear's insanity, actors, and costumes. Extracts from German criticism translated by his father, a bibliography of the play prepared by Norris, and an index to the entire volume compiled by his wife made up the rest of the volume.

In addition to the increased editorial comment, this volume of the Variorum signalled a further innovation in the plan—refusal to modernize the spelling. Furness also edged closer to adopting the First Folio text instead of constructing his own text—a change he would make officially in *Othello*. Justifying himself to Ingleby, Furness wrote, "The modernising of Shakespeare grows more wearisome to me every day. My edition is essentially one for scholars and students & surely for them the Folio is the most satisfactory."[80] Corson had long argued the supremacy of the First Folio, and since all textual variants appeared on each page anyway, Furness virtually decided to drop his original plan of forming his own text with each disputed reading resolved according to the majority of the ablest editors. "Although we may not have in the Folio the very text, 'absolute in its numbers,' as Shakespeare 'conceived it,' yet with all its defects it is much better than that of the Quarto, which is evidently one of those 'stolne and surreptitious' copies denounced by Heminge and Condell," he wrote in the Preface. "Wherefore, in this edition the text of the FIRST FOLIO has been virtually followed, but without, it is to trusted, an absolute surrender to that 'modern Manicheeism, the worship of the Printer's devil.'"[81] In the later Variorums even that proviso would be dropped.

Letters of congratulation poured in for the next two months from the Shakespearians—Norris, Crosby, Hudson, Brae, Rolfe, Halliwell-Phillipps, Timmins, Collier, Furnivall, Fleay, Fanny Kemble, Ingleby, White, and Mary Cowden-Clarke; from the Germans—Leo, Ulrici, Schmidt, and Köhler; from old Harvard friends—Longfellow, Francis J. Child, James T. Fields, James Hubbard, librarian of the Boston Public Library, and Justin Winsor, Harvard College librarian; and from new correspondents like William Gladstone and Alexander

Carlyle, who wrote, "My uncle, Mr. Carlyle, desires me to say that he accepts with much pleasure and gratitude your volume on 'King Lear.' He remarked to me also that yours is decidedly the best edition of Shakespeare yet published."[82] These private letters of praise were complemented by two additional public notices of Furness's growing literary reputation.

The first had come on January 6, 1880, when Furness was still reading proofsheets for *King Lear*. A letter from Cadwalader Biddle announced that Furness had been elected a trustee of the University of Pennsylvania, an honor which he accepted the same day to begin twenty-five years of devoted service to the university. During the next two decades, as chairman of the trustees' Library Committee, he would oversee the building of the new University Library designed by his brother Frank Furness; and while serving on the trustees' Department of Arts Committee, he would help Felix Schelling organize Pennsylvania's new Department of English and give it an early lead among the newly developing English literature curricula in Ivy League universities. These achievements, however, lay in the future. At the beginning of 1880, the simple invitation to serve was honor enough as he took his seat with John Welsh, J. B. Lippincott, Bishop Stevens, Eli Kirk Price, Judge George Sharswood, Silas Weir Mitchell, George Dana Boardman, and other movers and shakers of academic and cultural life in Philadelphia.

The second honor came just a month after the publication of *King Lear*. On April 16, 1880, the American Philosophical Society nominated him for membership, and Furness proudly joined his father who had been elected to membership forty years before almost to the day. This honor, coming amid the congratulatory letters on *King Lear*, aptly marked the end of a decade devoted to Shakespearian study. From the trial *Romeo and Juliet* in 1871 through *Macbeth* in 1873, *Hamlet* in 1877, and then *King Lear* in 1880, Furness had grown from a serious, but unknown, Shakespearian student to an internationally recognized Shakespearian authority. On intimate terms with scholars from Boston to Bonn, from Cornell to Cambridge, and recipient of three honorary degrees and universal acclaim for his literary study, Furness had brought to fledgling American scholarship a new prestige and reputation during the decade of the 1870s.

MAN ABOUT TOWN

Good company, good wine, good welcome,
Can make good people.
—Henry VIII 1.4.6-7

I beseech you heartily, some of you go home with
me to dinner.
—The Merry Wives of Windsor 3.2.70-71

Nineteenth-century patrician Philadelphia was a city of gentlemen's clubs and fraternal camaraderie; and in spite of his increasing deafness, Furness held up his end with the best of the clubbable set. To the Shakspere Society, the Union League, and the Harvard Club of Philadelphia, he added during the 1870s and 1880s the Penn Club, the University Club, the Social Arts Club, the Triplets, and the Fortnightly Club, which later became the Wistar Association. He remained most proud of the Shakspere Society, even though after *Romeo and Juliet* his enthusiasm flagged as he far surpassed the other Brothers in Shakespearian scholarship. At the end of the

112

society's study of *Antony and Cleopatra* on April 23, 1873, Furness resigned as secretary and in 1876 at his own request was placed on the retired list, confining his attendance, with the rare exception, to the annual dinners. "I no longer attend the meetings of the Shak. Soc. for two reasons," he confided to Ingleby in December 1873, "first because I am deaf as forty thousand posts, and secondly, because their study is of the smallest and most desultory kind; though I am always kept advised of their doings through their chief Officer & mainstay, Fish, who always dines with me the evenings of their meetings."[1]

The long friendship with Fish, legal colleague, co-founder of the Harvard Club, and fellow Shakespearian, came to a sudden end with Fish's death on May 5, 1879 (Shakespeare's birthday O.S.). At his bedside the day before, Furness was probably the last person that he recognized. "We have been loiterers & workers in the Shakespeare field for twenty years," Furness wrote that night in his journal, "and I shall miss him very sadly."[2] Publicly, Furness presented the memorial resolutions at a meeting of the Philadelphia Bar on May 8, honoring Fish for his learning, his grasp of legal principles, and his broad culture. Privately, he confessed to Ingleby, Halliwell-Phillipps, and White his doubt that the Shakspere Society would survive without Fish's persistent and unflagging enthusiasm, which had held the Shakspere Society together for twenty-seven years and made it the oldest Shakespeare society in existence.

As next oldest member, however, Furness stepped into the gap, and at the next meeting on May 20 he was elected Dean, a position he held until his own death in 1912. *King Lear* was chosen for the next year's study, and when the Society resumed its meetings on October 14, Furness read as the prolegomena for the year's study a large part of the appendix to the Variorum *King Lear*, then going through the press. Furness faithfully attended the readings during the winter's study. Then, apparently assured that the society would continue under the leadership of the Vice-Dean, Richard Ashhurst, he again pleaded his deafness and resumed his custom of attending only the annual dinner, never omitting to send copies of the Bill of Fare to his English Shakespearian friends.

Although the Shakspere Society was his first and oldest club, the Penn Club carried more prestige. Located in rooms rented from Furness at 720 Locust Street, the Penn Club, perhaps more than any other, was Furness's club. He joined the club as a charter member at its first reception on March 25, 1875; served as its second president from 1877 to 1887; and continued on its board of directors until 1905. Organized by members of the Penn Monthly Association with the original intention of entertaining literary and scientific guests of the Centennial Exhibition in 1876, the club soon occupied a permanent place in Philadelphia society. The club membership, limited to two hundred prominent men of education and culture, proclaimed as its purposes "the association of authors, artists, men of science and the learned professions, and amateurs of music, letters and the fine arts; and by receptions given to men or women distinguished in art, literature, science or politics and other kindred means, to promote social intercourse among its members."[3] Informal receptions, held every month or two, entertained visiting dignitaries and celebrities. During Furness's years the guest list read like a roll call of nineteenth-century actors and authors: Edwin Booth; Joseph Jefferson; Sir Henry Irving; Augustin Daly; Lawrence Barrett; the Italian tragedian Tommaso Salvini; the French playwright and actor Dion Boucicault; James Murdoch, who played Romeo to Fanny Kemble's Juliet; Bayard Taylor; Walt Whitman; Edmund Gosse; Bret Harte; and Madame Henri Greville.

One of the most glittering of those receptions took place on December 17, 1886, when the Penn Club hosted Pennsylvania professors Easton, Clarke, and Klapp and the cast of *The Acharnians*, a comedy of Aristophanes produced in the original Greek by students of the University of Pennsylvania. The records of the Penn Club give the following account:

It was a gala night for men of the University, all the branches of whose interests were represented—its Board of Trustees, Faculties, Alumni and Undergraduates. The affair was rendered doubly pleasant by the presentation of silver cups, of simple but chaste designs of Greek art, to the three prominent guests of the evening, and the gentlemen upon whom most of the work of the play devolved—Doctors Easton, Clarke and Klapp. Mr. Furness opened the ball with a witty speech full of pertinent allusions, which were received with great applause, and moreover was so inspired by the intellectuality and Hellenism of those present as to indulge his Attic wit in jokes in the original Greek. At the conclusion of Mr. Furness's remarks, Provost Pepper arose, and turning to the three distinguished guests of the evening, with a few well-chosen words, made the presentation to them of the testimonials given in appreciation of their labors. These gentlemen had heard nothing of what was coming, and their faces witnessed their innocent surprise and gratification. It was the order of the evening that there should be no response, and after the chorus had sung some selections from 'The Acharnians,' all adjourned to the supper room.[4]

The Fortnightly Club, also noted for its intellectual and influential receptions, listed Furness among its charter members. Formed on December 10, 1884, for the purpose of holding receptions on alternate Saturdays between December and April, the club was limited to twenty members, including prominent Philadelphians Henry C. Lea, Charles Platt, E. Coppee Mitchell, Charles Harrison, William Sellers, Fairman Rogers, Thomas McKean, Francis W. Lewis, Caspar Wistar, J.S. Newbold, William Pepper, George and Craig Biddle, and William F. Norris. The club regulations were modeled after the then defunct Wistar Party: "The number of invited citizens shall not exceed one hundred in addition to the members of the Club. Members shall have the privilege of introducing Strangers visiting the City. The entertainment shall not exceed oysters in two styles with one kind of Salad; ices and fruit; two kinds of light wine (sparkling wines excluded) and beer if desired."[5]

On October 30, 1886, Moncure Robinson and Isaac Lea, the two surviving members of the Wistar Association, elected to the Association Furness and the seven other members of the Fortnightly Club who were also members of the American Philosophical Society. The club then officially changed its name to the Wistar Association, removed from the Association's by-laws the provision that members had to belong to the American Philosophical Society, and formally revived the seventy-year-old tradition of the Wistar Party. Members took it in turns to give the receptions, and Furness was host of the dinners on March 5, 1887, March 15, 1890, and February 25, 1893, before resigning from the Association at the end of the 1893 season. Guests during those years included Mark Twain; the explorer Stanley; Pennsylvania Chief Justice Mitchell; James Russell Lowell; Attorneys-General Benjamin Brewster and Wayne MacVeagh; and Edmund Gosse, Clark Leturer in English Literature at Trinity College, Cambridge, who was a guest of Furness on January 3, 1885.

The formal cultural associations fostered by the Wistar Parties and the Penn Club were carried on more informally at a dozen other gentlemen's clubs throughout the city. It was Judge Biddle who had declared that "Saturday night was a gentlemen's night out,"[6] an epigram for which Furness added the gloss that "usage, profane not sacred, has consecrated Saturday evening to mirthful festivities, attuned thereto by the serene contemplation that we 'have tried all the week to be good.'"[7] Such indulgence awaited Furness at the Social Art Club (later the Rittenhouse Club) of which he was a member from 1875 to 1891, the University Club on whose Board of Governors he served between 1881 and 1882, and the Journalists' Club to which he was elected an honorary member in March 1883.

Significant among these clubs was the Triplets, a private eating club begun in 1879 by Furness, John Foster Kirk, editor of *Lippincott's Magazine*; and Lucius Clarke Davis, editor of *The Inquirer*. Years later Furness recalled how the club began:

> It was about twenty-five years ago that Kirk and I had an exceedingly pleasant dinner at Davis's home. Davis at that time was night editor of 'The Inquirer,' and after dinner as Kirk and myself accompanied Davis on his way to 'The Inquirer' Office, we spoke of the pleasure we all three should find in a repetition, at stated intervals of just such an informal dinner where there would be good talk. Whereupon we then and there decided that we would start a little club, untramelled by any organization whatsoever, and would at once begin it by naming, each of us, a man, who, if he were entirely unobjectionable to the others, and would join us, would become a fellow-diner. And inasmuch as all good things go by threes, we decided to meet every three weeks and call ourselves 'The Triplets.'[8]

The club met variously in the upper story of a restaurant at Broad and Chestnut Streets, at the Penn Club, and at the Continental Hotel. Over the years members of the Triplets included the sculptor Howard Roberts, Henry Reed, William Clark, Victor Gillou, John Bach McMaster, Morton McMichael, George Riché, the archaeologist Daniel G. Brinton, Simon Stern, Fairman Rogers, and Furness's brother Frank.

At one of the early dinners of the Triplets, on March 12, 1879, Furness met Walt Whitman. Struck then and afterward more by his appearance than by his poetry, Furness later described the meeting in his journal.

Last Wednesday our ninefold dinner took place & we had a delightful time. Our guests were Atherton Blight, Col. Forney (who was only a vehicle for the sake of getting our third & last guest) Walt Whitman.[9] I sat between the two latter. Walt, as he likes to be called, awed us all by his grand presence, his large bulk, his snowy hair, and his majestic beard, spreading over his broad chest, uncovered by aught else, his collar was unbuttoned, (if it had a button) & thrown back, exposing his bare chest Everything about him was exquisitely neat and clean— his hands irreproachable & he was very fond of leaning back in his chair & folding them across his breast. He is inclined to be shy & reserved, so that he may seem very different upon further acquaintance, but what I should say was his most striking characteristic at first sight is an entire absence of humour. I don't think he once smiled even & some droll things were said both by Kirk & Nicholls. He talked about Tennyson whom he greatly admires as the true exponent of the present age, draping the past in folds of beauty, counteracting the hard unyielding matter of fact of democracy. etc. etc. We were not greatly impressed by what he said & after his departure Kirk said that Walt was like little children who should be seen and not heard. In sooth he is great to behold, a head, hair & shoulders like an original of Rubens. I'm not sure that there isn't a strong tinge of Silenus about his looks.[10]

Furness could muster only tepid enthusiasm for Whitman's poetry—on one occasion he even urged Whitman to expurgate at least some of his books for the sake of a wider audience—yet he never tired of praising Whitman's looks. "I had meant to have talked to you about Walt Whitman whose writings I admire with a 'but,'" he wrote to Sir Edward Strachey after Whitman's death. "I found more pleasure from his Olympian-Jove like appearance than from anything he ever wrote."[11] On March 29, 1892, the day before Whitman's funeral, Furness confided to Edmund Gosse,

I'm not sure that the very best of Walt was not his Jovian looks. Latterly when I used to see him in his room, with that majestic avalanche of a beard flowing in snowy luxuriance over his chest, it was not hard to convert his blue wrapper into blue sky and the vast & innumerable newspapers piled knee deep around him into the clouds of Olympus. And oh, the lot of funny stories about him, gossip pure & simple but nourishing, which 'twould take so long to write & must be reserved for the pleasant time when you & I can ha'e a crack thegethir.[12]

One such story he did recount to Strachey: "I once met him in the street and said 'My dear Walt, you must allow me to thank you personally for being so handsome. I hope it don't offend you.' 'No, Horace,' he replied, 'I like it.'"[13]

The friendship appeared to be mutual. In the early days of the Triplets Club, Whitman often joined the club for dinner and evidently enjoyed himself. On March 27, 1879, he wrote to John Burroughs, "I am as usual—was over to Phila: last evening to a nice dinner party, all men, artists, &c, Horace Furness, (a good fellow)— his brother Frank, architect—my friend Forney—Kirke, (of Lippincott's Mag:) & eight or ten others—a jolly time."[14] When Whitman was too ill to get out, Furness visited him in Camden. Whitman mentioned to Richard Bucke one such visit in 1890: "Horace Furness and his father the old doctor (88) here to see me this afternoon—a splendid antique, but looks like a cadaver tho—Horace very deaf, gets along sort o' with ear trumpet—both real friends of mine."[15] About a year earlier Whitman had discussed Furness and his father with Horace Traubel: of the elder, Whitman had said, "I do not think he takes to Leaves of Grass. The Doctor's theories are all arranged with reference to Dryden, Bryant—as he was tutored in his early days;" and of Horace, Whitman had added, "'I am persuaded he is an absorber, a considerable reader, of Leaves of Grass: more radical: has newer ideas: friendly not only as a person but professionally, so to speak.' Then: 'Curiously, I have never found his deafness a bar: I have talked with him now and then: we seemed to get along very well together.'"[16]

Furness did everything that he could to alleviate the supposed poverty of Whitman during his Camden years. More than once he contributed to anonymous collections for the poet, adding on one occasion to the fund organizer Thomas Donaldson, "I am personally grateful to you for the privilege of aiding in the gift to 'the good grey poet.' How admirably you managed it. Pray always count me in whenever there is anything to be done for the ease or comfort of Walt Whitman."[17] In 1886 Furness, along with S. Weir Mitchell, George Childs, and Richard Watson Gilder, organized a lecture and poetry reading at the Opera House to benefit Whitman, and three years later he arranged an anonymous gift of $100 for an autograph copy of "O Captain! My Captain!" for S. Weir Mitchell, commenting, "A kinder or more delicate way of helping the grand old man cannot be devised." [18] During the last six or eight years of Whitman's life, according to William Thayer, Furness and George Childs, co-owner of the Philadelphia *Public Ledger*, subscribed "an annual sum for his upkeep; and when he grew too lame to walk, they supplied a horse and phaeton and paid a young man to act as his driver and valet."[19] As a final gesture to the poet Furness served as one of twenty-three honorary pall bearers for Whitman's funeral at Harleigh Cemetery in Camden on March 30, 1892.

Only after Whitman's estate had been settled and the truth about the poet's private life and his slyness in money matters became known, did Furness's attitude change. Even seven years after Whitman's death, however, Furness's disillusionment with the poet was tempered by his romantic memory of Whitman's appearance. When sending to Gosse a copy of *Calamus: A Series of Letters Written During the Years 1868-1880 by Walt Whitman to a Young Friend (Peter Doyle)*, Furness wrote,

> In one way, these Letters may do good,—albeit no good to Walts fame. They may reveal what an out and out poseur the 'Good Grey Poet' was all his life. He posed as poor, and he died with thousands of dollars in the Bank; he posed as a writer of absolutely spontaneous lines, and his MS reveals the utmost fastidiousness; he posed as a child of nature indifferent to food or clothes, these Letters show that he adored buckwheat cakes and salmon. We have his brains in alchohol at the University, and when dissection has taught us more about the most subtile organ, look out for revelations of character. But don't tell this about his brains—he had friends who have so little, that if they knew it, they might make it unpleasant for us. No, your phrase is perfect: his is poetry in solution & when to this you add that he was one of the handsomest, grandest looking men that ever strolled down from Olympus you have all I care to remember about him.[20]

Although Furness passed easily among the prominent of Philadelphia society, making the acquaintance of the great and the near great, and although for years the family was listed in *Boyd's Blue Book; a Society Directory Containing a List of the Names and Ad-*

dresses of the Elite of the City of Philadelphia, Furness preferred to spend a quiet life centered on Shakespeare and his own family. "We are the humblest of mortals, with a perfect aversion to general society from which we keep aloof by every devisable art, and yet it seems to me that we cannot get an evening to ourselves; it is the plague of living in a city," he once complained to Ingleby when discouraged with the slow progress on *Hamlet*.

> Strangers are eternally here whom we have to ask to dinner and then bang! goes an evening. And then I grind my teeth with rage, to think that the pleasantest work on earth has to be postponed for such evanescent pastime. We breakfast at 8:30. I teach my three boys from 9:30 till 2 p.m.—lunch and then transact business down town till about four, then take a brisk walk, rain or shine, with my two dogs (a huge Newfoundland weighing over 100 lbs & a superb setter) of about four miles, then home, and dress for dinner at six, and on happy evenings at work at Shakespeare at eight and on till two a.m. That is the happy life at which I aim & which I can compass when we are let alone. Mrs. Furness works at her desk not far from mine all the evening till about eleven when she retires & leaves me alone with my books and my pipe.[21]

Such complaints about entertaining strangers resulted in part from genuine scholarly frustration with interruptions; nevertheless, the occasional evening at the Walnut Street Theatre and the quiet chat with theatrical or literary friends were welcome distractions from study. The wine cellar of 222 West Washington Square was well stocked with wines from France and sherry by the cask from Spain, and many a pleasant evening of convivial Shakespearian gossip was spent with J. Parker Norris, A.I. Fish, then editor of *The Atlantic* James T. Fields, Hiram Corson, John S. Hart, and, whenever he was playing in Philadelphia, Edwin Booth. A humorous exchange of letters between Furness and Bayard Taylor suggests the cultured and witty tone of those evenings.[22]

222 West Washington Square
27 February 1876

Dear Bayard Taylor:

An thou hast no choicer hostelrie, wherein to doff thy habergeon when thou comest here next month to speak brave words, dismount, I prithee, at our door, and tirl the pin, and the portcullis (or thingum-bob, what-ever it is) shall stand as open to receive thee, as is already the heart of thine old friend

Horace Howard Furness

142 East 18th St. New York.
March 1, 1876.

Now, by my halidome! Sir Knight de Fournaise, I did not mistake me: it *was* the clank of thy destrier's hoof! I had even seated myself at my board, with a chine of beef, *gules, couchant*, twain demisoddon eggs, *regardant*, and manchet of bread, when McCann, the seneshal, tendered me thy missive on the point of his mace. Gadzooks! was my first word. "The saints forfend, an it be an evil tiding!" cried my good dame. "The play of blades is never evil," quod I, "whether on boss of steel or trencher of silver: but beshrew thy fears, good lass, this is venison, not malison!" Whereat she greeted, as is woman's foolish habit.

Yet I bethink me, worshipful friend and brother, that I am only free to partake of thy junketing between nones and compline, and must even depart with curfew; sith it hath been agreed upon by previous missives, that a clerk learned in the law, by whom certain feoffs of mine have been engrossed, hath engaged to confer with me after the multitude have had speech of me. Wherefor I have bidden him unto an hostel with a stony name, in the which, our conference being ended, it behooveth me to take shelter for the night, for I depart with the first stroke of matin chimes. Nathless, we shall have space for much courteous parley; and as for the ancient bins in thy castle cellar, *splendeur de Dieu!* I mind me well of them. Until then, St Dunstan and St. Veronica have thee in their good keeping!

Thine,
Bayard de Taillefer.

Aside from Shakespeare and his circle of literary friends, Furness's family commanded most of his attention. The birth of Caroline Augusta on July 3, 1873, completed the family, then consisting of Walter, age 12; Horrie, age 8; and Willy, age 7. Beyond the immediate family, parents, uncles, bothers, sisters, and in-laws produced a close-knit and congenial group. His father and mother still maintained the family home at 1426 Pine Street, next door to his uncle, James T. Furness, and his eight children at 1420 Pine Street. Furness's brother, the architect Frank Furness, lived across the street from 222 West Washington Square at 711 Locust Street in one of several houses belonging to Furness. His sister Annis Lee, married to medical doctor Caspar Wistar, lived at 1303 Arch Street, and his brother-in-law, Fairman Rogers, lived at 202 West Rittenhouse Square. Holidays, often celebrated together at 1426 Pine Street, were filled with merriment, good conversation, and children.

Devoted to his children, Furness spent much of his time with them when not working on Shakespeare. "It's a blessed thing to have a lot of little children around you—it's a great means of education & grace," Furness wrote to Norris, congratulating him on the birth of his second son, and then added philosophically, "But I find it's a blesseder thing to have big ones around you, & you can't have 'em big, without having 'em little first. The amount of pure pleasure and not to say royal fun, that I get out of my boys is simply incalculable."[23]

Perhaps for that reason Furness undertook to tutor his own boys. Although at one time he had daydreamed to Halliwell-Phillipps about putting them to school in Geneva or Vevey and spending his winters in England, in reality he spent his winters in the schoolroom of 222 West Washington Square, devoting four to five hours every day to their lessons. In 1877, he hired a Miss Case to teach the younger boys and Mr. Hodge, a law student at the University of Pennsylvania, to prepare Walter, then sixteen years old, for Harvard. When Hodge died unexpectedly on February 21, 1878, Furness again took over the lessons until a replacement could be found. "All this week I have been busy attending to the boys lessons," he noted in his journal. "Time is too precious before their examination in June to permit of any holydays. It sent me to the Dictionary and Grammar again in handsome style."[24] On the recommendation of William Goodwin, Professor of Greek at Harvard, James N. Byrne, a recent Harvard graduate, was engaged to fill Hodge's place. For the next year Byrne tutored Walter until he took his Harvard entrance examinations in June 1879 and was admitted with conditions in chemistry, physics, and Latin. Although the old-boy network and Furness's close friendship with his cousin Goodwin, Lowell, Longfellow, and Childs almost guaranteed Walter's admission, it did not help once classes began that September. After two years in the freshman class and one year as a sophomore, Walter left Harvard to dabble in architecture and work for his Uncle Frank. During Walter's last year at Harvard, not wishing to make the same mistake with the younger boys, Furness sent Horrie and Willy off to St. Paul's School in Concord, New Hampshire, where they studied from 1881 to 1884.

From October to May the Furness family followed their literary and social life at 222 West Washington Square, but from May to October they led the farmer's life at Lindenshade, their country estate in Wallingford. The rare books were secured in the fireproof vault, curtains and ornaments were packed away, and the house in town was left in the charge of Edward Archer or one of the other servants. Lindenshade served as summer headquarters for the entire Furness clan, hardly a week passing without visits from relatives or close friends like Atherton Blight and Norris. The formal evening dinner in their winter quarters, at which Furness never appeared without a dress coat, gave way to country manners and high tea at seven o'clock.

Since the first summer at Lindenshade in 1864, Furness had steadily added to the original estate: twenty-one acres in 1867, nineteen in 1871, eight in 1872, one in 1873, and six in 1874, until he owned in excess of eighty acres. The farm, greenhouse, and orchard supplied the family year around with food and the horses with fodder. The summer records for 1874, for example, show eighty-nine bushels of oats, forty-seven of wheat, and twenty of rye thrashed in September and forty-three full two-horse loads of hay barned in July. Ten bushels of Early Rose potatoes were sent to 1426 Pine Street, and ten bushels of Early Rose and forty bushels of Early Goodrich went to Washington Square in October. Two barrels of pears and one barrel of apples went to Pine Street, one barrel of pears to Arch Street, and eight barrels of apples to Washington Square. One hundred and twenty pounds of honey were gathered in August 1875. Rather modestly Furness described the estate to Ingleby: "Our establishment at Lindenshade is very humble compared with yours at Valentines. We only spend the summer months there, and generally take a jaunt to the seaside or mountains besides; its main purpose is to raise hay & oats & corn for our horses in town during the winter and our green houses there are merely for the propagation of the summer bedding plants, and our winter vegetables, such as cucumbers, salad, radishes & beans. I superintend the operations myself & prefer to have a gardener who doesn't know as much as I do myself, so you can readily conceive that our operations are on a very sober scale"[25]—an obvious understatement since the gardeners, grooms, farmers, household servants, and other retainers reached in 1877 a total of fifty-four.

Furness never tired of planning and planting bigger and better gardens. "Last Monday the apple and pear trees &c arrived from West Chester at about 3 p.m.," begins the journal entry for November 3, 1878.

> After dinner Kate & myself went out to help plant them, and a most delightful time we had. While James Murray & Sam Hutton were plying their shovels & spades we were distributing the trees in their proper places. It was a rare sight to see Kate struggling through the rough corn stubble with a long trailing bundle of apple trees, her face aglow with pleasure. We all worked bravely and shortly after sunset we finished planting the sixty eighth apple tree. It was one of the most delightful afternoons we have ever had. The weather was most delicious, clear & cool. The next morning we finished the cherries and the pears, and began upon a huge box of trees and shrubs.[26]

The formal gardens surrounding the salmon-colored house grew more elaborate every year. Terraces were added in 1875 and a fountain in 1878. In June 1876 several thousand roses were in bloom, and the greenhouse in 1878 boasted a lemon tree bearing twenty-six lemons, a passion vine with over four thousand blossoms, lilies of great variety, mushrooms year around, and cut flowers transported by the score to Washington Square.

Thus passed the summers at Lindenshade. The distractions of winter work left safely behind in town, surrounded by his flowers, Furness delighted in the life of the country gentleman devoted to his family. Vacations, spent in New York, Boston, Newport, or Cape May, invariably included the entire family. "When we travel our name is Gad: a troop cometh," he explained to Ingleby in 1875, declining Ingleby's invitation for an extended visit. "We go nowhere without our children & we love them too well to have our friends sigh for the memory of the 'much calumniated King Herod.'"[27]

The happiest outings and occasions, however, happened right at Lindenshade. Birthdays were celebrated by the whole family in high style with the person of honor enthroned in the parlor to receive his presents. "18 Aug. Willie's Birthday," reads a sample journal entry.

> After breakfast the Procession filed in, as follows: Polly with a Puppet, Horrie with a Game, Walter with a large tin ship, Mother with an Aquarium, Lily with a ball, Father with a tent, Aunt Nannie with a frightful Crocodile, Grand Mother with a Japanese Monkey and a Birthday Cake, surrounded by nine candles & bearing the inscription in red sugar 'General W.H. Furness 9 years old,' Grand Father with a Knife.[28]

Family outings, like this trip to the races, often included aunts, uncles, cousins, and friends.

> Yesterday was the day of the Races at the Rose-Tree. Walters friend, Stevie Crothers came out on Friday p.m., & Willie Lyman stayed over all for the purpose of attending the thrilling scene. Our luncheon before we started was enlivened by the presence of Willie Dick & a friend of his named Meigs, thus reinforced we started at 2 p.m. for the racecourse. Mother, Willie, Clyffe, Polly & myself in the Fox cart, Walter & Crothers in the Dog-cart, & Willie Lyman & Horrie in the Dolly cart. . . . On the race course we found Fairman and his drag already there, with Nannie & Frank among his outside passengers. The races were duly exciting & all the children were intensely interested, especially in the hurdle races, which by the way were enlivened by the bolting of a horse which knocked down two men, one of them senseless. We reached home safe & sound with ferocious appetites all round for supper.[29]

And interspersed between descriptions of the weather and records of the farm appear in the summer diary accounts like the following:

> Day before yesterday (13 Oct.) was a perfect day, cloudless sky, broad sunshine, the landscape hazy and the temperature like June. We walked to the Persimmon tree, Polly, Willy, Clyffe, Horrie, Walter & we old folks. After getting a delicious feast of the luscious fruit we strolled along the road to the Fairman's field sloping to Crumb Creek, there while Kate & myself leaned on the fence basking in the heavenly light & warmth the children tumbled & frolicked in the grass, it was an ideal hour never to be forgotten.[30]

The Lindenshade journal ends with the November 14, 1878 entry: "The happiest summer of our lives. Laus Deo." Looking back five years later, Furness added the sad postscript "and the *last*." During the happy decade of the 1870s two ominous shadows had gradually gathered and darkened the Furness family. The partial deafness that had excluded Furness from joining the Union Army a decade before increasingly isolated him in a private, silent world— good for Shakespearian scholarship but devastating to business and social intercourse. In September 1875, claiming deafness and the difficulty of riding on horseback from Lindenshade to town on Sunday mornings, Furness resigned his position as Superintendent of the Sunday School. In the same year he gave up his law office at 520 Walnut Street, and after 1880 he was no longer listed in the *Philadelphia Directory* as a lawyer. The law books were sold at auction in January 1885, and with the exception of the occasional family will or property deed, Furness no longer practised his chosen profession.

The forced retirement from the bar, cushioned by his new career in Shakespeare and the family fortune inherited in 1870, did not trouble him nearly as much as his social handicap. Although he often joked about being "as deaf as forty thousand posts" or "forty thousand adders," he keenly felt his disadvantage on social occasions. Conversation at the dinner table he managed with difficulty using his ear trumpet, but public meetings progressed in a dull buzz. To White he wrote in 1880, "My ab-hominable deafness has obliged me to lay down the inviolable rule of never dining away from my own table where if I eat or do not eat or flourish my ear trumpet in an unseemly fashion no one is annoyed or embarrassed but myself."[31] The difficulty with which he negotiated public events appears, for example, in his journal account of the Congress of Authors held at Independence Hall during the Centennial Exhibition on July 1, 1876.

> The room was sombre and dark—the scaffolding outside covered all the southern windows, and awed by the place every one seemed to speak in subdued tones—to my deaf ears it was even more hushed and the scene became ghostly; noiseless figures glided around among the relics of the past—until I could scarcely distinguish Frank Etting from a stuffed Continental soldier. It was really a good gathering of the lesser lights of literature—after a while a loud voice called out

'The Authors of America will please enter Independence Hall.' . . . A venerable gentleman next called over the names of those present, who advanced and laid on the table the memoirs that they had prepared of the members of the First Continental Congress. Fearful lest I should miss hearing my name I asked Charles Hart to tell me when my name was called. As time wore on & Geo. Hunter was by my side I made the same request of him. When at last my turn came Frank Etting repeated it in stentorian tones, it was caught up by George Hunter and yelled by Charles Hart. Every one was startled to find that Horace Howard Furness was in such intense and enthusiastic demand.[32]

Humor aside, his deafness turned even pleasant chats with Shakespearian friends into unpleasant trials. "My deafness is an insuperable barrier to all pleasurable intercourse," he wrote to Ingleby, declining Ingleby's invitation for a visit during their 1880 European holiday. "You can't gossip 'with a man in the tone with which you would hail the masthead."[33] When Ingleby insisted, Furness warned, "Never forget that you have brought upon yourself the trouble and the bore of talking to a deaf man, a class that I hate and shun like the plague."[34]

The other shadow, more serious and insidious, blotted forever Furness's happiness and snuffed short Kate Furness's literary career and her life. Her chronic illness, diagnosed as acute neuralgia, that for years had often confined her to her bed worsened steadily during the last years of the decade. Literary projects were set aside. After completing the index to the notes in the Variorum *Hamlet*, she had begun a list of solitary words in Shakespeare which Norris had agreed to publish in installments in his "Shakespearian Gossip" column in *Robinson's Epitome of Literature*. The list never appeared, nor did she finish reading the works of Mrs. Inchbald and extracting examples of words defined in their context for the *Oxford English Dictionary*, a task undertaken in 1879. Repeated requests from James Augustus Murray for progress reports in August 1880 and January 1881 apparently went unanswered.

Dr. Calvin Knerr, the family's homeopathic physician,[35] ordered a change of climate and scene during the winter of 1879, and by spring 1880, when the last proofsheets for *King Lear* had been returned to the publisher, plans were laid for the long delayed European trip, albeit a trip not for pleasure but for health. To Fanny

Kemble, then living in London, he explained, "I go on account of the
ill-health of my wife, who needs change of scene & mode of living—
it is with her, not, perhaps so much ill-health as lack of good health,
she is very pale & far from strong, although she protests that she is
perfectly well. However that may be our physician has told us to go,
and go we must."[36] The four best staterooms were reserved on the
steamship *Gallia* which sailed on June 30. The entourage included
Furness and his wife, the four children, their maid Anette, and Dr.
Knerr. After several weeks in London, the family planned to travel
through Germany, see the Passion Play at Oberammergau, and
perhaps spend the winter on the Nile, all contingent upon Kate's
health.

At the first news of the trip, however, the English Shakespearians began to plan his itinerary. Halliwell-Phillipps wrote twice in
March urging Furness to visit him in Brighton and announcing that
Timmins would be his host in Stratford: "If you don't make use of me
in every way you possibly can when in this country I will never
forgive you."[37] Ingleby refused to take no for an answer, and even
Collier at age ninety-two wrote three times requesting dates and
times for Furness's visit. Everything, however, depended on Kate's
health, and Furness gracefully tried to bow out of these insistent
invitations. "I go for Mrs. Furness's health, everything yields to that,"
he wrote in April to Ingleby.

> No single day is certain until I see how the voyage has affected her
> and how much fatigue she can undergo. As for really coming down
> like Assyrians upon your fold at Valentines I love you too well for that.
> Why, man dear, we have four children, my oldest boy, Walter is six
> inches taller than I (he's six feet) and Polly is six years old—and such
> a trail as we make all spread out would reach almost from London to
> Valentines, and by the time the rear reached you the van would have
> worn its welcome out."[38]

To Halliwell-Phillipps he wrote in May, "As I do not go to England on
a pleasure trip but for Mrs. Furness's health, I cannot form an hour's
plan beforehand. Our only fixed point is Liverpool—all after that is,
and will remain, vague. . . . As we go this summer for health, if all
goes well with us we shall go next summer for pleasure and then be
sure we'll go straight to Brighton."[39] Privately Furness complained
to Grant White, who himself had just returned from England,

What you say of Timmins sends a shudder through me. Of course he's one of the best fellows on earth—but dost thou not know—hast thou not heard that it is these same best fellows that can make you weary of life and long for the silent tomb? Of course he quotes poetry & I'll wager my life he knows all Byron. What shall I do? what shall I do! I don't want to see any sights. I only want to breathe the air of Warwickshire & gaze my fill at all the landscape. And what about Ingleby? Did you meet him? And Furnivall? and all of 'em, and all of 'em? I wish they'd let me alone. . . . We sail in the 'Gallia' a fortnight from today. I take my whole family. Mrs Furness, four children, maid and Physician. I humbly request to prayers of the congregation with such a convoy. Don't you think I can trust to that array frightening off all the zealous Shakespearians?[40]

The family sailed on June 30, accompanied by Edwin Booth, who was engaged to play *Hamlet* in the New Princess Theatre that autumn. Having arrived in Liverpool on July 9, they settled in Fenton's Hotel in London where they were met by Rebecca and Fairman Rogers. "We are so snugly fixed here," Furness wrote to Ingleby on July 31,

that I think we shall stay at least a fortnight longer, making this our headquarters with excursions to Brighton & Salisbury & Stratford etc. etc. Your railways bother me much, and usually reduce me to a state of drivelling idiocy. But blessings on your English climate. It has infused new strength in Mrs. Furness; if it only continue I shall be the happiest of men and wouldn't call the Queen me cousin.[41]

Furness did meet Furnivall, and Ingleby did come up to London for a day, but on the day appointed to visit Ingleby in Ilford, Kate's neuralgia worsened, and she was confined to bed. Deciding to leave at once for a warmer climate, the family headed for the West Country on August 9, stopping in Salisbury and Bath, before crossing the English Channel to Paris, Chalons, Strasbourg, Basle, Berne, Lucerne, Zurich, Stuttgart, Heidelberg, Mainz, and down the Rhine to Coblenz, Cologne, and Brussels.

Kate's health steadily deteriorated, and by September 14, the Furnesses were again established in Fenton's Hotel in London where Kate was confined to her bed or her room for eight weeks. As soon as she could be moved, they left for Liverpool on November 19 and returned home on the *Scythia*, after a rough crossing reaching New York on December 4 and Philadelphia on December 6. Furness had told no one of their return to London, and when safely at home in 222 West Washington Square, he explained to Ingleby,

> Had there been anything on Earth that you could have done for me I would assuredly have called on you, but there was absolutely nothing. Our admirable Homaeopathic physician Dr. Wilson of Brook St. came twice a day, and the Hotel people, at Fenton's and at Claridge's were devoted to us, and I scoured London from St Swithin's lane to Hyde Park in search of delicacies to tempt an invalid's appetite. Bailey, the poulterer, of Mount St, was my daily counselor & Mansbridge, the butterman, of Welbeck St was my bosom friend. I bought Greek & Latin Grammars and opened school for my boys. (the oldest, Walter, returned to America in September, at the end of his College vacation) and I got a spelling and reading book for Polly. It was a most miserable nightmare of a time. I never want to see London again.[42]

In the bracing winter air of Philadelphia, the deadly neuralgia subsided, leaving Kate slowly improving but very weak. As the search for her health intensified, all thought of Shakespeare disappeared. "As for Shickspur—who was Shickspur? I've forgotten how to spell his name—a poet, wasn't he? & wrote extravaganzas?"[43] Furness joked with Furnivall in January 1881; but it was a weak attempt at humor. *Othello*, begun in 1879, lay unfinished and untouched as the shadows hovering over the Furness family thickened into darkness.

THE PENN YEARS

Seyton
 The Queen, my lord, is dead.
Macbeth
 She should have died herafter:
 There would have been a time for such a word.
       —*Macbeth* 5.5.16-18

For the next three years Furness thought of little else but Kate's health. With each apparent recovery his spirits rose, and with each setback the darkness grew closer as she slowly grew weaker. Spring came late to Philadelphia in 1881, but as the warm weather returned, Kate showed some improvement. Breathing more easily for the moment, Furness turned to his neglected library table. "Throughout this sad winter I have had neither heart nor time to write to any of my friends," he wrote to Collier on April 30. "Kate has been such a sufferer that I have not left her night or day. She is now a little wee bit better and I seize the chance just to scratch a few lines to you to assure you of our affectionate remembrance."[1] To Ingleby he gave the encouraging news that she was driving in the carriage every sunny day, and to F.A. Leo, then president of the German Shakespeare Society, he added on May 3, "I place great hopes in the balmy air of our country seat whither we shall go in a few weeks."[2]

Summer faded into fall and fall faded into Indian summer as Furness lingered at Lindenshade with only flitting thoughts of Shakespeare or Shakespearian friends. "Poor Corson seems to have vanished from my horizon as well as from yours," he wrote to Norris on August 8.

> I have not heard from him for very, very long. But then I can say the same of half a dozen other Shakespearian Correspondents. I have written no letters to any of 'em for months, I had almost said years. I lead a life of absolute indolence. I don't read a line from morning to night & I spend my days wandering among the shrubs & flowers, thanking Heaven that I am at home & not in Europe. Mrs. Furness is slowly, very slowly gaining.[3]

On September 12, Furness broke his silence again to give much the same report to Ingleby: "Ever since I saw you I have led the idlest of lives, and when this indolence is to end I cannot say. Mrs. Furness still engrosses all my attention. Although she is not so well as when you saw her in London, yet she is better than she was during the winter."[4] Still at Lindenshade on November 28, he wrote to Corson, "Mrs. Furness is, I trust, slowly improving. I am doing nothin, utterly lazy & worthless."[5]

By the following spring Kate had passed several weeks free from pain, and Furness once again turned to things Shakespearian, thanking C.E. Flower for his edition of *Much Ado about Nothing*, sending White the latest Shakspere Society Bill of Fare from the annual dinner, and forwarding to the Shakespeare Birthplace Trust a complete set of the Variorum and Kate's *Concordance to the Poems*. In May he prepared a report on the Barton Collection of Shakespeariana for the Boston Public Library, and for the December 7, 1882 issue of *The Nation* he reviewed Halliwell-Phillipps's second edition of *Outlines of the Life of Shakespeare*. "Thanks heaped up, pressed down, and running over for these 'Outlines of the Life of Shakespeare.' I have read it with great enjoyment," he had written to Halliwell-Phillipps the previous December, and then turning to what would become a favorite theme, he continued,

I grow so weary of the attempts to extract Shakespeare's inner life from his works. If his inner life is there recorded it can possibly be discovered and eliminated, but were it really there, his works would cease to be the miracles that they are. It is because it is not there that these dramas stand alone in literature, with not a character in them from Doll Tearsheet to Hamlet that is not itself with no trace of William Shakespeare in it. And to say that when the Poet was sad and gloomy he wrote a tragedy & when he was merry he wrote a comedy, seems to me, childish, besides being generally false to human nature; the reverse would more likely be the case. When will people cease measuring Shakespeare by themselves! Has the world never yet digested AEsops fable of the frog and the ox[6]

Valuable as these projects might have been, Furness was just dabbling and marking time. Again for Kate's benefit the family remained in the country until just before Christmas, and *Othello* lay packed with the other books in the library in town. Rumors appeared from time to time in *The American* and *The Academy* that Furness had resumed his work on *Othello*. Hudson encouraged him to go on, writing, "Now that you have grown so ripe and mighty in the work, it would be a thousand pities, not to have you do more."[7] But the light had gone out on *Othello*. "Let me just drop out of your present thoughts," he wrote to Ingleby in November 1882. "In happier days when Mrs. Furness is strong & well again, then we'll take up the broken thread & I am quite sure that no traces of frayed ends or of splicing will be discernible when once it is joined. I have entered my fiftieth year & my work is done—that is, my literary work. I don't care for it, nor think of it from one week's end to the other."[8]

During her last year Kate's strength rose and fell. Through the winter she suffered, and in March the neuralgia in her head had increased so sharply that Furness telegraphed Willie and Horrie to return home at once from St. Paul's. Night after night for over three months he sat by her bedside through the night, snatching what sleep he could whenever she dozed. By July, however, she had rallied and, though far from well, was coming to dinner and driving every afternoon in the country. So encouraged was Furness that he even resumed work on *Othello*. Describing Kate's recuperation as "little short of a miracle," he wrote to Ingleby on September 2,

Now, week by week I can see that she is slowly gaining. Every afternoon we drive out for a couple of hours, and, what will be better proof to you than anything else, I have flittings across my memory that such a drama as 'Othello' was once written, and I have brought from the city some books labelled 'Shakespeare' . . . If I get to work again I shall be ready for the printers by this time next year. Heigho! What may not a year, at our time of life, bring forth![9]

But the year did not bring forth *Othello*. The end for Kate Furness came swiftly in late October 1883. On Saturday, October 27, Furness again summoned the boys from Concord, and on the morning of October 30, surrounded by her husband and children, she died at Wallingford and was buried at Laurel Hill Cemetery on November 1.

From Halliwell-Phillipps, Corson, Fleay, and White came words of condolence, and from Mary Cowden-Clarke a poem titled "Helen Kate Furness," written when the news reached Genoa on November 16, and published in the January issue of *Shakespeariana*. "If I could stretch my hand over the broad Atlantic I would grasp yours and sit silent with you as Job's friends did when they showed most sympathy with him," wrote Aldis Wright from Cambridge. "I would commend you to the soothing influences of the two great consolers, memory and hope, trusting that these will enable you to bear patiently the loneliness that death has made in your household and in your thoughts."[10] Public notices of her death appeared in *The Athenaeum* and the *Shakespeare Jahrbuch*, but perhaps the most fitting expression of sympathy came from Norris in the December issue of *Shakespeariana*.

The announcement of the death of Helen Kate Furness, which sad event took place at her husband's country seat, in the suburbs of Philadelphia, on the 30th of October last, was heard with profound regret and sorrow by the fraternity of Shakespearian scholars, of which she was so distinguished a member. With many social charms, varied accomplishments, and refined tastes, which an ample wealth enabled her to cultivate and gratify, she was not unlike that "fair maid of Belmont," of whom the great poet, whom she dearly loved, has written. She was a sympathetic companion and an invaluable co-laborer of her distinguished husband, Horace Howard Furness, and her Concordance of Shakespeare's poems fitly supplements that of her sister Shakespearian, Mrs. Cowden Clark. Had she given to the world as the fruit of her life nothing more than this Concordance, she would have placed the fraternity under a debt of the heaviest obligation. Her death was not unexpected and was a happy release from continuous pain.

"Then she is well and nothing can be ill,
Her body sleeps—
And her immortal part with the angels lives." [11]

Heartfelt as these words of sympathy were, they could not lighten the black shadow that had plunged Furness into darkness. Desolate and brokenhearted, he passed through the long days, hiding the agonizing ache under a calm face before the children, and suffered through the lonely darkness of the night, crying out for unconsiousness, for death, for one comforting touch or word of assurance. Days faded into weeks and weeks into months, but the anguish lingered. "Is it real, ·Walter? Am I not dreaming? Shan't I wake up & find that I have had a nightmare?" he wrote from Cape May the following July where he had taken Polly for the usual family vacation; and when Kate's birthday passed on July 26, he wrote again to Walter, "I stumbled and staggered through the day, and cried myself to sleep at night. God help us all, dear boy." [12]

By the first anniversary of her death his own agonizing pleas for death had subsided to a dull, but constant, heartache. "This day has passed, but one day is as black as another, and tomorrow must be lived through, and the morrow after, until in God's good time we are all reunited," he wrote to Willie and Horrie on October 30, 1884. "My chiefest consolation is that our darling has been saved from this bitter grief at any rate, for if she lives again she has the assurance that we too shall live again, & she knows that our reunion is sure."[13] As doubt strove with faith, he clung to that hope of reunion to stave off the ever threatening surge of sorrow. The encouragement he could not find in his Unitarian faith he discovered in Robert Browning's poem "Prospice."[14]

> Fear death?—to feel the fog in my throat,
>   The mist in my face,
> When the snows begin, and the blasts denote
>   I am nearing the place,
> The power of the night, the press of the storm,
>   The post of the foe;
> Where he stands, the Arch Fear in a visible form,
>   Yet the strong man must go:

For the journey is done and the summit attained,
    And the barriers fall,
Though a battle's to fight ere the guerdon be gained,
    The reward of it all.
I was ever a fighter, so—one fight more,
    The best and the last!
I would hate that death bandaged my eyes, and forbore,
    And bade me creep past.
No! let me taste the whole of it, fare like my peers
    The heroes of old,
Bear the brunt, in a minute pay glad life's arrears
    Of pain, darkness and cold.
For sudden the worst turns the best to the brave,
    The black minute's at end,
And the elements' rage, the fiend-voices that rave,
    Shall dwindle, shall blend,
Shall change, shall become first a peace out of pain,
    Then a light, then thy breast,
O thou soul of my soul! I shall clasp thee again,
    And with God be the rest!

To Edmund Gosse he wrote in May 1885,

I think you once told me that you know Mr. Browning personally
Would you mind telling him, sometime when you see him, from me of
whom he never heard & one of the most insignificant of his readers
how deeply how fervently I bless him for writing 'Prospice'? Though I
cannot read it but in a blinding mist of unutterable agony, and though
I have no faith whereon to build any assurance of its truth yet the
vision is so heavenly sweet, and the haven so well worth every
conceivable tempest, and the tempest so inconceivably welcome that
drives thither that I thank Mr. Browning from the very depths of my
soul for giving me, even in fancy such divine comfort. And when an
intellect so grand as Mr. Browning's can have so firm a faith, may I not
trembling dare to trust a little? Dear Gosse, may you never know what
it is to be alive and yet utterly, utterly dead.[15]

In the Spring of 1884 Furness created memorials to his wife at
Vassar and Smith. To each college he sent the sum of $500, the
interest from which formed the Helen Kate Furness Prize for the best
essay on a Shakespearian or Elizabethan subject. "My only objects,"
he wrote on May 19 to Dr. Caldwell, President of Vassar College, "are

to encourage, throughout the coming years, the study of Shake-speare, and to perpetuate, in a Woman's College, the memory and the example of a woman, who, while fulfilling with scrupulous exact-ness all the duties of a Mother, a Housekeeper, a Manager of several Charitable Associations, and the demands of Society, yet found time for literary culture, and for enduring scholarly work in Shakespear-ian literature."[16] The gifts, to which he later added an additional $500, were accompanied by a copy of the *Concordance* and an enlarged and framed platinotype to be hung in the library. "I should like to think that fresh young faces would sometimes look up at that face with pleasure."[17]

The months of grief stretched into a year and more devoid of literary work. "I am too unutterably weary with everything to stick to one purpose for longer than a half hour," [18] he wrote to Rolfe in April 1884. That October he refused a request from President Gilman to lecture to the Shakespeare classes at Johns Hopkins, and in Febru-ary 1885, he turned down a similar invitation from Corson for a "Shakespearian Conversation." "My life is done," he wrote. "I cannot get up any interest in anything beneath the sun. I strive and struggle the very hardest and work myself into a momentary excitement but the flush dies away, and everything is 'Dust and ashes. Dead and done for.'"[19] And to college classmate John Chandler Bancroft, he wrote that March, "Thanks for your words of sympathy—but my life, and my work, is over. 'The wine of life is drawn, and the mere lees is left this vault to brag of.'" [20] The thought of *Othello* only intensified the agony; an aside to Corson in a discussion of *Romeo and Juliet* tells all.

It is not a tragedy—Good God! Were they not married & supremely happy? Could length of years, to the span of Methusalah, have added more? To me 'Othello' is the only real tragedy. Hamlet isn't, he was a weak vacillating fool, who blundered into success. 'Macbeth' isn't, he was a villain that deserved his fate. 'Lear' surely is not. The poor old gent. was half crazed at the start, & hanging was too good for that selfish minx Cordelia. But 'Othello' is pure, unalleviated, black tragedy, too bitter bad to be read twice—for all that it will be the next I edit if I ever touch work (or play) again. [21]

In the end not Shakespeare, but the routine round of duty, restored to Furness his lively wit, his love for literature, and his life's work. Even during the early years of Kate's illness, Furness had faithfully attended meetings of the Trustees of the University of Pennsylvania and participated in its committee work. In 1880 he had been appointed to the Committee on the Department of Arts, followed in 1881 by the Committee on the Library, whose chairman he became in 1882, and in 1884 by the Committee on the Department of Law. Although he attended no meetings between January 1883 and April 1884, as he emerged from his grief, he increasingly immersed himself in the diverse affairs of the university—a welcome diversion to fill up the "daily round, the trivial task." With the Reverend George Dana Boardman, Dr. William Hunt, and John Clarke Sims, Furness during his tenure on the board considered every essay submitted for the Henry Reed Prize, the competition in honor of Henry Reed, friend of Wordsworth and for twenty-three years Professor of Rhetoric and English Literature at the University. In October 1884, he was busy writing to Harvard, Johns Hopkins, and other Eastern universities for their policies on board and lodging, as well as walking the streets to inspect boarding rooms in West Philadelphia. "I have been busy on a Committee of our University appointed to investigate the Boarding and Lodging of our Students, "he wrote in his weekly letter to Willie and Horrie on October 26.

> We find that parents at a distance in the Southern States, Cuba & elsewhere, are unwilling to send their sons to a University in a large city where they know nothing of the Boarding houses or of the company into which their children will be thrown. They also like to know beforehand the prices that are to be paid &c. Accordingly I had resolutely to set to work and find out all the statistics on these subjects. Consequently, provided with a list, I began last Monday and on that day and two succeeding ones I visited no less than sixty three of these dreadful places of abode. Half the time Walter went with me & with him, for ears, I got on finely. The students were exclusively Medical & Scientific, with only one or two exceptions the Undergraduates live at home in the city. Alack and alack! I unearthed some startling developements; chiefly that two thirds of those students sleep two in a bed! They prefer it! and insist on it! In not one instance did I find that they had a separate room as a parlor or study, and I found the average board extremely low, much lower than in Cambridge. It is clear that Dormitories cannot compete with those Boarding Houses.[22]

The dormitory question having been investigated, a month later in November 1884, Furness was busy with the other members of the Committee on the Department of Law—Eli Kirk Price, John Welsh, Samuel Dickson, and Frederick Fraley—revising the university statutes, and on December 29 that year, he wrote to Corson that "university business is now running me pretty hard." [23]

The chief university business that occupied Furness during the difficult months of mourning was the Seybert Commission for Investigating Modern Spiritualism. In February 1883, eight months before Kate's death, Henry Seybert had endowed the Adam Seybert Chair of Moral and Intellectual Philosophy at the University of Pennsylvania on the condition that the university would undertake an investigation of the truth of modern spiritualism. Accordingly, the Trustees appointed in July 1883 a committee, consisting of William Pepper, then Provost of the University and Professor of the Theory and Practice of Medicine; George S. Fullerton, the first incumbent of the Seybert Chair of Philosophy; Joseph Leidy, the eminent biologist and anatomist; George A. Koenig, Professor of Chemistry, Mineralogy and Metallurgy; Robert E. Thompson, Professor of History and English Literature; and Furness, who served as Acting Chairman. To this group were later added the engineer Coleman Sellers, Physical Director of the University J. William White, homeopathic physician Dr. Calvin Knerr, and fellow Trustee and medical doctor Silas Weir Mitchell. In early 1884 the committee began its investigation of independent slate writing by which spirit messages were purportedly written by a medium on the inside of a sealed slate. From there the committee turned to spirit rapping, sealed letters, materialization of spirits, and other manifestations of spiritualism. The full story of the committee's three-year investigation was told by Furness in the *Preliminary Report of the Seybert Commission for Investigating Modern Spiritualism* (1887).

At the outset of the investigation each member had expressed his freedom from prejudice and his willingness to accept any conclusions warranted by the facts. Among them only Furness, apparently drawn by his desperate desire for assurance of reunion with Kate, confessed a leaning toward the truth of spiritualism. "I do not hesitate to acknowledge that I have been throughout sincerely and extremely anxious to become converted to Spiritualism," he wrote in the *Preliminary Report*. "In whatever direction my judgment is warped, it is warped in favor of that belief. I cannot conceive of the texture of that mind which would not welcome such an indisputable proof of immortality as Spiritualism professes to hold out." [24] Again in a letter written to George Putnam after the Commission had concluded its investigation, he added,

> And I so hoped that Spiritualism was true! I entered in the investigation almost a convert, and at this hour I would give almost all I possess to be one. But not a sound or a vibration or a thrill comes from beyond the grave; there is no crevice in that wall. To my infinite regret I have become convinced that all the manifestations of Spiritualism, however mysterious they may be, find their cause in the unknown capacities of the mind, and that they are all *diesseits* and not *jenseits*. [25]

As hope turned to disappointment and disappointment turned to disgust at the devious fraud he encountered at every turn, Furness gradually regained his ironic sense of humor, baiting the spirits with literary and Shakespearian questions no doubt unsolvable in this world.

At the outset, however, he wanted to believe, and as Chairman of the Commission he devoted hours to arranging séances, often travelling to New York and Boston to visit mediums who could not come to Philadelphia. Many séances were held at 222 West Washington Square where Furness entertained as house guests the likes of Dr. Henry Slade, Harry Kellar, and Margaret Fox Kane, one of the founders of the Modern Spiritualist Movement in 1848. His sessions with the latter Furness recounted to Willie and Horrie in November 1884.

> She came late in the p.m. only a little while before dinner, at which we had a pleasant sociable time, with only Polly & Miss Logan present. After dinner, and while Miss Logan was still at the table, I thought it best to make due arrangements for the session of the Seybert Com. in the evening and to that end asked Mrs. Kane if she thought the spirits would find the dining room convenient. Whereupon a most vigorous succession of raps began on the table under our very hands as an indication of the spirits' pleasure. Miss Logan sat unmoved, until I turned to her & said "Do you hear the spirits rapping?" And then you should have seen her jump. I laughed till the tears came. She had thought that I was drumming on the table with my fingers but when

assured that the noise came from the spirits she bounded from her seat with horror & astonishment on every feature ejaculating "Bless me! bless me!" We tried the study, the parlor and the library in succession & found the raps especially loud in one corner of the latter. But after all the dining room was the best & there the Committee met in the evening. We put the spirits bravely through their paces for an hour, and held another session the next evening. With neither of those meetings was Mrs. Kane satisfied but we heard enough to serve as a groundwork for our conclusions. . . . The next evening, Friday, your Aunt Nannie gathered a group of eight or ten friends & they had a high old time with Mrs. Kane & the spirits, the latter certainly showed an intimate acquaintance with the family affairs of some of the guests, but made a terrible mull of it in sending a message to your Uncle Frank from his Father![26]

The spirit rappings were confined entirely to Mrs. Kane's person (Furness even detected their source in her ankles), and the Commission declared her a fraud, a judgment confirmed by Mrs. Kane's own confession to Furness four years later.

Similar deception was discovered in the field of independent slate writing. "Dr. Knerr has unmasked the slate writing of Mrs. Patterson!" Furness confided to his sons two weeks after Mrs. Kane's visit.

By a long course of apparent credulity Dr. K. has grown to be looked upon by Mrs. P. as one of her firmest believers. So last week Dr. Knerr carried with him to the séance a small hand mirror, which he so adroitly manipulated under the table that he had the satisfaction of seeing the medium open the slate, write on it, take out the little pencil close the slate & put the bit of pencil on top. All the while his attention was supposed by her to be absorbed in deciphering the written communications from departed spirits. He watched her repetition of the feat three times & then came away but without intimating to her his detection of the trick. He is now anxious to have me follow his example, & perhaps I shall. If I do I'll let you hear further. I hate to waste so much time. What abhorent deceit is met at every turn in this spiritualism. The very name is becoming a stench in my nostrils.[27]

It was this same medium, Mrs. Patterson, who at the very first séance held by the Commission had assured Furness through a spirit communication signed by Elias Hicks that he was "endowed with great Mediumistic powers." [28] Furness, in the spirit of true scientific inquiry, did try to develop his spiritual potential; for six months he wore under his hat magnetized blotting paper secured from a medium, and for half an hour each night he sat in the darkness with a sealed slate on his lap waiting for a spirit message. Needless to say, he learned more about independent slate writing in one lesson from the conjurer Kellar and the magician Yost, who was instructing Polly in the magical arts, than he had in six long months of "mediumistic development."

Perhaps most humorous and incriminating to spiritualism were the Commission's attempts to divine the identity of the skull in Furness's library, the skull used by tragedians Edmund Kean, Edwin Forrest, Henry Irving, Edwin Booth, and others whenever *Hamlet* was performed at the Walnut Street Theatre. Furness placed his question to the spirits in a sealed envelope, carefully secured the flap and four corners with wax seals, and dispatched it to a medium who, without opening the letter, would allegedly not only read the question but also produce an answer from the spirit world. To the first question—"What was the name, age, sex, color or condition in life of the owner, when alive, of the skull here in my library?"—one Dr. J.V. Mansfield of Boston reported that a conference of six eminent, scientific ghosts—Hare, Combe, Fowler, Spurzheim, Gall, and Rush—had concluded that the skull probably belonged to a black woman about forty years old, but that its name could not be known. Mansfield's calling card carried the legend "From the bright stars / And viewless air / Sweet Spirit, if thy home be there, / Answer me.—Answer me." Close inspection of the envelope returned to Furness, however, revealed that the seals had been cut out, the letter extracted, read, and returned to the envelope, and the seals restored to their position with mucilage.

Similar fraud appeared wherever the sealed letters were submitted, and the identity of the skull became increasingly complex. Dr. Eleanor Martin of Columbus, Ohio, related in verse the tragic story of Sister Belle, a tall, fair woman with jet black eyes and golden hair one yard long, whose unfortunate corpse had been sold to three medical doctors, leaving only a lonely skull. Mrs. Eliza Martin of Oxford, Massachusetts reported that it belonged to a French girl, named Marie St. Clair, whose life of dissipation and sin had resulted in an untimely death. And when Furness returned to Dr. Mansfield with the question "Has Marie St. Clair met Sister Belle in the other world?" the solution took yet another turn when he received a reply from Marie St. Clair signed "Your sister." "To our purblind vision the joint ownership of one skull by two different persons presents a physiological problem more or less difficult of solution," concluded Furness wryly in the *Preliminary Report*. "But all difficulty vanishes as soon as 'the river is crossed.' I derived no little comfort and much light from a Materializing Seance which I attended shortly afterwards in Boston, where both Marie St. Clair and Sister Belle appeared together, at the same time, and greeted me with affectionate warmth. To my inexpressible relief they were each well provided with skulls."[29]

The materializing séance with its darkened room, comforting music from the melodeon, and the white robed apparition appearing through the curtains of the dark cabinet also disappointed then amused Furness with its patent fraud. Having attended some twenty to thirty séances, Furness soon discovered that the spirits would answer to any name from life or literature—from Fair Rosamund to Olivia in Tennyson's *Talking Oak* to Marie St. Clair. Of the latter Furness wrote, "To be sure, she varies with every different Medium, but that is only one of her piquant little ways, which I early learned to overlook and at last grew to like. She is both short and tall, lean and plump, with straight hair and with curls, young and middle-aged, so that now it affords me real pleasure to meet a new variety of her; but in all her varieties she never fails to express her delight over my guarding with care that which was 'the last thing on her neck before she passed over.'"[30] The crowning delight came whenever William Shakespeare (usually dressed as in the Chandos Portrait) materialized from the cabinet. Humbly, but perhaps unfairly, Furness would ask the meaning of the misprint "Vllorxa" in *Timon of Athens* or the mysterious "dram of eale" in *Hamlet*, only to have the spirit hastily draw the curtains of the cabinet in his face.

Shakespeare, however, did have the last word. When the *Preliminary Report* appeared in June 1887, the spirit world was not pleased. The American Spiritualist Alliance undertook a thorough investigation of the Seybert Report and three months later published its scathing attack on the Commission's three-year study. More clever, however, and illustrative of the fact that Shakespeare, like the Bible, can be quoted to serve any occasion was a curious book by A.B. Richmond, Esq., who advertised himself to be, like Furness, a member of the Pennsylvania Bar, a book called *What I Saw at Cassadaga Lake: a Review of the Seybert Commissioners' Report*. Apparently written at the spiritualist enclave in Western New York, the book contains "An Open Letter to the Seybert Commission," dated 31 October 1887, asserting that the author had received a spirit message through an independent slate writing medium at Lily Dale from none other than Henry Seybert: "Sir, do all you can to combat the error into which my Commission have fallen. They were untruthful and unfaithful. H. Seybert." [31] The letter begins with Hamlet's exhortation "There are more things in heaven and earth, Horatio, / Than are dreamt of in your philosophy" and continues with Shakespearian quotations liberally sprinkled throughout in an extended attack on Furness and the Seybert Commission.

From despair to disillusionment to disgust to ironic delight the investigation of Modern Spiritualism had carried Furness through the difficult years following Kate's death. By the time the *Preliminary Report* was published, *Othello* had been in print for more than a year and the *Merchant of Venice* was almost two-thirds finished. Aside from exposing spiritualism in all of its departments as a fraud, the Seybert Commission did what Shakespeare could not do; it recalled Furness from his mourning, from those agonized cries to Kate in the darkness of his grief, and restored him to the land of the living, of laughter, and of literature.

In addition to the Seybert Commission, other University business filled the days of Furness's mourning and expanded into the two decades following. In January 1885 he was elected one of the Managers of the University Hospital, accepting duties that ranged from checking mundane details to overseeing the expansion of the medical school from the oldest in the country to one of the finest and most modern. "On Wednesday P.M. I gave my weekly inspection of the Univ. Hospital," he wrote to Nannie several years later,

> and as I am the only member of the Com. of three who attends to this duty, it falls to me to examine the accounts, and add up long columns of figures, approve with my signature sixty or seventy bills ranging in am't from twenty-five cents to six hundred dollars, count all the cash in hand (and it must come out to a penny), then go through every part of the hospital, peer into linen closets, cupboards, refrigerators, walk through the huge kitchen, sniff into ice-boxes, and look grimly at

every speck of dirt. The Hospital is really fast becoming a model. The antiseptic doctrine has changed every table from wood to glass, and floors and walls of the bath-rooms &c, to snowy tiles. [32]

From 1890 to 1895 Furness also served on the Committee on the Department of Philosophy, and in 1894 he was elected to the Board of Managers of the Department for Women. His most significant achievements, however, came in two other committees: the Committee on the Library and the Comittee on the Department of Arts.

On February 1, 1881, Furness had been appointed to the Committee on the Library, and in the following January he became its chairman. Preoccupied with Kate's illness, Furness at first took little interest in the committee, but after her death the committee served to fill the empty hours. The first order of business was the appointment of a permanent librarian, and the second was the cataloguing of books. Robert Ellis Thompson, then John Welsh Centennial Professor of History and English Literature, had been serving as a part-time librarian. No books had been catalogued since the publication of the *Catalogue of the University Library* in 1829; no record of withdrawals had been kept, and no inventory had been taken. Reported Furness to the Trustees in December 1883,

> In its present state the Library cannot be said to fill its proper position as an indispensable adjunct to the University, as an aid to Education. In this regard we are far behind other Universities of equal rank, and each year we are drifting farther to the rear. We have no complete Catalogue and can have none until we have a Librarian to make one. Our resources in books are unknown, and, therefore, except in especial branches the Library can hold out no allurement to students to avail themselves of its benefits. [33]

The Trustees authorized Furness to find a librarian, and in January he began interviewing candidates. Having unsuccessfully tempted first the librarian of the College of Physicians and then his friend J. Foster Kirk, editor of *Lippincott's Magazine*, Furness settled on James Barnwell, who was elected by the Trustees in February 1884 and served until 1887, when he became librarian at the Library Company and was replaced by Gregory Keen. Each month Furness reported to the Trustees the number of books received and catalogued, and by January 1888 Barnwell and Keen had catalogued some 20,000 books, represented by over 71,000 handwritten cards housed in cabinets donated by Furness.

The college library then occupied two rooms in College Hall plus ten additional storage rooms scattered around the building to house its 40,000 volumes. Circulars, written and paid for by Furness and sent to friends of the university in June 1885 and again in June 1886, had attracted gifts of some 58,000 pamphlets, magazines, catalogues, and reports. As the library expanded, the available storage space shrank, and in his annual report, dated October 1885, Provost William Pepper finally called for a new fireproof library. "Our restricted and inconvenient accomodations are a source of continual anxiety," reported Furness to the Trustees in November 1886.

> All our shelves are crowded, on some of them we have to put double rows, one behind the other, a heart-breaking necessity to every genuine librarian; the wall space is covered with shelves to the ceiling, books are piled up on the tops of alcoves, every corner is occupied, the window sills are utilised to the last inch, and even the floor is used for the storage of our books—a state of affairs which impedes all library work, and so far thwarts the library's use, in that valuable time is lost in searching and shifting.[34]

In December, when the library was designated by the Secretary of the Interior as a depository for all the publications of the United States government and eleven sacks of public documents arrived, Furness reported, "The floor is the only place where the volumes can be put, and even there they would have to be stacked."[35]

In February 1887 the Trustees authorized plans for a new library, and in March a Joint Committee on Library and on Building, Estates, and Property requested Furness to gather plans and information from other university libraries and elected Frank Furness (later appointed one of nine architects in the University's School of Architecture) as the architect for the new building. Furness consulted with Justin Winsor, librarian at Harvard, and with Melvil Dewey, then at Columbia. By June 1888 the plans had been approved, the site selected, and over $130,000 raised toward the goal of $150,000. At their July meeting the Trustees directed Furness to prepare proper ceremonies for laying the cornerstone.

On a chilly, gray Monday afternoon, October 15, 1888, some

three hundred invited guests joined the Provost, Trustees, and officers of the Grand Lodge of Free and Accepted Masons of Pennsylvania on a platform surrounding the cornerstone for the appropriate
ceremonies. Students and spectators lined the unfinished walls of
the building, sat on the scaffolding, and watched from windows of
nearby buildings. *The Pennsylvanian* gives the following account of
the proceedings:

THE LAYING OF THE CORNER-STONE OF THE LIBRARY BUILDING

The Provost and Trustees of the University, together with the Right
Worshipful Grand Lodge of Free and Accepted Masons of Pennsyl-
vania, assembled in the Chapel and proceeded to the site of the
Library building. The Grand Lodge took its place on the platform, and
the Officers and Trustees of the University took their places on the
north side. The Provost presided. The Grand Master thanked the
Trustees "for the honor paid to the Craft, in their invitation to the
Lodge to lay the corner-stone," and then the Lodge proceeded to
perform that duty according to their ancient usages and customs.
The ceremonies commenced with an Invocation by the Grand Chap-
lain. The documents, coins and other valuable articles, including the
"Library Issue" of THE PENNSYLVANIAN, were then placed in the
cornerstone, and all was sealed up. The imposing ceremonies of
testing the work and stone with the golden square, plumb and level
were then gone through with, also the spreading of the cement with
the golden trowel and the striking of the stone with the gavel, and the
stone was declared by the Grand Master of Masons to be "duly laid
according to the Ancient Usages, Customs and Landmarks of Free
Masonry." The corn, oil and wine were then poured out, the actions
being accompanied with the set words of the Masonic Liturgy. The
Architect of the new building was then presented to the Grand
Master, who in turn handed him "the designs from the trestle-board
and the tools of the workmen." [36]

The ceremony then concluded with an address by Furness, remarks
by the Provost, and a hymn by the university chapel choir. After
paying tribute to the educational interests of the ancient Brother-
hood, Furness continued,

The founding of a Library *is* a momentous, even a solemn event. It
consecrates a building to the preservation of the intellect of the past
and of the present. It gives a permanent habitation to the fleeting

thoughts that have stirred or soothed men's minds, and are here garnered for the service of all. It is the wealth here stored that is indestructible; all other wealth that can be heaped up may take to it wings and fly away. Intellectual wealth is alone permanent, and affords the standard of a nation's power. A nation without libraries is a nation without books; and a nation without books vanishes from the earth, and we have to send forth expeditions with shovel and spade to exhume its scanty traces. The fight of light against darkness, the battles of knowledge, the wings whereby we fly to heaven, against ignorance which is the curse of God, are all fought outside in the world, but a library is the armory where the weapons are stored, and where the campaigns are planned. If we are the heirs of all the ages, it is in libraries that our inheritance is recorded, and to them must we resort to enter on possession.[37]

The address, one of the earliest public speeches of Furness, already showed the rhetorical polish that would make him a speaker in demand at every formal occasion in Philadelphia by the turn of the century.

September 1890 saw Furness, back from flights of rhetoric, supervising the moving of books to the new library, discussing with Pepper the installment of gas fixtures, authorizing the payment of bills for current expenses of the library, and naming the alcoves after donors of books. During the autumn semester the library was opened to students, and five months later, on February 7, 1891, the formal opening ceremonies took place in the spacious, lofty reading room. Before the scholars, patrons of the university, and invited guests gathered under the Romanesque arches and barrel-vaulted ceiling, Furness, as Chairman of the Building Committee, presented the library to Provost Pepper, who received it on behalf of the Trustees. After describing the fireproof book stacks, the card catalogue (arranged according to the new Dewey system), and the museums on the second and third floors for the Assyrian, Babylonian, Egyptian, and American collections, Furness went on to list the major collections in the library: the original volumes presented to the university in 1784 by Louis XVI, the Henry C. Carey Library of Political Economy, the Allen Library of classical literature containing over 30,000 volumes, the Pott Library of philology, the Stillé Medical Library, the Thomas Cochran Library containing all publications of the United States Government, the MacCartee Library of Chinese and Japanese literature—and the list went on.

When the cornerstone was laid, the Building Committee had promised that the "best appointed library building in this Western World" would rise above it. Due in part to Furness's energetic chairmanship of the Committee on the Library, the Library of the University of Pennsylvania was securely established as a major research library. Furness chaired the Committee on the Library until January 1896, when he relinquished the gavel to W.W. Frazier, but continued to serve on the committee until his resignation from the board in 1904. While the records show his continued active interest in the library—discussions of book purchases, establishment of departmental libraries, and personal gifts of books and donations to current library expenses—the presentation of the University Library remains the high mark of his career on that committee.

The administrative skill and knowledge of books that Furness brought to the University Library, he also exercised on the Library Company Board of Directors. The Library Company of Philadelphia, founded in 1732 by Benjamin Franklin, had long been *the* Philadelphia Library, located on Chestnut Street below 5th and in Furness's day also at its new Ridgeway Branch at Broad and Christian Streets. Elected on May 6, 1889, Furness joined another congenial group, most of whom he knew from the Penn Club or the Wistar Association. S. Weir Mitchell, Henry C. Lea, and James Hutchinson served with Furness as University trustees, and James Barnwell, then librarian at the Library Company, had just left the University Library two years before. Soon an informal Library Dinner Club added its monthly engagement to Furness's social calendar. Almost immediately after his election, the Director's Minutes show various proposals to print a new catalogue, and Furness, as chairman of the Catalogue Committee, directed not only the University Library cataloguing, but also the updating of the Library Company's old printed catalogue of 1857. With James Biddle, Edward Buckley, Charles Platt, Francis Lewis, and Ellis Yarnall, Furness was also elected to the Book Committee, on which he served until his resignation in November 1904. To this committee Furness brought his expertise in literature and knowledge of second-hand and rare book dealers. In October 1890, for example, he was authorized to spend one thousand dollars on literary reference works; in December 1897, he spent another thousand on Bibles and prayer books, four hundred on Milton, and three hundred on early Quaker tracts. Good sense, however, did not always prevail on the board. After the February 1899 meeting, he wrote the following letter to Maurice Conway who had offered the Library Company a collection of books on Thomas Paine.

> The Directors of the Phila. Library are all old men and what with coughs, colds and engagements only six of the twelve attended the meeting on Thursday. The Report of the Book Committee in favour of purchasing your Paine Library was presented, and I spoke earnestly in favour, and then another Director spoke most viciously against it. And then alas! just as victory was in my grasp, and they had actually empowered me to close with you, on the basis of $800—this cantankerous Director raised the point that there was no quorum, and we were powerless to act. So there was no help for it. The question must go over to the next meeting, which is the first Thursday in March. In the meantime this opposing member who has a violent prejudice against Paine and his Works will organise all the antagonism against the purchase, in his power,—and as the Directors are timid I'm afraid he will prevail. If he raises the cry of economy and lack of funds, as 'tis most likely, I'm afraid we're dished. That always is a bugaboo to the timid.[38]

While guiding the development of two important Philadelphia libraries, Furness also wielded great influence on the University of Pennsylvania Committee on the Department of Arts. Engaging Furness in activities as diverse as editing the 1885 University Catalogue and advising the Provost on the appointment of a new Greek professor, the committee during the late 1880s and early 1890s directed at Furness's urging a reorganization of the entire Department of Arts and, in particular, the formation of a new Department of English. English had been taught at Pennsylvania since 1755, when William Smith, the first Provost, had joined the faculty; and the teaching of Henry Reed, Professor of Rhetoric and English Literature from 1834 to 1854, was still remembered and honored with the Henry Reed Prize in Composition. Some literature, as illustrative of rhetorical style, was taught during the 1880s by John McElroy, then Professor of Rhetoric and English Language, but Robert Ellis Thompson, the John Welsh Centennial Professor of History and English Literature, ignored his literary title and devoted his time to teaching political economy and history in the Wharton School. Dissatisfied with the haphazard study of English at Penn and spurred, perhaps, by accounts of Horrie's courses in Shakespeare and nineteenth-century

English literature at Harvard, Furness expressed his concern to Pepper about the instruction in Greek, Latin, and English and proposed a separate chair in history so that the John Welsh Centennial Professorship could be returned to the English department. At their November 1885 meeting, the Trustees requested Furness to examine the faculty rosters and to report what, in his opinion, could be done. About the same time Edward Steel, President of the Board of Education of Philadelphia, had asked Furness to help select a teacher for the chair of English literature at the Philadelphia High School. This double request gave Furness the ideal chance to speak for reform of the English curriculum.

During the last quarter of the nineteenth century both universities and secondary schools had begun to shift from a classical curriculum that emphasized the study of Latin to a modern curriculum that emphasized the historical and grammatical study of English. Victorian pragmatism questioned whether any practical advantage could be gained from years spent in study of the classics. "It has become quite apparent to me that during the last fifteen or twenty years a decided change has come over the public estimate of the relative importance of the study of Latin and English," wrote Furness to Steel on May 2, 1886, in a letter that subsequently was made public in the Philadelphia newspapers. "In this driving, practical world, and in schools that are to fit young people to enter into its competitive struggles, thoughtful men are beginning to question the value of the time spent in studying a dead language. If the time be not well spent it is a loss in dollars and cents; the gain must be very positive and clear if we are to be sure that we are not misspending our money." [39] While noting that at one time the easiest way to learn English grammar had been to study Latin grammar, Furness contended, in spite of his own classical education, that the goal could now be reached faster and with greater benefit to the students through a study of English. The slowly accumulating volumes of the *Oxford English Dictionary*, the editions of the Early English Text Society, and the work of other literary societies had opened the possibility for the systematic study of English literature. "Within the last quarter of a century," continued Furness,

> there has been awakened a great and healthy and growing interest in the early structure and history of our own language, and experience

has shown that we can therein find all the requirements for teaching grammar that are afforded by Latin, and that, in addition, while we are studying it, are we not acquiring at the same time a knowledge of the bone and sinew of our own strong, sturdy English? a knowledge that will help us throughout life to express our thoughts in honest, home-spun, vigourous phrases? . . . To be a tolerably good English scholar is within the capacity of any High School boy—surely a goal far prefer-able to that of being a decidedly poor Latin scholar.[40]

Love of learning inspired by the excitement of "our own strong, sturdy English" formed Furness's *raison d'etre* for English study. His report to the Trustees, later made public in the March 1889 issue of *Education*, proposed a course of study that worked backward from modern literature in the freshman year to Anglo-Saxon in the senior year. Modern literature, being the more familiar, would be taught to freshmen, and sophomores would read Milton and the eighteenth-century authors. Juniors would study the Renaissance poets and dramatists, and seniors would read Chaucer and Beowulf. Only during the sophomore year and the first term of the junior year, after extensive reading, would the study of rhetorical style be added to the curriculum; and philology and grammar would be reserved until the junior and senior years, when historical examples could be drawn from Old and Middle English.

College curricula, however, are not changed lightly, and Fur-ness faced disdain from Thompson, whom Furness had removed from his position in the library, and open opposition from McElroy, who had been teaching rhetoric since 1867 and since 1876 had directed the Department of English. Rhetoric, consisting of practical rules for writing and speech, argued McElroy, must be taught throughout the college course beginning in the freshman year. Liter-ature illustrative of rhetorical principles could be taught along with rhetoric, but literature was secondary and any proposal to defer rhetoric, grammar, and philology to later in the college course would irreparably harm the instruction of English. Furness did, however, find an ally in Felix Schelling, a young Instructor of English Literature, who had been appointed in 1886. Furness quickly recog-nized Schelling's scholarship and promise and became his patron on the Board of Trustees, consulting with him on the organization of the department and urging his promotion to Assistant Professor of English Literature in June 1888. Through the spring of 1888 a Special

Committee on the Re-organization of the College Faculty considered proposals by Furness and Schelling and counter-proposals by McElroy, but little substantive reform took place until McElroy's illness and death two years later in November 1890.

The Provost, casting about for a replacement for McElroy to finish the term, opened negotiations with Richard Moulton, who was then giving lectures that winter on *Faust* for the University Lecture Association. Furness grasped his opportunity, and in a series of letters to Pepper dictated the details of his reform.

222 West Washington Square

Dear Pepper:—

In re. Moulton. Please make no arrangement with him which may at all interfere with Schelling, to part with whom will be, on our part suicidal. He has a future before him, which is just about dawning—witness the fact that Boston has sent to him to edit Ben Jonson's 'Discoveries' for a popular school series—a great and merited compliment. (We must not forget that Schelling is to have additional pay for his additional work this term.)

In speaking to Moulton, I think it should be borne in mind that whatever subject he takes up with his classes, be it Goethe's Faust, Aeschylus, Sophocles, or Cervantes, it is all to be considered as within the English Department. Let Moulton range over the whole field at will. Let Schelling be restricted to the Elizabethan or modern field, whichever he prefers (I think he'll prefer the modern which will be all the better) and for heaven's sake let us stop that hideous waste of talents & learning in making Easton [Morton William Easton, Adjunct Profesor of Greek and Instructor in French] teach elementary French and put him to comparative Philology including Anglosaxon. There you have Early English, Middle English & Modern English provided for, with Moulton to awaken refined enthusiasm for all that is best over the whole field.

Also we need a man to teach both elementary French & German—one man could easily do it—and then Seidensticker [Oswald Seidensticker, Professor of German Language and Literature] who is a real scholar, could devote himself to the highest German Literature—Perhaps Koenig [Walter Koenig, Assistant Librarian], in the Library, would be a good man for this elementary work.

If you will devote your energies to raising funds for this English Department you'll be doing vastly, *vastly* more permanent & effective good for the University than by connecting it with all the Free Li-

braries that could be built between here and Florida. I speak the
words of soberness & wisdom. Heed them.

Yours ever
H.H.F.
21 Dec. [1890][41]

These were strong words to a man about to endow the Free
Library of Philadelphia, but Pepper valued Furness's advice and did
heed it. A further request for a detailed proposal provoked an even
more direct response.

222 West Washington Square

Dear Pepper:

In re. English Dep't. (for Undergraduates solely—we have no money
for Post graduates) Three branches must be taught:—
    (a) Literature,
    (b) Themes,
    (c) Elocution.
————————————————
    (a) Literature—Early
                    Middle (Elizabethan)
                    Modern.
Early (i.e. Anglosaxon & Chaucer can be adequately taught by Lec-
tures, ten in the year, once a fortnight and only to the Seniors.
Middle (i.e. Elizabethan & Milton & a touch of Dryden) should claim
the greatest time & attention & be continuous from the middle of the
Sophomore to the end of Senior—'Tis the spinal column of our
Literature.
Modern (i.e. Pope to Carlyle) should be taught in the Freshman &
Sophomore years, heavily. And concurrently during these two years
there should be *every week*:—
    (b) *Themes*—very short, not more than a page or two—and
solely for style, spelling & punctuation, paraphrases of Johnson,
Macaulay, Carlyle &c &c and translations from what the class is
reading in Latin & Greek—sometimes they must be in rhythm or
rhyme. For the Junior & Senior years—one theme each month will be
sufficient—and these should be exercises in *thinking* or *disputations*.
    (c) *Elocution* may be taught only in the Senior year (once a
week) as a preparation for Commencement & to break down the
dreadful monotony which predominates on that occasion.

If it be conceded that this scheme would make a tolerably good English course—let's see for means:—
We now spend about $5000— per annum (the exact figure is, I think, $4750— but make it the larger sum).

First: Let Schelling take the Elizabethan & middle English (I don't use 'middle English' in the technical sense but merely the '*middle*' of my own division above). I have great faith in Schelling. If his health holds out, he has a good name & a fine fame before him. Give him not a doit less than $2500— Let him take the Themes of the Sophomore Year).

Second: Secure a teacher of Modern English who shall also take the Themes of the Freshman Year. His classes will be Freshmen & Sophomores. Let his salary be $1500—

Third: Secure a Lecturer in Anglosaxon & Chaucer—Ten Lectures in the Senior Year (including a Final Examination) at $50 per Lecture $500—

Fourth: Secure a teacher of Elocution for the Seniors @ $500— per annum.

Thus:—Schelling $2500—
      Modern English   1500—
      Chaucer   500—
      Elocution   500—
               $5000—

If Thompson can share any of these labours I should give him the Junior & Senior Themes (In fact I was thinking of him when I restricted Schelling to the Sophomore Themes) and a share of the English writers of today.
There dear Pepper, here is something to chew on & ruminate. 'Tis the second letter I've written to you on the subject & I'll be _____ if I write a third. With good teachers—such a course ought to turn out boys with a *good general knowledge* of English. Alongside of it should go lectures in Greek & Latin Literature, obligatory on all the students of English.

Yours ever
H.H.F.
10 Feb. '91[42]

This time Furness virtually had his way. At their June 1891 meeting the Trustees appointed Schelling head of the department and authorized a special Committee on English, consisting of Charles Harrison, Walter Smith, and Furness as chairman, to interview and hire an additional instructor. In March 1892 the Trustees voted to place $7000 at the disposal of the Committee on English to provide for the department, and in June 1892 the Trustees voted to remove Thompson from the John Welsh Professorship of History and English Literature and place the endowed chair at the disposal of the Committee on English. The final triumph came the following year when the Trustees voted in May 1893 to make Easton the Professor of Comparative and English Philology and to transfer the John Welsh Professorship to Felix Schelling.

Not content just to write the script or to direct the English Department from backstage, Furness also played before the audience. Between January and March 1888 Furness delivered a course of lectures to the juniors and seniors in the College and Wharton School, and at their May meeting the Trustees requested that the course be made part of the curriculum. Accordingly, the following January Furness again gave four lectures first to the upperclassmen and then to the public through the University Lecture Association; two of the lectures—"The Study of Shakespeare" and "On the Text of Shakespeare"—subsequently appeared in the pages of *Poet-Lore* for March 1889 and June 1891. Describing the lectures as having the highest value and having been received with the greatest applause, Pepper proposed that the Trustees elect Furness to an Honorary Professorship of English Literature, and at their May 1889 meeting Furness was declared duly elected. When McElroy died in November 1890, Furness not only pursued the re-organization of the department, but also stepped into the classroom to read through a Shakespeare play one hour a week with the senior class. To Schelling he wrote on November 7,

> I am merely frightened at my own temerity, which has been bolstered up solely by the fear lest the additional work thrown on you should prove too much for your most courageous spirit in your over taxed frame. All I can offer is to read Shakespeare to the boys—in the full assurance that an hour spent in hearing him is not misspent—and with your permission I'll take the liberty of drilling them somewhat in elocution or at least in modes of expression. I can reach the University punctually at twelve o'clock. From then till four I am at your service any day except Saturday. [43]

The enthusiasm with which these and subsequent Shakespeare readings were received at the University, eventually leading to his later career as a Shakespearian reader, may be gauged accurately by a front page story in *The Pennsylvanian* after a reading of *Hamlet* in March 1893.

Dr. Furness' Readings

Friday afternoon saw the college chapel crowded until every seat was full and the walls lined with students and visitors who were willing and glad to stand for two hours listening to the reading of Hamlet by Dr. Furness. This was the last of the course of four readings kindly given by Dr. Furness, and in no way did it fall below the mark of interest to which the former readings had risen. When Dr. Furness entered the chapel he was greeted with a round of applause from the college men who have learned in such a short time to welcome him as one who has a great deal in common with the students of a university. In introducing his subject he first called the attention of his audience to the fact, that as long as human beings are interested in the mystery of a human soul, their interest could not fail to be stirred by Shakespeare's picture of the character of Hamlet. That Hamlet was driven by frenzy and ecstacy to extravagant acts, but that his mania was entirely different from an ordinary madness or insanity, and his character well worthy of deep study. Proceeding then to the reading, Dr. Furness called forth repeated applause by his attractive and descriptive reading, as well as by his apt, and at times, brilliant comments on the text. These readings have brought the students out in far greater numbers than any lecture or reading of the year, and will long be looked back to as a rare literary treat that probably can never again be offered to the students by Dr. Furness.[44]

The popularity of these readings and lectures, no doubt, also accounted for his election as an Honorary Member of Phi Beta Kappa when the Pennsylvania Chapter of the fraternity was chartered on September 7, 1892, and for his service as President of the Chapter from 1896 to 1897, succeeding his father who had served from 1893 until his death in 1896.

As well received as were these lectures, Furness's friends soon grew concerned about the increasing demands of teaching on Furness's time. "Shakespeare students may well bear a grudge against those interrupting and time-consuming Shakespeare lectures he has been prevailed upon to give during the past winter, in just so far as they have interfered with his vastly more important regular work,"

observed Charlotte Endymion Porter in the May 1889 *Poet-Lore*
"Charming as those lectures have been,—making Shakespeare's
time or Shakespeare's art and meaning live in many a genial
anecdote and enlightening touch of comment,—they may have
caused the judicious partly to grieve on the score of their obstruc-
tion to the even flow of his normal library work."[45] Furness himself
admitted as much in a letter written from Wallingford to Rolfe
several years later. "Decidedly I must resign from the University
and the Phila. Library and move out here, if I am ever to go on
with my Shakespeare work—and I must go no more philander-
ing about giving Readings. 'Tis no sin, Hal, to labour in one's
vocation but Shakespearean Reading is not my vocation." [46]
But the University had been good to Furness. From the investigation of spiritualism to the inspection of the University Hospital,
from cataloguing books and building a library to designing the English Department and teaching Shakespeare, the affairs of the University of Pennsylvania had carried Furness from Shakespeare
through sorrow and despair to resignation and had restored him
once again to Shakespeare. Where Furness, at first, grasped only
for duty to fill the lonely darkness of his bereavment, he gradually
discovered, as the years passsed, a renewed interest in literary
work.

Even while the Seybert Commission held its seances, while the
crowded library stacks spilled over onto the floor with uncatalogued
books, and the instruction in English received its first critical
glances, Furness had turned to his own library and slowly began to
pick up the threads of *Othello* that for almost five years had lain in a
tangled mass too emotional to unravel. Furness dated the revival of
his literary work from the visit of Edmund Gosse in early January
1885. "You will never know how much good your brief little visit
gave me," he wrote to Gosse on March 22.

> It half revealed to me that there were some folk in the world who
> really did care whether or not I worked for them. And for the first time
> for many a long year, after you went away, I opened my book cases of
> my own accord and looked over my notes on 'Othello'—Since then I
> have actually worked an evening or two every week. It has been
> agony but I have done it. If ever I buckle to, again in earnest, I shall
> date the change from your evening's invigorating talk. Awares and
> unawares I entertained an angel.[47]

Throughout the spring and summer Furness corresponded with Furnivall, with Arthur Knapp at the Boston Public Library, and with Edwin Booth, who was writing out for Furness his stage interpretation of Iago. On April 29, Hudson wrote to encourage Furness to press on. "For more than a year past, I have been presuming that you were at work on *Othello*; and I am hoping and trusting that in due time the results of that work will be forthcoming. I have sometimes found absorption in literary work a wholesome and grateful refuge from painful thoughts and pressures too near the heart."[48]

Hardly had Furness begun to work again, however, when his mother, now eighty years old, became seriously ill, her strength gradually waning through the spring months until her death at Lindenshade on June 11, 1885. Again the shadow descended, reviving and intensifying his own sense of loss. Describing his father the day after the funeral, Furness wrote, "Of course, he cannot possibly begin to feel his loss for some time to come—he will find that the second week is worse than the first, the second month worse than the first month and the second year infinitely worse than ever before. Do you get less hungry by fasting?"[49]

Describing himself that October as "still within the heavy shadow of my Mother's death,"[50] and refusing all but the necessary social engagements, Furness worked quietly through the summer and fall on the appendix to *Othello*, corresponding with Halliwell-Phillipps about the date of the text and gathering opinions from Mitchell and other members of the Pennsylvania medical faculty concerning the nature of Desdemona's death (Did Othello stab or smother her? How could she speak after her apparent death? If she could speak, why could she not revive?). On October 18, he announced to Wright, "After days and weeks of alternating work and inaction, and all of misery, I have finished 'Othello' and sent it to the printers, and the First Scene is stereotyped."[51] By December the printers had reached Act III, and on April 3, 1886 the first copy reached Furness.

Enthusiastic reviews and letters of congratulation hailed the resumption of the Variorum, and Columbia at its centennial commencement the following year awarded Furness the honorary L.H.D. degree; but this time the praise seemed to matter little. To Gosse he had written in March 1886,

'Othello' is finished. I had my last proofs today. In three weeks a copy will start for Delamere Terrace. I can't think of anything in it to which to call your especial attention. I have been 'sassy' throughout. However, turn to Desdemona's death, where I have gathered the opinions of the Faculty, and they disagree! The various translations of 'not poppy nor Mandragora' &c gave me a little flickering interest which lasted for a few hours—But what weariness and horror it has been to me throughout. The only solitary page which I care for is the Dedication. But that way madness lies. I am learning to wait, not patiently but simply waiting."[52]

IN MEMORIAM
'—Neither present time, nor years unborn
Can to my sight that heavenly face restore.'

THE VARIORUM RESUMES
(1886-1901)

> Come what come may,
> Time and the hour runs through the roughest day.
> —*Macbeth* 1.3.147-48

Time and the hour did carry Furness along through the middle period of the Variorum, fifteen years punctuated at regular intervals by the appearance of a new Variorum volume: *Othello* (1886), *The Merchant of Venice* (1888), *As You Like It* (1890), *The Tempest* (1892), *A Midsummer Night's Dream* (1895), *The Winter's Tale* (1898), *Much Ado About Nothing* (1899), and *Twelfth Night* (1901). After the six agonizing years with *Othello*, except for *Antony and Cleopatra* in 1907, Furness turned exclusively to the comedies for respite and relief, completing as well during the final years of the Variorum *Love's Labor's Lost* in 1904 and *Cymbeline* in 1913. "You see I cling to the Comedies," he wrote to Rolfe in November 1899 after finishing *Much Ado About Nothing*. "When I finished 'Othello' I almost swore I'd never again edit a tragedy. To live for a year or two, day and night, in a tragic atmosphere, is almost too much for my weak nature. I think I said somewhere in my notes on that play, that Shakespeare should never have written it. I think so still. It horrifies me to open its pages."[1] To Leo he added, while seeing *As You Like It* through the press, "Life itself is enough of a tragedy. We need not go to the world of imagination for it—it lies all around us in our daily life."[2]

Othello and its painful associations never ceased to haunt Furness. "Its gloom is unrelieved from beginning to end," he wrote to Charles Adams one year before his death. "Were I ever again obliged to read 'Othello,' I would immediately, at the conclusion, read 'As You Like It' five times consecutively."[3] Yet even through the idyllic Forest of Arden or the moonlit midsummer madness of lovers and fairies his own grief pursued him, breaking through in the un-guarded moment in the letters to his closest friends. "As I cannot possibly live to complete all the plays, it seems to me best to aim at finishing all the Comedies," he declared to Wright in August 1895, when beginning *The Winter's Tale*, and then added,

> And I certainly hope I shall not live to complete even those. If you are not weary, dear Wright, I am. A heart shattered like mine never heals. I do so deeply regret that you did not see her when we were in England—but the shadows were even then dark around me and I could not leave her side nor take her whither I would. Ah well, though time does drag still it passes. Thank God, for that! How fine and full of meaning that phrase is in the Bible: "it came to pass." Nothing comes but to pass. But I must not think in that direction. "That way madness lies."[4]

In March 1898 a letter to Charles Eliot Norton concerning an inser-tion in the next edition of *The Tempest* suddenly breaks off with the cry "Oh Norton, dear Norton, to think that out of my ten volumes, that Dedication must appear in six. I never thought 'twould appear but in one. Have I not been stretched long enough on the rack of this tough world. I'll concede every attribute to the over ruling Pow-er but that of Love."[5] And when Corson lost his wife in October 1901, Furness wrote words of sympathy that reveal not only his desire to console but also his need, even after eighteen years, to be consoled.[6]

Wallingford,
    Delaware County,
        Pennsylvania.
    Dearest Corson,
I have, only this day, received your letter and from it learned, for the first time, of your shattered life. My heart bleeds for you. No mortal imaginaton can prefigure the utter desolation that settles down on life after such a blow—the awful silence of it all! With your exquisitely sensitive nature you must be cut to the brains. Dear boy, how I grieve for you. There are no words of comfort. Were I with you I could only hold your hand and look into your face in silence. The sole comfort will lie in re-union, and until that happy blessed morn we must grimly bear the 'Dull deep pain and constant anguish of patience.'
    Time brings no relief, it gives merely the power to hide the wound. The agony of the separation grows fiercer every day—Do we grow less hungry by fasting? You are not an hour out of my thoughts.
    God be merciful to us all.
Yours, dear Corson affectionately
H.H.F.
18 October

Neither did time blur Kate's memory. Although he resolved never to let the shadow which had darkened his life fall on his children, he constantly kept her memory alive by recalling the happy years of their childhood and the words of their mother. Not a meal passed, when the children were present, without some mention of her name. Her place was always laid at table, and her chair sat vacant, occupied on occasion only by Caroline. Even his two granddaughters—Helen Kate Furness born in 1887 and Kate Jayne born in 1895—kept the memory of her name green and growing. Never once, evidently, did he consider remarriage. Years later when Gosse sent him a copy of *Coventry Patmore* (1905), Furness's comment on Patmore's three wives testifies to his singlehearted devotion to Kate's memory. "Indeed I was shocked to learn that he married again! and yet again! And yet after a remarriage I don't see why a man shouldn't marry forty wives if he has the opportunity. It's the second step that costs in this case."[7] What, one wonders, did

Furness think in 1886—less than three years after Kate's death—when his close friend Weir Mitchell remarried after the death of his wife?

To Shakespeare and to comedy, then, Furness turned not so much for their own sake as to fill the time and to heal the wound that he himself kept fresh and throbbing. "I am kept busy, night and day," he wrote to Fleay in November 1889. "'Tis my only resource. It doesn't drown thought—it merely passes the time. In sitting still with folded hands madness lies. And so I drive ahead through storm."[8] With each new play the excitement of discovery faded into drudgery as proofsheets dragged on day after day. While reading proof for *The Winter's Tale*, Furness wrote to Nannie, "Not one throb of interest has it stirred in me while going through the press. I sigh when I open the proofs, I groan while I read them, and I smile when I finish them. They seem so empty and barren—a mere waste of time to labour over them. But for what else is my time good for? I must do something with these long weary days."[9]

When he had finished a play, Furness immediately lost interest in it. Three years after its publication he had still not cut the pages of *A Midsummer Night's Dream*, nor, he announced to Nannie after finishing the proofsheets for *The Winter's Tale*, did he intend to cut the leaves of that play either. Yet he drove himself incessantly onward, beginning the next play before the one at hand was fairly finished. The very day that the last proofs of *The Winter's Tale* had returned to Lippincott's Furness began numbering the lines in *Much Ado About Nothing*, and a month after the first copy of the former reached Lindenshade, he had finished the collation of the quartos and folios of the latter. Thus, in spite of the ever present pain, Furness pressed on, and the row of Variorum volumes stretched further along the shelf as the years pushed toward reunion with Kate. "How wise and noble it is of you to persevere thus in diligent literary labour," wrote Mary Cowden-Clarke to thank Furness for her gift copy of *A Midsummer Night's Dream*. "It is the best possible means of relieving the ache of heart that *will* haunt one, and would otherwise dull every hour that one breathes."[10]

As volume followed volume Furness adopted certain other changes that set the comedies of the middle years apart from the tragedies of the earlier years. First among these stands his decision, first demonstrated in *Othello*, to print the First Folio text without change, even in accidentals, with the variants and emendations of some forty subsequent editors, including his own, listed below. In *Romeo and Juliet, Macbeth, Hamlet,* and *King Lear* Furness had created his own modernized text and, following the principle first laid down in the preface to *Romeo and Juliet,* "as a general rule, adopted the reading of a majority of the ablest editors."

For most Shakespearian editors and textual critics of the eighteenth and nineteenth centuries, such a course seemed eminently reasonable. In the days before bibliographical criticism revealed the distinctions between good quartos and bad, fair papers and foul, and generally investigated the relationship between the printed text and the manuscript that lay behind it, Heminge and Condell's charge of "diuerse stolne, and surreptitious copies, maimed, and deformed by the frauds and stealthes of iniurious imposters" had tainted virtually all of the Shakespearian quartos. And their claim, obviously unsupported by the text of the First Folio itself, that these imperfect copies "are now offer'd to your view cur'd, and perfect of their limbes; and all the rest, absolute in their numbers, as he conceiued them" further called into question the reliability of any Shakespearian text. In 1756, Samuel Johnson, for example, had stated the prevailing view of the hopeless corruption of Shakespeare's words:

> Copied for the actors, and multiplied by transcript after transcript, vitiated by the blunders of the penman, or changed by the affectation of the player; perhaps enlarged to introduce a jest, or mutilated to shorten the representation; and printed at last without the concurrence of the authour, without the consent of the proprietor, from compilations made by chance or by stealth out of the separate parts written for the theatre: and thus thrust into the world surreptitiously and hastily, they suffered another depravation from the ignorance and negligence of the printers . . . It is not easy for invention to bring together so many causes concurring to vitiate a text.[11]

Since, according to the prevailing wisdom, Shakespeare's text was hopelessly corrupt, the editor's main task was to select and explain the best of the bad readings or, if that became impossible, to emend the text.

Furness, like most eighteenth- and nineteenth-century editors of Shakespeare, had a classical education and was influenced by the practice of textual criticism of classical texts where any manuscript, no matter how corrupt, could represent a line of descent from the original and hence preserve some correct readings of the archetype.[12] As a result, editors of Shakespeare freely chose their readings from good and bad quarto and folio alike with little or no regard to the authority of a given text or to its relationship to Shakespeare's manuscript. In the 1604 quarto of *Hamlet*, for example, Claudius observes of Hamlet: "The termes of our estate may not endure / Hazerd so neer's as doth hourely grow / Out of his browes" (3.3.5-7). The First Folio reads "dangerous" for "neer's" and "Lunacies" for "browes." If, as modern bibliographical criticism has conjectured, the good quarto was set from Shakespeare's foul papers with some reference to the 1603 bad quarto and the folio was set up from the good quarto collated with the promptbook, itself a scribal transcript, then the quarto readings "neer's" and "browes" have higher authority, being closer to Shakespeare's autograph manuscript, than the folio's "dangerous" and "Lunacies." One cannot, as did Furness and a majority of editors before him, chose "near us" in one line and "lunacies" in the other. Or, to chose a more widely known case, in the famous crux in *Hamlet* 1.2.129 "O, that this too too (solid/sullied/ sallied) flesh would melt," Furness followed every other editor before his time in choosing the First Folio"s "solid" over the quartos' "sullied" (misprinted "sallied") even though the second quarto was probably printed from Shakespeare's foul papers and hence closer to Shakespeare's original intention than the First Folio which was probably printed from a scribal prompt book and hence of lesser authority. Although Furness introduced few emendations of his own, yet in the beginning he readily followed the practice of earlier editors of Shakespeare, reinforced by his own classical training, of choosing what seemed the best reading from the various printed texts available without regard for their authority.

While editing *Othello*, however, Furness departed from this editorial tradition to reprint exactly the First Folio. In so doing he joined the few nineteenth-century pioneers of conservative textual criticism that staked out the territory to be explored and mapped in detail by W.W. Greg, A.W. Pollard, and R.B. McKerrow, founders of the new bibliographical criticism of the early twentieth century. In the years before Pollard published his *Shakespeare Folios and Quartos* (1909), those pioneers were few. In the 1850s Tycho Mommsen had published critical editions of *Romeo and Juliet* and *Hamlet*, arguing that the first quartos were corrupt, pirated editions and that editors should base their texts on the good quartos of 1599 and 1604. In 1887, Halliwell-Phillipps, in his seventh edition of *Outlines of the Life of Shakespeare* publicly called for a re-evaluation of the First Folio, arguing that the "stolne and surreptitious copies" referred only to the bad quartos of *Hamlet, Henry V, Romeo and Juliet*, and *The Merry Wives of Windsor*, and that for all the imperfections of the First Folio, Heminge and Condell had faithfully gathered the best possible copies of the plays that could be found. "There cannot, indeed, be a doubt that according to their lights they expressed a sincere conviction when they delivered the immortal dramas to the public as being 'absolute in their numbers as he conceived them.'"[13] As early as the 1870s during Furness's editing of *Hamlet*, Corson too had argued so strongly for First Folio readings and against all emendations where any sense could be made out of the readings of Heminge and Condell that Furness had accused him of "firstfoliolatry."

Furness's did not follow these few pioneers entirely for reasons debated in The Bibliographical Society and approved in the pages of *The Library* after the turn of the century. Nevertheless, his decision to reprint the First Folio reproduced the authoritative text for six of the subsequent plays that he would edit, and his increasingly conservative textual criticism provided a necessary check on the freely emended texts edited by some of his predecessors. While editing *King Lear*, Furness had begun to side with Corson, refused to modernize the spelling, and had virtually followed the First Folio in constructing his own text. In June 1880, before beginning *Othello*, Furness then consulted White for his advice.

> This opens a subject over which I am greatly perplexed. Don't you think it would be better to adopt for my text the first folio? This edition of mine is not for babes; it is for persons who think for themselves, and wish to have all the apparatus for a critical study. With this edition study doesn't end, it begins. And for this purpose would it not be more satisfactory to have in full the ipsissima verba of what is alleged to be a copy of the authors MS? The text which I prefer can be stated easily in the footnotes. It would increase my labour in some directions so much that I have hitherto shrunk from it. The discussion of the metre, alone, would lead me a pretty dance, and life is short.[14]

White's reply has not survived, but apparently he agreed, for with the support of those other prominent American Shakespearians, Rolfe and Corson, Furness in *Othello* reproduced letter for letter the First Folio reading from his own copy. His argument he set forth in the preface to that play.

> When reading Shakespeare, we resign ourselves to the mighty current, and let it bear us along whithersoever it will; we see no shoals, heed no rocks, need no pilot. Whether spoken from rude boards or printed in homely form, the words are Shakespeare's, the hour is his, and a thought of texts is an impertinence. But when we study Shakespeare, then our mood changes; no longer are we 'sitting at a play,' the passive recipients of impressions through the eye and ear, but we weigh every word, analyse every expression, sift every phrase, that no grain of art or beauty which we can assimilate shall escape. To do this to our best advantage we must have Shakespeare's own words before us. No other words will avail, even though they be those of the wisest and most inspired of our day and generation We must have Shakespeare's own text; or, failing this, the nearest possible approach to it. We shall be duly grateful to the wise and learned, who, where phrases are obscure, give us the words which they believe to have been Shakespeare's; but, as students, we must have under our eyes the original text, which, however stubborn it may seem at times, may yet open its treasures to our importunity, and reveal charms before undreamed of. . . Can any good reason be urged why, in this present play at least, we should not, in the hours devoted to study, be it remembered, have the text of the First Folio as our guide?[15]

Some dissenting voices were heard, but most scholars and reviewers subsequently agreed on the wisdom of the new plan, still essentially followed in the modern Variorums—although purely typographical features are now modernized owing to the general availability of photographic facsimiles of the First Folio when a close study of the actual printing is desired. *The Saturday Review* issued the most outspoken criticism.

> After five volumes of his Variorum edition had appeared, Mr Furness altered his plan; he ceased to form a text of his own, reprinted from the First Folio with all its errors, and threw upon the student the task of constructing a better text than that of 1623. We regret his decision. No one who seriously cares for Shakespeare can find any difficulty in procuring a facsimile of the First Folio; in the case of certain plays the earlier quartos are no less important. There cannot be a doubt that in

a thousand instances any good modern text comes nearer to what Shakespeare wrote than does the careless handiwork of Heminge and Condell. We want to have before our eyes the words of Shakespeare, not the blunders of a compositor, and it is certain that there is less of Shakespeare in the text which Mr. Furness now prints than in the text which a critic as judicious and as conservative as his present editor could himself exhibit . . . 'Who am I,' asks the most modest of scholars, 'that I should thrust myself in between the student and the text, as though in me resided the power to restore Shakespeare's own words?' But the truth is that he thrusts the compositors of 1623 between us and Shakespeare; they were not sacred persons, nor is their work of sacrosanct authority. . . . it is surely best to start from what the poet wrote, and if the editors have not helped us to discover this, where is the justification of the weary task of collation and commentatorship?[16]

Ingleby too disagreed, and Joseph Knight, reviewing *Othello* in *The Athenaeum*, cautiously gave his approval although he lamented the disparity with the earlier volumes. "It is none the less to be regretted that a change which more or less resembles, to use an illustration that must be familiar to Mr. Furness, 'swapping horses in the middle of a stream,' has had to be made. It is at least to be hoped that the new system will be maintained."[17]

Most reviewers, however, then and later applauded Furness's shift to the First Folio. Rolfe in *The Literary World*, Norris in *Shakespeariana*, Leo in the *Shakespeare Jahrbuch*, Ernest Whitney in the *New Englander and Yale Review*, and Charlotte Porter in *Poet Lore* all noted the change with approval. George Lyman Kittredge succinctly summed up the debate in *The Nation*, "The advantages of the change are manifest, and it is hard to see any objection to it. The student has under his eye, in a marvellously condensed and legible arrangement, a collation of some forty texts, and he can choose for himself. The reading preferred by the editor is indicated in a note."[18] Sending his congratulations for *Othello*, Rolfe added,

It seemed to me that it was a happy thought to give the Folio text *literatim*. I had my doubts about it when you first mentioned the plan, though I believe I gave it my approval. Now that I see the book, all doubts vanish into air. It is a real comfort to have the old original text right under one's eye, with all the tinkering and torturing of the crickets properly subordinated thereto . . . No, my boy, you've hit it at last. . . . It's a pity that the other volumes couldn't be made uniform with this in this regard.[19]

In a purely mechanical sense the new plan eased Furness's task by making the collation of the quartos, folios, and subsequent editions much easier. Furness had a photographic memory, and by reprinting exactly the First Folio text, he could easily detect all variations. A letter to Nannie, written during the editing of *Much Ado About Nothing*, explains what he called "the curious play of my memory."

I read over about sixty or seventy lines in the First Folio, and these lines I can remember, down to the most insignificant comma, for hours or as long as I am at work on them. When they are finished and I turn to a fresh column, every trace of them is vanished. While they are present I could write down from memory every divergence in any subsequent edition. This goes from me utterly the minute I turn to another set. I wonder if it is so with everyone. Perhaps I may thank this peculiarity, if it be one, for my accuracy. Aldis Wright is probably the only man who has ever verified my work—and I think he did it only in *As You Like It* and therein he detected only six errors (I think that is the number) and these were probably errors in proof-reading. Surely, not a large percentage when you consider that the two thousand lines of the play must be multiplied by forty—to give the number of lines collated. Ay de mi! what a humbug the world is! This mechanical drudgery is called 'scholarship!' And of such 'scholarship' is nine-tenths of the German learning composed![20]

In addition to reprinting the First Folio instead of constructing his own text, Furness made a second change that emphasized his growing textual conservatism. Instead of simply recording the explanations of his predecessor, he increasingly spoke out in the variorum volumes of the middle years, arguing for First Folio readings, in spite of their manifold errors, whenever any sense could be squeezed out of the passage in question. His longest notes consisted of attempts to explain the First Folio readings, and in the preface to *A Midsummer Night's Dream* this growing conservatism solidified into a statement of editorial practice.

Never for a minute should we lose sight of that star to every wandering textual bark which has been from time immemorial the scholar's surest guide in criticism: *Durior lectio preferenda est.* The successive winnowings are all forgot, to which the text has been subjected for nigh two hundred years. Never again can there be such harvests as were richly garnered by ROWE, THEOBALD, and CAPELL, and when to these we add STEEVENS and MALONE of more recent times, we may rest assured that the gleaning for us is of the very scantiest, and reserved only for the keenest and most skilful eyesight. At the present day those who know the most venture the least.... Moreover, by this time the text of SHAKESPEARE has become so fixed and settled that I think it safe to predict that, unless a veritable MS of SHAKESPEARE's own be discovered, not a single future emendation will be generally accepted in critical editions.[21]

This preference for explanation over emendation was later ratified by W.W. Greg, who wrote in *The Library* in 1924,

Explanation is safer and less heady work than conjecture, and even when perverse it has served both to define the possibilities of interpretation and to help the formation of a severer code of emendation. Only through the discipline of endless trial and failure can be won the sure sense of where explanation becomes impossible and alteration of the text necessary. It is the fine flower of criticism, and few attain it.[22]

When no sense could be made of the First Folio readings, Furness defended the mystery of ignorance over the labored enlightenment and emendation of the learned. "What 'scamels' are, or are not," he wrote about the delicacy offered to Trinculo by Caliban in *The Tempest* (2.2.180),

may be learned from the portentous mass of notes on the word, extending to two of the following pages, wherein there has been proposed as a substitute every article of food known to man which begins and ends with *s*, from 'shamois' to 'sea-owls.' For my part, I unblushingly confess that I do not know what 'scamels' are, and that I prefer to retain the word in the text and to remain in utter, invincible ignorance. From the very beginning of the Play we know that the scene lies in an enchanted island. Is this to be forgotten? Since the air is full of sweet sounds, why may not the rocks be inhabited by unknown birds of gay plumage or by vague animals of a grateful and appetising plumpness? Let the picture remain, of the dashing rocks, the stealthy, freckled whelp, and, in the clutch of his long nails, a young and tender scamel.[23]

While most reviewers praised his editorial policy, the occasional critic chafed under such textual conservatism, usually when a favorite emendation fell to the barbed wit of the editor. When reviewing *A Midsummer Night's Dream* for *The Nation*, Kittredge accused Furness of "excessive reverence" for the First Folio; and when reviewing *Twelfth Night*, *The Nation* again took note of the increasing textual conservatism that had marked the successive volumes of the Variorum and, while defending his use of the First Folio, raised the spectre of "firstfoliolotry" just as Furness had with Corson years before.

> Occasionally, however, Dr. Furness carries his respect for the venerable too far, and defends a manifest error. . . . The druidic mist that enshrouds the 'true original copies' of Heminge and Condell's title-page covers a multitude of their sins. Folio-worship is a form of religion that is not quite free from superstitious taint. Among the Baconians, indeed, it has grown to be a kind of melancholy madness.[24]

With such increasing editorial conservatism in the text came a contrasting outspokenness in the commentary. As comedy followed comedy, more and more entries signed "—Ed." appeared, often summing up the evidence and deciding an editorial dispute or dismissing the foolishness of some dryasdust scholar with a witty comment. When Antigonus objects to Leontes' imprisonment of Hermione in *The Winter's Tale*, for example, he says, "You are abus'd, and by some putter on, / That will be damn'd for't: would I knew the Villaine, / I would Land'damne him" (2.1.171-73). Two pages of commentary follow speculating on the meaning of "Land-damne": taking away a man's life (Hanmer); to pit, bury, or stop up with land (Capell); to rid the country of him (Johnson); to bury him alive and stop him up with earth (Rann); to poison him with laudanum (Steevens); to lamback or beat him (Collier); to live-damn or damn him alive (Walker); to lambaste him (Keightley); or to lan-dan him, done by rustics walking from house to house blowing trumpets and beating drums, pans, and kettles to proclaim the parties discovered in adultery (Thorncliffe). At the end of this critical cacophony Furness wryly concluded, "We can all grasp the meaning of the last half of 'Land-damne,' and I would add, that to understand half of Shakespeare's meaning in a difficult passage is something to be not a little proud of.—Ed."[25] Regarding the famous "seacoast of Bohemia" where Antigonus makes his exit pursued by a bear, Furness attended for three pages both to those critics who went to great lengths to excuse Shakespeare for his geographical blunder and to those who maintained that the line needed no excuse since at various times in history the King of Bohemia had held possessions on the coast of the Adriatic. Again gently poking fun at the learned commentators, Furness summed up the debate, "Indeed it is not easy to decide, in reviewing the whole question, which to admire the more, the ingenuity which supplies excuses where none is really needed, or the diffusion of geographical knowledge.—Ed."[26]

Such summing up, which came to be an expectation at every crux, also began with *Othello*. In that volume he modestly explained to his readers "In the Commentary I have, in many a place, put ED. where I should much prefer to have omitted it. But I beg to have it understood that is present not as a claimant, but as a safeguard, that upon none of my betters may be fathered my folly."[27] Privately he confided to Corson after he finished *Othello*, "In the way of editing I have done just what I pleased, followed no rule, but every whim, and have been obtrusive, personal and flippant. . . . As I have worked solely for my own sake, the verdict of the public is absolutely indifferent to me."[28] And later he returned to the subject in a letter written to Nannie as he read proof for *The Winter's Tale*.

> You speak of *Macbeth* and few 'Ed's' therein. Down to *Lear*, I was still wincing under old Josh. Lippincott's sneer that my proposed edition would be mighty good for the Editor but mighty poor for the publishers, implying that I was self-seeking in wishing him to undertake the publication. I can tell you, 'twas hard work in editing the plays to hold my tongue in many and many a place. But in *Lear* or rather when Lear was finished, Kate said she wanted me to break loose altogether and speak my mind freely. So to her I owe my emancipation.[29]

The public verdict approved and asked for more. In thanking Furness for *A Midsummer Night's Dream*, Gosse wrote, "You have a wonderful skill in the luminous arrangement of your data, and you make all the elephantine commentators dance with a grace which would surprise themselves."[30] Said John Foster Kirk after *The Tempest*,

> The preface is certainly the most delightful you have ever written; I seemed in reading it to hear it from your own lips and to catch the twinkling of your eyes. Then your control over your rebel rout of commentators is more complete than even before . . . I am in danger sometimes of confounding you with Shakespeare, and imagining that it is he himself who, in his own style, settles the questions, as to what he said and what he meant.[31]

Furnivall, too, approved, writing after *The Tempest*, "I'm glad to see more of your Ed.s in the book. Don't fear to increase them in future vols. If your opinion isn't worth more than 3/4ths of the men whose dicta you record, I'm a Dutchman."[32] *Notes and Queries* noted his "sane, lucid, and suggestive comments,"[33] and the *Birmingham Daily Post and Journal*, when reviewing *As You Like It*, reported, "All possible questions, from the pronunciation of 'Jaques' to the history of the 'Seven Ages,' and the more complex 'cruxes,' are fully and learnedly set forth, often with much quiet humour, and always with perfect fairness and genuine good faith."[34] Henry Austin Clapp, reviewing *The Winter's Tale* for *The Atlantic Monthly*, added,

> Over and over again in these volumes Dr. Furness, with a dozen pen strokes, quietly overthrows some old accepted blunder, and substitutes an explanation of his own which carries complete conviction. On the other hand, when, as occasionally happens, he finds a passage hopeless, he is neither afraid nor ashamed to say so, and to leave the student wandering in a bog, with eyes confused by twenty will-o'-the-wisp lights from the pens of as many commentators. The readers of The Atlantic scarcely need to be reminded of Dr. Furness's quaint humor, which not only cooperates charmingly with his fine faculty in the discussion of nice points of taste, but often serves as a watering cart when the editor is involved in the dust of textual and verbal criticism.[35]

If Furness was accused of "excessive reverence" for the First Folio in regard to his textual criticism, in regard to Shakespeare's life and the date of composition of the plays he was accused of "heresy"—not the Baconian heresy of his day, but rather a complete indifference to the order of the plays, to the dates of composition, or to attempts to trace Shakespeare's intellectual development by reference to the correct order of the plays. Baconian heresy Furness had dismissed in a characteristically witty comment in the variorum *The Merchant of Venice.*

> One is sometimes inclined to say to those who dispute the authorship of these plays, as the Cockney did to the eels, 'down, wantons, down!' but a little calm reflection reveals to us that this attempt to dethrone Shakespeare, so far from being treason, or *lésé majesté*, is, in fact, most devout and respectful homage to him. In our sallad days, when first we begin to study Shakespeare, who does not remember his bewildering efforts to attribute to mortal hand these immortal plays? Then follows the fruitless attempt to discern in that Stratford youth, the Emperor, by the grace of God, of all Literature. In our despair of marrying, as Emerson says, the man to the verse, we wed the verse to the greatest known intellect of that age. Can homage be more profound? But, as I have said, this we do when we are young in judgement. The older we grow in this study, and the farther we advance in it, the clearer becomes our vision that, if the royal robes do not fit Shakespeare, they certainly do not, and cannot, fit any one else. Wherefore, I conceive that we have here a not altogether inaccurate gauge of the depth, or duration, or persistence of Shakespearian study, and, measuring by a scale of maturity, or growth, in this study, I have come to look upon all attempts to prove that Bacon wrote these dramas, merely as indications of youth, possibly, of extreme youth, and that they find their comforting parallels in the transitory ailments incident to childhood, like the chicken-pox or the measles. The attack is pretty sure to come, but we know that it is neither dangerous nor chronic, that time will effect a cure, and that, when once well over it, there is no likelihood whatever of its recurrence.—ED.[36]

His orthodoxy wavered, however, when the biographers began to probe for Shakespeare the man. "I don't even care who wrote the plays," he once wrote to William Everett. "If I care about it at all—it is to rejoice that we know so little about the divine Williams."[37] Even when Charles Wallace discovered in 1909 the legal deposition with Shakespeare's signature and submitted his discovery to the *Century,* Furness advised R.U. Johnson to print it, but added, "I personally take very little interest in any facts which relate solely to the everyday occurrences of Shakespeare's life ... The older I grow, the less I care about Shakespeare's outer life. No outer life could come up to the grandeur of the plays."[38] His reasons he succinctly summarized in a letter to Owen Wister.

Very early I abandoned all investigations of the order in which the divine Williams wrote his Plays, for two reasons. First: indifference to the whole subject which seems utterly alien either to true enjoyment of the Plays themselves or to true art. The Plays were written for the eye and ear, and while, through these, the brain is busy with infinite suggestions in every realm of thought, no care arises as to where the plays were written, when they were written, or even by whom they were written. Artistically, too, such questions are impertinent; in listening to a piece of Music, if your mind wanders into speculations as to the composer, the music is a failure as a work of art; or in looking at a picture do you think of the canvas under the paint? I accept the Plays, as I look at jewels,—the colour and the brilliancy charm and dazzle, and never a thought enters my mind of where it was found or by whom it was cut. My second reason is that soon as you seek to know more of the order of Composition than is afforded by the external evidence supplied by dates of publication, etc., you unloose a babel of tongues which no rule can combine into harmony. Every son of Adam will be guided by his own temperament; consequently, proofs which are utterly irrelevant to one mind, will be confirmations strong as holy Writ to another. For instance Furnivall, Dowden and others believe that Shakespeare, in general, wrote Comedies when he was merry, and Tragedies when he was sad— Comedies in youth, Tragedies in age & maturity. On the other hand, I incline exactly to the reverse. And all of us, found our reasons on the monstrous assumption that there is a parallelism between Shakespeare's mind and our own,—an assumption, whereof the existence is indubitable, which ought to shake Olympus with Homeric laughter. Unquestionably, on broad lines Shakespeare's character is revealed in his Plays—but the lines are so broad that they are about coequal to the Four Cardinal Virtues. I doubt further individualising. Of course, if your temperament leads you to take a deep interest in the Order of Composition,—all that I have said, is to you justly, moonshine. The book for you is Dowden's 'Shakespeare, his Mind and Art.'[39]

Such contempt for chronology and biographical criticism ran counter to the enthusiastic efforts of the New Shakspere Society, founded in 1874 by Furnivall with the express purpose of establishing by scientific tests, mainly metrical, the chronological succession of Shakespeare's plays and then studying the plays in revised order to reveal the inner man Shakespeare. The Society had floundered for a time with the largely inaccurate and contradictory conclusions of the the metrical tests designed by Frederick Gard Fleay, but eventually realized its objective in the book by one of its vice presidents, Edward Dowden's *Shakspere: A Critical Study of His Mind and Art* (1875). This subjective biography, which had immense influence on the Shakespearian world of the late nineteenth century, divided the poet's career into four periods—In the workshop, In the world, Out of the depths, and On the heights—and, while ignoring the known facts about Shakespeare as a playwright and businessman at the Globe and Blackfriars Theatre, concentrated entirely, and often questionably, on Shakespeare's inner mind and intellectual development as supposedly revealed in the plays.

Perhaps as a corrective to this search for the man Shakespere at the expense of his plays, Furness erred, if indeed it was an error, by elevating the plays at the expense of the man. In May 1877 Furness wrote to Fleay,

> I'm afraid I'm too old and too much sunk in my original wickedness & sin to adopt with all the enthusiasm and zeal on which you insist your views of the importance of studying the order of Shakespeare's plays. Shakespeare always has been & I'm afraid always will be, to me such an impalpable myth, such a very shade of shades that I cannot orient, adjust myself to the thought that there was any growth in him. At his lowest estate in his weakest plays he is so high above my intellectual reach that I cannot ascribe his weakness to immaturity but to some chance indifference or haste. Every now & then after reading some of yours or Dowden's or Furnivall's arguments in favour of this new school of study I feel as though after all it is the true way & that I must devote myself to it. But the metal cools & I congeal into a backslider.[40]

In 1882, when reviewing for *The Nation* the second edition of Halliwell-Phillipps's *Outlines of the Life of Shakespeare*, Furness praised the factual and objective scholarship of Halliwell-Phillipps, but disparaged Dowden's subjective biography, charging that the world was "going Shakespeare-mad": "a life has been manufactured for him out of a supposed chronological order in which he wrote his plays—that he wrote tragedy when he was sad and comedy when he was merry—and this chronological order has been founded on the number of syllables in his lines."[41]

This disdain for any attempt to establish the order of the plays and to construct thereupon the intellectual development of Shakespeare's mind Furness repeated in the preface to *As You Like It* in 1890 and with increasing virulence in *The Tempest, A Midsummer Night's Dream, The Winter's Tale, Much Ado About Nothing,* and *Twelfth Night.* "Stress has been laid in these later days on the Chronological Order in which SHAKESPEARE wrote his plays," observed Furness in *As You Like It,*

> and attempts have been made to connect their tragic or their comic tone with the outward circumstances of SHAKESPEARE's own life. . . . For my part, I believe that SHAKESPEARE wrote his plays, like the conscientious playwright that he was, to fill the theatre and make money for his fellow-actors and for himself; and I confess to absolute scepticism in reference to the belief that in these dramas SHAKESPEARE's self can be discovered (except on the broadest lines), or that either his outer or his inner life is to any discoverable degree reflected in his plays: it is because SHAKESPEARE is *not* there that the characters are so perfect.[42]

In the appendix to *A Midsummer Night's Dream* Furness devoted twenty pages to discussion of the date of composition. Everyone from Malone (1790) to Verity (1894) had his say, and among the twenty-nine critics summarized, every date from 1590 to 1598 had its champion. Again Furness made plain his own view in the preface.

> In this whole subject of fixing dates of these plays I confess I take no atom of interest, beyond that which lies in any curious speculation. But many of my superiors assert that this subject, to me so jejune, is of keen interest, and the source of what they think is, in their own case, refined pleasure. To this decision, while reserving the right of private judgement, I yield, at the same time wishing that these, my betters, would occasionally go for a while 'into retreat,' and calmly and soberly, in seclusion, ask themselves what is the chief end of man in reading SHAKESPEARE. I think they would discern that not by the discovery of the dates of these plays is it that fear and compassion, or the sense of humor, are awakened: the clearer vision would enable them, I trust, to separate the chaff from the wheat; and that when,

before them, there pass scenes of breathing life, with the hot blood stirring, they would not seek after the date of the play nor ask SHAKESPEARE how old he was when he wrote it. . . . the dates of the plays are purely biographical, and have for me as much relevancy to the plays themselves as has a chemical analysis of the paper of the Folio or of the ink of the Quartos.[43]

For the biographical critics these were fighting words, and the reviewers came out swinging. "I can hardly say with Dr. Furness, that facts which are 'purely biographical' have for me as much relevancy to the plays themselves as has 'a chemical analysis of the paper of the Folio or of the ink of the Quarto,'" retorted Edward Hale in *The Dial* review of *A Midsummer Night's Dream*. "For my own part, on appreciating its place in Shakespeare's life, I read 'Hamlet' with an increase of pleasure which could never be given me by the contemplation of a chemical formula."[44] "Hurrah! here is your new volume after all," wrote Furnivall and then added, "but you still chaff us about the dating of the plays, & will not give us credit for the only reason for which we care for them & that is, to get them into the right order of Shakspere's development, & so let us better understand the growth of his mind & art, his soul. Surely it *does* matter infinitely to any real student & lover of Sh. whether he wrote the *Tempest* before the *Dream*, or after it, whether the *Winter's Tale* is at the end of his writing life, or, like *L.L.Lost*, at the beginning of it; whether his genius is a hodge-podge or an orderly development."[45] *The Saturday Review* had one word for it—"heresy."[46]

Furness, however, remained unrepentant and in *The Winter's Tale, Much Ado About Nothing*, and *Twelfth Night* restated his case with growing conviction. In the preface to *Much Ado About Nothing* Furness marvelled at the mystery that surrounded "the divine Williams," and a few pages later, after discussing Fleay's assertion that Shakespeare had in all probability visited Denmark, Saxony, and Italy with a troupe of travelling players, directed his sarcasm at the "probably's" and "likely's" with which the subjective biographers probed the mystery of Shakespeare's life.

This 'probable' transportation of SHAKESPEARE into Germany and Italy incites me to say that profound as are my veneration and gratitude to SHAKESPEARE as a poet, they are deeper to him as a man. With that prophetic glance, vouchsafed only to the heaven-descended, he foresaw the inexhaustible flood of imaginings which would be set abroach to account for any prolonged obscurity enveloping his life. Clearly, with this end in view, he evaded all public notice for seven long years. From 1585, when his twin children were baptised (common decency must assume that he was present at that ceremony,) until 1592, we know absolutely nothing of him. For one momentary flash, in 1587 when the terms of a mortgage given by his father, had to be adjusted, we may possibly catch a glimpse of him; but for all the rest a Cimmerian midnight holds him. And what a priceless boon! What an unobstructed field wherein to prove that he so devoted himself to the study of every trade, profession, pursuit, and accomplishment that he became that master of them all, which his plays clearly show him to have been. It was during these seven silent years, while holding horses at the doors of the theatres for his daily bread, that he became, if we are to believe each critic and commentator, a thorough master of law and practice down to the minutest quillet, a thorough master of medicine, with the most searching knowledge of the virtue of every herb, mineral, or medicament, including treatment of the insane and an anticipation of Harvey's circulation of the blood; he became skilled in veterinary medicine and was familiar with every disease that can afflict a horse; he learned the art of war, and served a campaign in the field; he became such an adept in music that long afterward he indicated prodigies and eclipses by solmisation; he went to sea and acquired an absolute mastery of a ship in a furious tempest, and made only one slight mistake, long years afterward, in the number of a ship's glasses; he studied botany and knew every flower by name; horticulture, and knew every fruit; arboriculture, and knew the quality and value of all timber; that he practised archery daily, who can doubt? and when not hawking, or fishing, he was fencing; he became familiar with astronomy and at home in astrology; he learned ornithology through and through, from young scamels on the rock to the wren of little quill; a passionate huntsman, he was also a pigeon-fancier, and from long observation discovered that doves would defend their nest, and that pigeons lacked gall; he was a printer and not only set up books, but bound them afterward; as we have just seen he was a strolling actor in Germany, and travelled in Italy, noting the tide at Venice and the evening mass at Verona; he got his Bible by heart, including the Apocrypha; he read every translation of every classic author then published, and every original in Greek, Latin, Italian, and French (of course he learned German while strolling) and, finally, he read through the whole of English literature, from Chaucer down to every play or poem written by his contemporaries, and as he read he took voluminous notes (sly dog!) of every unusual word, phrase, or idea to palm it off afterward as his own!

My own private conviction is that he mastered cuneiform; visited America; and remained some time in Boston,—greatly to his intellectual advantage.[47]

In spite of his increasing outspokenness, however, Furness always treated the biographical critics and speculators with meticulous fairness and objectivity in the appendix, accurately summarizing each argument, plausible or implausible, for the record. Perhaps, for that reason, most reviewers resigned themselves to forgiving seventy times seven. *The Atlantic Monthly* review of *Twelfth Night*, for example, noted, "Once more the editor has his fling at those who find the chronology of an author's works a valuable aid in the study of his genius," but, after quoting a passage from the preface, added, "Respect for the writer forbids the natural exclamation on such a passage. It is surely too late in the day for it to be worth while arguing against it. In any case, it is satisfactory that Dr. Furness none the less faithfully presents all the data available for the discussion which he regards so contemptuously."[48] When thanking Furness for *Twelfth Night*, Rolfe admonished,

> The preface is delightful as usual, but don't you think you've run about all the funny variation on the well-worn theme of your indifference to the chronology of the plays? We should miss em dreadfully but look out that some critic doesn't snub you for the iteration. Of course I agree with you perfectly. I don't care a picayune whether William wrote *Hamlet* in 1492 or 1776; but I don't go round town once a week proclaiming that I don't.[49]

Furnivall, too, writing after *Twelfth Night* struck a conciliatory tone: "I've read your Introduction; & it kept me in a continual chuckle at its delightful chaff of us chronological & 'probably' men. My dear boy, I do love it & you. . . . We all honour & bless you for it [the Variorum]. Long may you live to continue it!"[50]

That wish for a long and productive life echoed with increasing sincerity over the middle years of the Variorum as one by one the old names passed off the Variorum gift list and new names took their places. Each year, when Furness joined the Shakespeare Brothers for the annual dinner of the Shakspere Society of Philadelphia, he found fewer of the original fraternity that had inspired the Variorum. George Allen had died in 1876, Fish in 1879, and Furman Sheppard, who had helped defend the Variorum against Wright's charge of piracy, in 1883. When sending Edward Strachey a Bill of Fare from the 1895 Annual Dinner, Furness noted, "The flight of time is brought home to me, not painfully because I am glad to grow old, when I reflect that I am its oldest living member, and have been its Dean for more than twenty years."[51]

Among other American Shakespearians only Norris, Rolfe, and Corson lived to see *Othello* finished in 1886, and only Norris would outlive Furness himself. White had died in 1885; Hudson, the dean of American editors of Shakespeare, died in 1886; and Crosby, one-time Shakespearian from Zanesville, Ohio, had fallen into financial disgrace in 1884, sold his Shakespearian library at auction in March 1886, and faded from the Shakespearian scene. About White, Furness had written in December 1885 to his widow,

> Our loss in the Shakespearian world is irreparable; there is absolutely no one to take his place. Personally my loss is extreme. The world grows very small and narrow to us as we grow older and 'the public' while it dwindles in number increases in volume. My 'public' for which I work & to which I look for sympathy has diminished to four or five names, and chiefest among them stood his. Without his approving nod or criticising frown much of the zest is gone.[52]

Rolfe, too, felt the loss. "Go ahead with the *Merchant* without any delay or fooling," he advised Furness after the publication of *Othello* in April 1886. "Would that you could live to give us all the rest, and take three years for a volume! On whom will your ponderous mantel fall? Where is the *young* man that could hope to bear up under the "ponderous and marble" load? The giants are dying off—except you and a few *old* fellows on the other side of the pond—and the breed seems to be extinct."[53]

Indeed, as Furness emerged from his years of grief to resume the Variorum, almost all the giants "on the other side of the pond," with whom he had argued emendations and from whom he had sought advice in the early Variorum years, had also died. When Furness began the Variorum, he had corresponded with Halliwell-Phillipps and the other members of the Old Shakespeare Society—

Alexander Dyce, Charles Knight, and John Payne Collier—but by the time Furness was working on *As You Like It* and the other comedies, these editors and many other English Shakespearians were gone: Alexander Dyce and William Harness had both died in 1869 while *Romeo and Juliet* was going through the press; Thomas Keightley died in 1872; Charles Knight, in 1873; Howard Staunton, in 1874; Andrew Brae, in 1881; Collier, in 1883 at the age of ninety-four; Blanchard Jerrold, in 1884; Ingleby, in 1886; and finally, in 1889, Halliwell-Phillipps. Only Aldis Wright and Furnivall, among those original correspondents still remained. "Dear me! how old I feel when I look back at those old days when I first wrote to you, and you answered me so kindly," Furness had written to Halliwell-Phillipps in June 1887. "Those were the days of Dyce and Knight, and Harness and Collier, and Staunton, from nearly all of whom I had such kind letters. Since then a new school has sprung up, whose ways are not as our ways. Ah, well, the world certainly moves, but motion can be backward as well as forward."[54] And a year later, thanking Furness for *The Merchant of Venice*, Halliwell-Phillipps had replied, "Pray accept my warmest thanks for your splendid & admirable book, one of your very best if not the very best. I am delighted with it. It is the first Shakespeare book I have gone through for many weeks. . . . Old age is telling on me dreadfully, I, though *apparently* pretty well, feel that my former energy is gone for ever."[55] It was the last letter to Furness from his earliest English Shakespearian friend. Among his German friends, too, the old order had passed. Writing to Corson two months after Halliwell-Phillipps's death, Furness lamented, "Of German scholars, my correspondents, there is scarcely one now alive—Schmidt, Hertzberg, Delius, Ulrici, Elze alas! alas! all gone! Leo of Berlin in the only one left."[56] And to Leo he added a month later, "Now that death is so rapidly thinning our ranks, it behooves us who remain to draw closer to each other, while we can."[57]

This sense of the old order passing—prompted both by his personal grief and the losses in the Shakespearian world—emerges again and again in the letters of this period. "Dear me! how old I am!" he exclaimed to Rolfe in January 1900 while reminiscing about the beginning of the Variorum.

Dyce and Harness died when R. and J. was going through the press. But I had most kind notes of encouragement from Charles Knight and

Keightley, and with Collier and Staunton I corresponded on most familiar terms for years—so also Halliwell. As for Aldis Wright . . . he and I are the only survivors of that old group. By touching hands with Collier, I reach back through Malone to Stevens, to Dr. Johnson, to Capell, to Theobald, and to Pope. 'I feel chilly and grown old.'[58]

One almost catches the echo of Tennyson's Sir Bedivere, "First made and latest left of all the knights," telling the story of the Round Table "In the white winter of his age, to those / With whom he dwelt, new faces, other minds." And in some ways Furness was presiding over the passing of an age in the Shakespearian world—from the textual criticism that occupied the eighteenth- and early nineteenth-century editors to the biographical and interpretive criticism of the late nineteenth and twentieth centuries.

But unlike Sir Bedivere, the quest was not over for Furness; the Variorum adventure had just entered another phase with new friends, new correspondents, and new scholarly battles to fight. Several new correspondents entered Furness's life about this time— J. Appleton Morgan, founder of the Shakespeare Society of New York which Furness joined in April 1884; Edmund Gosse, whom Furness had entertained during his American visit in January 1885; Felix Schelling, who had joined the University of Pennsylvania Department of English in 1886; Charles Eliot Norton; Sir Edward Strachey; Joseph Knight; and Henry Clay Folger, to whom Furness now turned with the bibliographical questions that he had once directed to Halliwell-Phillipps. Furness seemed particularly drawn to Folger and his wife Emily, and some one hundred letters from the 1890s and 1900s, many of them dinner and house party invitations, from Furness to the Folgers survive to suggest the warmth of their friendship. Furness even undertook to lay out a course of Shakespearian study for Mrs. Folger, and with wistful backward glances at what might have been, he praised her for her assistance in her husband's Shakespearian work. "It is quite impossible that I should attempt to set forth any detailed course of study in Shakespeare," he wrote on July 25, 1894.

I can merely say that any one who can so far master the following books so as to stand a fair examination in them ought to be an A.M. in the Dep't of Shakespeare:—The Variorum of 1821, Dyce's Second Edition, Staunton's Second Edition, Collier's Second Edition, Collier's

Dramatic History, Wards Dramatic History, Sidney Walker's Versifica-
tion and Criticisms, and Abbotts Shakespearian Grammar. I take no
doit of interest in The Order of Shakespeare's Plays, The Date of his
Plays, nor the facts of his life. They are to me as extraneous as the
quality of the paper on which the Folio is printed. But this is merely
my individual opinion and worth no more. How delightful is the
glimpse that you give me in saying that your study aims at helping
your husband. Pray give him my deepest congratulations. One most
important item I overlooked, viz: Take Booth's Reprint of the First
Folio, and read a play every day consecutively. At the end of the
Thirty seven days you will be in a Shakespearian atmosphere that will
astonish you with its novelty and its pleasure, and its profit. Don't
read a single note during the month. If after finishing all that I have
suggested you find you still have time to spare, I can suggest many
more books to fill up, but 'twill not be necessary. You will by that time
know your own needs so well that you can add them yourself.[59]

Two days later he wrote again to add Knight's edition of Shakespeare to the list, and the following June he wrote to congratulate
her on her progress and to suggest Lady Martin's *On Some of the
Female Characters of Shakespeare's Plays* for further reading. Again
in a letter on the same subject, dated 12 June 1896—his wedding
anniversary—the comparison with Kate once more rises to the fore.
"The picture you draw of working with your husband moves me
deeply, and I thank Heaven that such happiness still exists, somewhere on 'this huge rondure.'"[60]

Among the new friends and the old who persisted during the
middle years of the Variorum, those from the stage, rather than
those from the study, had the most influence on the Variorum. Chief
among them stood the prince of players, Edwin Booth. Furness's
friendship with Booth dated back to the early years of the Variorum
and continued strong through the 1880s and early 1890s. On two
different occasions—April 17, 1885 and December 8, 1887—Furness
entertained Booth at a reception in his honor at the Penn Club
where the literary and cultured elite of Philadelphia gathered to
welcome him. On May 22, 1888 Furness became a charter member of
The Players, a New York club organized by Booth, Augustin Daly,
Mark Twain, Laurence Hutton, Brander Matthews, and others to
provide a meeting place for men from the theatrical, literary, and
artistic worlds. On March 30, 1889, Furness attended a supper at

Delmonico's given by Daly to honor Booth's gift of the house at 16 Gramercy Park to The Players, and during Booth's declining years in the early 1890s Furness visited him there often. On June 9, 1893, with Thomas Aldrich, David Bispham, and Joseph Jefferson, Furness served as an honorary pallbearer at Booth's funeral.

Behind these public displays lay a close personal friendship. Whenever Booth played in Philadelphia during the 1870s or 1880s, he dined at 222 West Washington Square and exchanged Shakespearian gossip with Furness, who then often accompanied Booth to the theatre. "Have just returned from a visit to Furness, who was out;" Booth wrote to his daughter Edwina on one such occasion in April 1885,

> but by agreement I sat in his library and smoked his pipe. His father (whom I never met before) came in and chatted awhile, and then the eldest son. While I was there Furness called *here* and left his skull, which I shall use tonight. This skull has been used by all the great actors since Kean. There being some doubt as to my having ever used it, we will make it sure to-night.[61]

Booth was playing in *Hamlet* and *The Merchant of Venice* with Madam Ristori at the Academy of Music, and after he left, Furness wrote this account to Horrie and Willie:

> The outside record of my week might be summed up in almost one word: Booth. His visit here terminated last eveg and we have all greatly enjoyed him. He dined here everyday, except yesterday when he had a matinee, and each evening I spent with him in his dressing room, smoking & laughing and criticising. When he went on the stage, a chair was put for me at the wings & there I sat, believing myself to be one of the participants in the scene, very much tempted at times to emerge as a Deus ex machina and set things all straight, to tell Hamlet to peg away at his old Uncle without the least compunction & to jog Shylocks elbow & suggest the word 'blood' in his bond. Booth seemed to enjoy having me at hand & I think my friendly presence stimulated him, in fact he said that one of the actors asked him why it was that ear trumpets helped a performance, and on Booth's asking for an explanation the actor said that they noticed his acting was enlivened by the presence of an ear trumpet at the wings.[62]

On Sunday, April 12, 1885, as Booth dined with Furness and spent the evening with him, the talk turned from the week's performances of Shylock and Hamlet to Iago, for Booth had undertaken to write out his stage business for the variorum *Othello*. "I arose very late, having sat up with *Othello* till nearly daylight," Booth wrote to Edwina on Tuesday April 14, "it being my moody time for keeping faith with Furness on the Shakspere subject, and at such times, when I begin, I can't stop till I have had my say."[63] Before leaving Philadelphia that week Booth gave Furness an interleaved copy of his promptbook inscribed "Some Notes for ye Novice, H.H.F." A few days later on May 12, he wrote Furness a long letter from Boston clarifying a troublesome passage.

> Ever since I left you I have been pacing the 'Rialto,' my gaberdine wrapped about me, but with eyes fixed on the 'Sagittary.' In other words, I have been thinking more of *Iago* than of *Shylock*. In Act III I made some remark regarding *Desdemona's* boldness which, I'm sure, does not express *my* opinion of her. I was *Iago* when I wrote it. . . . She was not the darling 'daisy' we see upon the stage, in white satin of the latest cut, and wax pearls, gabbling the precious text by rote; but a true woman, with a mind of her own, a deathly devotion to the man of her choice, and as pure and artless as a baby. 'Tis absurd for me to say this to you, who know more of Shakspere in a moment than I've learned in thirty years; but that note of mine (or rather *Iago's* comment on it) distresses me, and I want you to understand me rightly.[64]

No sooner had Booth finished with Iago than, at Furness's urging, he turned to Shylock. "In a few days I shall be at work, I hope, with *Shylock*, for Furness," he wrote to Edwina on May 24, and the letters to and from Furness on the subject mark the stops on Booth's western tour during the following season—Cincinnati, Louisville, San Francisco. On January 31, 1887, Booth wrote from Cincinnati,

> Hold on! The *Jew* came to me last evening, just as I was leaving Pittsburg, and stayed with me all night, on the sleeping-car, whence sleep was banished, and I think I've got him by the beard, or *nose*, I know not which; but I'll hang on to him a while, and see what he'll do for me. I'll have his pound of flesh if I can get it off his old bones.[65]

In February a marked promptbook, postmarked Memphis, arrived along with a lecture on Shylock which Furness included in the appendix in a section devoted to the acting of Shylock by Burbage, Dogget, Macklin, Kean, and Irving. As in *Othello* Furness placed Booth's acting directions in the commentary at the foot of each page of text. "The result," wrote Charlotte Porter in *Shakespeari- ana*,

> is like catching the instant flash of light emitted in the living flitting dramatic action of the piece, in a permanent lens. It is what the careful critic tries hard to follow quick enough to remember and register, and almost always fails to picture. . . . here is an actor's own word for his interpretation. If a few more of the gifted ones would take the same trouble to spell us out their art methods dramatic criticism would find at hand its data for a worthy task of comparison and judgment.[66]

The increasingly close relationship between editor and actor during the middle period of the Variorum did not end with Booth's death. Lawrence Barrett, fellow member of The Players, whom Furness had also entertained at Penn Club receptions in his honor, wrote enthusiastically to Furness on June 14, 1888.

> I thank you most heartily for the copy of the "Merchant." I am in the midst of it and shall go to the close with increasing interest. It will be of great use to me in the oncoming revival of the play which we give this season through the country. Please remember that I was the first Bassanio . . . to adopt your division of Antonio's letter into two parts.[67]

At the end of that season Barrett sent to Furness his stage prop letter of Antonio to Bassanio, a letter which still resides among Furness's Shakespearian relics in the Furness Memorial Library.

As Furness turned to the comedies with their romantic hero- ines, he continued his innovation of including stage interpretations in the commentary and the appendix. With Ellen Terry and Lady Helena Faucit Martin, he discussed the acting of Rosalind, Miranda, Hermione, and Beatrice. Concerning the latter actress he wrote to Nannie on October 24, 1897,

You speak, dear, of having read Mrs. Jameson. Isn't it delightful, but a far finer book is Lady Martin's 'Some of Shakespeare's Female Characters.' Mrs. Jameson looks at the characters as a highly intelligent sympathetic nature would look at them. Lady Martin is the character itself, and interprets to you its every emotion. You do not look at Portia, or Rosalind, or Hermione, but through Lady Martin, Portia, Rosalind, and Hermione speak to you themselves and tell you all that passes in their souls. In my opinion Lady M.'s book is the finest that has ever been written on Shakespeare, and outweighs tons of Commentaries.[68]

Ellen Terry and Henry Irving met Furness during their second American tour in 1884-1885. Irving and his troupe visited Philadelphia twice—December 8-20, 1884, when they played *Twelfth Night* and *Much Ado About Nothing*, and again February 9-14, 1885, when they performed *The Merchant of Venice*. Furness called on them, entertained them, and attended their performances. "I saw [Irving] in the Mer. of Ven. and was greatly pleased," Furness wrote to Horrie and Willie on February 15.

I went late, & saw the last three acts only. Of course, as I couldn't hear a syllable, it was merely a dumb show but I especially admired Shylocks bearing in the Trial scene; up to the critical moment, there was such a calm sense of power in Shylock's bearing, not only did he have Antonio in his power but he felt the whole authority of the Venetian law at his back; he did not need to rant, or show the least vehemence, his calmness was far more terrible and bloodthirsty than any emotion. And Portia was too lovely, her by-play is fascinating— and Alexander (Bassanio) is just as handsome as they make 'em. With the latter & his pretty little wife we grew very well acquainted; they are Cheston's friends and on his account I called on them. They are in a higher social position than the rest of the troupe, and are thoroughly charming; the wife is, I think, a kinswoman of Ruskin. They have left this noon for Boston, & stopped here on their way to the cars just to bid us good bye. If they had stayed here another week, I think they would have grown as much at home here, as you children. . . . On Miss Terry I called at the Aldine. She kept me waiting an abominably long time, and I had just resolved to shake the dust from my feet, when she came tripping gaily into the room strumming a banjo. You should have seen her look of horror and embarrassment at the sight of me! She stammered out 'Why—I—thought—it—was—Horrie—your—

son!' She had intended to show you that she too could strum on the banjo. I had a very pleasant chat with her.[69]

A telegram from Chicago after the troupe left Philadelpia testifies to the friendship established in so short a time.

> I received a telegram this eveg from 'L.F. Austin, Chicago' (is he not Irvings agent or secretary?) asking me to reply by telegraph whether or not I believed the first Quarto (the telegram spelled it 'quarter') of Hamlet was obtained by shorthand during representation. What a queer idea! to telegraph a question of that sort, on Sunday too! I suppose there had been some dispute & I am the referee. Has a note on Shakespeare ever been telegraphed before, I wonder? I have replied 'Aye' but it took thirty five words to say it.[70]

On Monday, April 6, 1885, at the close of Irving's tour, Furness joined Booth, Barrett, Thomas Aldrich, Oliver Wendell Holmes, W.D. Howells, Mark Twain, and some one hundred other eminent men to entertain Irving at a banquet at Delmonico's.

Years later in her autobiography *The Story of My Life* (1908) Ellen Terry fondly recalled her friendship with Furness and, in particular, her attendance in Sanders Theatre where Furness was reading *As You Like It* on March 6, 1901.

> Henry and I were so fortunate as to gain the friendship and approval of Dr. Horace Howard Furness, perhaps the finest Shakespearean scholar in America, and editor of the "Variorum Shakespeare," which Henry considered the best of all editions—"the one which counts." It was in Boston, I think, that I disgraced myself at one of Dr. Furness's lectures. He was discussing "As You Like It" and Rosalind, and proving with much elaboration that English in Shakespeare's time was pronounced like a broad country dialect, and that Rosalind spoke Warwickshire! A little girl who was sitting in the row in front of me had lent me her copy of the play a moment before, and now, absorbed in Dr. Furness's argument, I forgot the book wasn't mine and began scrawling controversial notes in it with my very thick and blotty fountain pen.
>
> "Give me back my book! Give me my book!" screamed the little girl. "How dare you write in my book!" She began to cry with rage.
>
> Her mother tried to hush her up: "Don't, darling. Be quiet! It's Miss Ellen Terry."
>
> "I don't care! She's spoilt my nice book!"[71]

The following day she wrote to Furness *"Didn't I pay for my pleasure* of yesterday in a blinding headache for the rest of the evening! but I would go through with it again for the pleasure of hearing you recite the lines 'Blow blow thou winter wind.'"[72]

Perhaps the most significant theatrical friendship Furness formed during these years was with Augustin Daly, playwright, dramatic critic, and manager of Daly's Theatre in New York. During the years that Furness devoted to Shakespeare's comedies, Daly was creating his own Shakespearian sensation with his revivals of Shakespeare in New York, Philadelphia, and London: *The Merry Wives of Windsor*, 1885-1886; *The Taming of the Shrew*, 1886-1887; *A Midsummer Night's Dream*, 1887-1888; *As You Like It*, 1889-1890; *Love's Labour's Lost*, 1890-1891; *Twelfth Night*, 1892-1893; *The Two Gentlemen of Verona*, 1894-1895; *Romeo and Juliet*, 1895-1896; *Much Ado About Nothing*, 1896-1897; *The Tempest*, 1897-1898; and *The Merchant of Venice*, 1898-1899. Although Daly and his colleague, New York drama critic William Winter, removed all vulgar and suggestive language, rearranged scenes, cut lines and added others, and embellished the bare Elizabethan stage with lavish scenery, costumes, and music, they did revive Shakespearian comedy when no one else was playing it, and in at least three instances—*A Midsummer Night's Dream*, *The Taming of the Shrew*, and *The Merchant of Venice*—produced landmarks of nineteenth-century theatrical history. Everyone in the theatrical world knew Augustin Daly, and all the best people frequented Daly's Theatre.

Furness had met Daly on May 6, 1884 at a Penn Club reception in his honor given during Daly's fifth annual visit to Philadelphia where the company was playing *Our English Friend* and *Seven-Twenty-Eight* at the Walnut Street Theatre. Furness and Daly quickly became fast friends. Later that month Daly presented a signed photograph of his players to the Penn Club (Furness had kept the first for himself and extracted another for the club), and Furness presented Daly with letters of introduction to the English Shakespearians just before Daly's company left for London in July, the first visit of an American company to England. "When in England shall you go to Birmingham?" he wrote Daly on June 22.

If so, I wish you could see my friend, Sam: Timmins, he is quite one of *the* men of the city, an ardent Shakespeare student & devoted theatre goer & critic—& one of the most genial of companions. Everyone knows him & he knows everyone. I'll write to him to be sure & look you up if you go there. 'May smooth success be strewed before your feet' wherever you go.[73]

Furness's friendship with Daly and with his four leading players—Ada Rehan, Mrs. Gilbert, James Lewis, and John Drew—stretched over the next fifteen years until Daly's death in 1899. When in New York Furness went to Daly's theatre, and when in Philadelphia Daly visited Furness. To Daly went gift copies of the Variorum comedies as they issued from the press, and to Furness went the lavish editions of Daly's productions, bound with a reproduction of the first quarto or folio, that Daly distributed to opening night audiences. On the one hundreth night of *The Taming of the Shrew*, April 13, 1887, Furness joined the cast and some fifty other guests, including William Winter, Mark Twain, General Sherman, Lawrence Hutton, and A.C. Milne, to celebrate the event. In a pavilion erected on the stage of Daly's Theatre the assembled guests gathered around a table twenty-eight feet across displaying in the center a bed of yellow roses, jonquils, and tulips and enjoyed a midnight supper.

The admiration seemed to be mutual. To thank Daly for his commemorative edition of *As You Like It*, Furness wrote on January 23, 1890,

> What a monument of the finest devotion to Shakespeare this copy, which you have sent me, is! It cannot but be a very great satisfaction to you to reflect that you will float down the tide of time for centuries to come as one who in this age had so lofty an ideal of art. Every breather in America should be grateful to you. At any rate I can answer for one.[74]

And Daly replied in kind to Furness on March 22, 1892, thanking him for the Variorum *Tempest*.

> It is a dreadful thing that we are *99* miles apart in the body and so near in spirit. I would so often like to have you drop in upon me *here* when I am doing things on this stage in harmony with your best likings: and I am often sad in the thought that so much must go off my stage which I am sure would brighten some of your hours.[75]

Even though Daly relied chiefly on William Winter for the cutting and editing of his productions, some collaboration evidently did take place between Furness and Daly. When Daly was cutting and rearranging *Twelfth Night* in January 1893, he sought approval from Furness, who wrote in reply,

> In the name of sanctity, why do you think I'll be shocked at any changes which a modern playwright thinks best to make in the omission or transposition of scenes in Shakespeare. His stage is not our stage, his audiences are not our audiences. 'Tis only additions like Dryden's Tate's, & Garrick's that are lese majeste. Your partial combination of the two Sea coast scenes strikes me as excellent. What you specially refer to in the omission of the scene between Mal. & the Clown I do not quite understand. Surely not the prison scene when the Clown is Sir Topas. However you are one in whom I put an absolute trust. Let me strongly advise you to end the play with the Duke's speech to Viola 'you shall from this time be your master's mistress.' We really do not want to see Malvolio again. The laugh has died out & it can with difficulty be revived.[76]

And when Daly opened with *Twelfth Night* at Daly's Theatre in London the following January, he cabled Furness with the news of its success. "Of the success of you and yours, in 'Twelfth Night' the cable has already apprised us," replied Furness, "and my heart did so joy thereat that I echoed Walt Whitman and gave a barbaric yawp over the roofs of the world. . . . And at the contemplation of it now I lie back in my chair and send out from my pipe great volumes of contented smoke." And then he added, "Some time or other you must give our dear Ada a chance to show her power in Shakespearian tragedy. I have said this to you before. There are tones in her voice that can reach the very font of sympathetic tears,"[77] a comment that may have led to Daly's production of *Romeo and Juliet* the following season. During the 1895-96 season Daly again consulted Furness about his plan to consolidate the two parts of *Henry IV*, cutting much of the political matter and starring James Lewis as Falstaff. Although Furness approved of the plan and advised Daly about the details, Daly eventually abandoned the plan as unfeasible and never produced the play.

Furness was particularly attracted to Daly's leading lady, Ada Rehan, and on several occasions advised her on her parts. "Give my love to the fair Ada & charge her not to act Portia till the conceited man who writes these lines has had a good talk with her," he wrote to Daly on April 12, 1896.[78] And again on October 11, 1896, as the company rehearsed *Much Ado About Nothing*, he again wrote to Ada Rehan about Beatrice.

> A letter from him whom Mrs. Gilbert (bless her) calls The Master tells me that you are to act Beatrice, and it delights me—a delight which is purely unselfish—for even if I see you therein, which is doubtful, I cannot hear a single word. Therefore, I am all the more anxious for Beatrice's sake that you should not malign her and Benedick by wrongly emphasising one little phrase, which as far as I know, is universally minunderstood. 'Tis in the scene in the Church when Beatrice and Benedick are left alone after poor Hero has been led away by the Friar. Benedick asks, 'May a man do it?' and Beatrice replied, 'It is a mans office, but not yours!' This is generally accepted as bitter sarcasm, which I think is utterly wrong. It is really a confession of Love, and should be uttered sadly—almost tenderly. Had it been sarcasm, Benedick would have been stung to the quick, whereas it elicits almost a declaration of love on his part. It was a mans duty, inasmuch as the quarrel should be taken up by a brother, or a cousin or a very near relation. The privilege of that relationship Benedick had not then but were he Beatrices accepted lover, then he might claim the right of vindicating Heros honor. And in Beatrices words there should be heard the faint echo of an exquisite confession of love. Of course I am gabbing like a tinker to one whose thorough dramatic instinct has detected all this at once, but I tremble lest this instinct should be overborne by tradition and hence the impertinence of thus writing to you.[79]

On October 6, 1898, Furness extended his offer of advice to the whole cast, then preparing for the revival of *The Merchant of Venice* in December 1898. "Do you still purpose to bring out 'The Merchant of Venice'?" he wrote to Daly.

> Because if you do, I am going to make a most brazenfaced offer. It is, to come to New York some day and read the play to your assembled Dramatis Personae, or only to you and Ada Rehan, as you think fit. I am arrogant enough to suppose that the interpretation of one who has cogitated as much on the play as I have, is not altogether valueless.[80]

In such ways over the years Furness encouraged and be-friended many an actor and actress with advice on their parts, gifts of the Variorum, letters and reviews in the newspaper, and cordial hospitality. When English actress Adelaide Neilson made her first American tour in 1872, Furness praised her acting of Juliet in the *Athenaeum* and presented her with a copy of the Variorum *Romeo and Juliet*. For fifteen years Furness advised and corresponded with Edward Smith Willard; one such visit by Willard to Wallingford Furness described in December 1897:

> Thursday P.M. Willard, the actor, came out to see me under Horrie's guidance, and we had a very pleasant time—I told him he was made to act Benedick; he bounded at my words & said he had already been looking into the part. I told him to come to me again in a year, and I'd go over the whole play with him. By that time, possibly, if I'm alive amd nothing happens (as Mother used to say), I should have finished it.[81]

With Tita Brand, one of Ben Greet's Players, he corresponded for several years, answering her questions on Gertrude, Juliet, Rosalind, Adriana, and Olivia. With Edith Matthison, Ben Greet's leading lady, and her husband Rann Kenndy, he became close friends. When Greet brought *Everyman* to Philadelphia in December 1902, Furness again befriended the troupe. Calling Mrs. Kennedy "an actress in ten thousand," Furness praised the performance in the local press. "I wrote a short letter to the Ledger urging every one to see it," he reported to Willie.

> I think this signed letter possibly turned the tide in favour of the play. The audiences afterward were fairly crowded, nay jammed, & Ben Greet wrote me a note of warm thanks. If my letter did good, I am heartily glad. I saw the play yesterday for the first and only time, and although I could hear no word I was mightily moved. Mrs. Kennedy is certainly one of the greatest of actresses.[82]

To repay Furness for such kindnesses extended over the years to the theatrical profession, the New Theatre, on April 12, 1910, presented Furness with a gold medal at a noon lunchon in his honor at the Bellevue-Stratford. The ceremony, originally intended to mark the opening of the New Theatre in New York in November 1909, but delayed because of Furness's illness, included tributes to Furness by Weir Mitchell, Talcott Williams, John Luther Long, Edith Matthison, and director of the New Theatre Company Winthrop Ames.

> As no scholar in the world has done so much for dramatic art in America as you," said Ames, "the players of the New Theatre bring this medal and this message to you. Profound in scholarship, exhaustive in research, ingenious and sane in interpretation, delightful in humor, and in grace of expression, [to you] the Founders of the New Theatre present this medal as a testimony of respect and honor.[83]

Nor was this the only honor that came to Furness as the Variorum continued. On April 13, 1887, at its centennial commencement, Columbia University conferred upon him the honorary L.H.D. degree. On June 27, 1894, forty years after his own graduation, Harvard University recalled him to receive the L.L.D. There in Sanders Theater former classmate, now President of Harvard, Charles W. Eliot pronounced him "the most famous interpreter, with skill and ingenuity, of the works of Shakespeare."[84] On May 12, 1897, the American Academy of Arts and Sciences elected Furness an Associate Fellow (the distinction between Fellows resident in Boston and non-resident Associate Fellows was discontinued in 1913); and on October 23, 1901, at its bicenntenial commencement, Yale University honored Furness with a third Doctor of Laws degree "in recognition of those elucidations of Shakspere wherein you have compassed the impossible task of gilding refined gold."[85] Two further honors came from England. From Stratford-on-Avon in 1893 came the nomination of Furness to be a trustee of the Shakespeare Birthplace Trust, according to the wishes of C.E. Flower, the late director of the Birthplace Trust. Only the English law prohibiting an alien from serving as a trustee prevented his election. Finally on June 13, 1899, the University of Cambridge conferred upon Furness the degree Litt. D., a degree reserved for those whose fame has been derived from purely literary work and an honor accorded only two other American men of letters before Furness—Oliver Wendell Holmes and Charles Eliot Norton.

The degree had been proposed by Wright, a gesture which Furness returned by proposing Wright for honorary membership in the American Philosophical Society, America's oldest learned society. When word reached Wallingford that the Council of the Senate had sanctioned a Grace for conferring on him the degree, Furness booked passage on the *Umbria* on May 27 and arrived in London on June 5. The ceremony he described in a letter to Folger on June 18.

Well, last Tuesday in the Senate House of the University, my name was duly enrolled on the Records—they give no diploma. The ceremony was simple and soon over. An 'Esquire Bedell' conducted me to a certain spot on the dais a few feet from the Vice-Chancellor who sat in his scarlet robes of office about four feet from the edge of the dais—(I, too, had on a bright red gown & carried in my hand a black velvet puffy hat with gold cord) Then the Esquire Bedell conducted the Public Orator to a corresponding spot on the left of the Vice-Chancellor; the Public Orator then pronounced his speech in Latin, setting forth the reasons for conferring the degree & when he had finished took me by the right hand and conducted me to the Vice-Chancellor who rising took my hand & pronounced the formula which as far as I could make out is exactly the same as that used at Harvard. And then I returned to my seat. The rest of the function was the listening to the 'Prize Poem' & the distribution of prizes and announcement of Class Honours etc. etc. Everyone was most kind and attentive. I dined 'in Hall' with the Fellows, but could hardly eat for gaping about me at the grand old portraits, the carved roof & the stained glass windows. I asked Aldis Wright, who was like a brother to me in devotion, to pinch my arm to be sure I was not in a dream and he did it with such zeal that my arm is black & blue from the elbow to the shoulder. Indeed, the whole visit was flawless from beginning to end.[86]

Almost flawless, that is, for throughout his years of editing Shakespeare's comedies, throughout his theatregoing and support of the theatrical profession, and in spite of his accumulating honors, even in the Senate House at Cambridge University, as he received the highest literary praise of the English speaking world for his life devoted to Shakespeare, his grief pursued him. "The occasion, to me, was really solemn, deeply tinged with sadness," he wrote to Sarah Wister when safely back in his library at Wallingford. "The Latin speech was so long that I had time to realise where I was, and to summon before me the faces, dearer than life, that would have so glowed with pleasure. Ay de mi, but this life lasts long. Will it never end?"[87]

THE PUBLIC YEARS

In limited professions.
There is boundless theft

Timon of Athens 4.3.423-24

A better speech was never spoke before.
Love's Labors Lost 5.2.110

As comedy piled upon comedy, pushing Furness to the peak of his profession as an editor of Shakespeare, he found himself enmeshed in the demands of three new professions: Shakespearian readings, biblical translation, and public speaking. First had come the lectures on Shakespeare, agreed to in an idle moment, before the upperclassmen at the University of Pennsylvania in 1888; then followed the second course of lectures in 1889, repeated for the University Lecture Association, the Honorary Professorship of English Literature, and the Shakespearian readings to the senior class in 1890. By the winter of 1893 Shakespearian readings had become customary at the university, received with enthusiastic acclaim by the students but, as the podium pushed the study into the background, with something less than enthusiasm by Furness himself. "The first three weeks of February are utterly ruined and consumed by some abhorred Shakespeare Readings for the Lecture Association,"[1] he complained to Lea; and to Daly's invitation to the opening night of *Twelfth Night* in January 1893 he replied, "Ah my dear Daly what wouldn't I give could I but accept it! But on the afternoon of that very day I am to read 'The Merchant of Venice' here in this city. Ugh! How I wish Shylock had gone for Antonio & finished the business on the spot. Then I could have had a delightful evening with you."[2] Nevertheless, the curtain had gone up on a new profession, and Furness was obliged to play his part until the closing lines.

In October 1893, President Gilman invited Furness to read at Johns Hopkins University, and on successive Wednesdays in December and January Furness travelled to Baltimore to read *The Merchant of Venice*, *As You Like It*, *Macbeth*, and *Hamlet*. In late January 1894 he read *Henry V*, *Richard III*, *A Midsummer Night's Dream*, and *Hamlet* at the Pennsylvania Academy of Fine Arts and reported to Thorpe on January 22 that "I have two Readings every week from now on until the 17th of February."[3] Four days later, when Charles Winston invited him to read at Richmond College, Furness excused himself with the plea that all his time was engaged for the rest of the season, yet early March found him travelling to Virginia to read *The Merchant of Venice*, *Macbeth*, *Henry V*, and *Hamlet* at Richmond College. The following season proved just as hectic—the Berkeley Lyceum and the New York School of Dramatic Expression in November, Baltimore again in January, and a whirlwind week in Boston, where, among similar engagements, Agnes Irwin, Dean of Radcliffe, had invited him to read *A Midsummer Night's Dream* to the women of the college. His deafness, which encased him in total silence, barred him from the usual social pleasantries on such occasions. Refusing most invitations for dinner or hospitality from his hosts, Furness composed himself at the nearest hotel before the reading and invariably caught the first train for Philadelphia after it, arriving at Wallingford where, too aroused to sleep, he would work over proofsheets until two in the morning. As proofsheets of *A Midsummer Night's Dream* vied with requests for his increasingly popular readings during the winter of 1894-1895, Furness in desperation turned to Nannie to schedule his readings, to handle all the arrangements, and to say no when Furness himself found it impossible to do so.

Thus evolved one of the most enjoyable intellectual entertainments available in Philadelphia. Seated alone on stage behind a desk or table with his large print Hanmer's Shakespeare before him, Furness would read through an entire play dramatically, interspersing it with critical, explanatory, philological, and analytical comments, or, as he explained to President Gilman, "Whatever occurs to me at the moment—and the difficulty is to keep a restraint upon my garrulous old tongue. . . . This seems to me the truest way of lecturing on Shakespeare, and I cannot but think that the eight or ten plays which I have thus read have been, as it were, revealed to the audience."[4]

The plays were abridged so that each reading lasted for two hours, although Hamlet took two hours and twenty minutes. For his abridgement Furness followed a marked copy of the plays from which Fanny Kemble had given her readings forty years before, and in Furness's own copy of Hanmer twenty-six plays are marked with her deletions and omissions. With a nod to Victorian respectability, the abridgement generally followed that earlier notorious edition of Shakespeare, by Thomas Bowdler, who purged from the plays all profanity, indecency, and "whatever is unfit to be read aloud by a gentleman to a company of ladies." In Romeo and Juliet, for example, Furness omitted act one, scene three, with its mildly bawdy anecdote of the garrulous nurse preparing Juliet for Paris's proposal; and in the next act, when Mercutio tries to summon the absent Romeo, he conjures by "Rosaline's bright eyes, by her high forehead and her scarlet lip," but Furness excised "her fine foot, straight leg, and quivering thigh, / And the desmesnes that there adjacent lie." Perhaps it was with such judicious cutting in mind that D.C. Heath & Company of Boston approached Furness in February 1889 about preparing an expurgated edition of Shakespeare, an invitation that Furness refused as "a manifest attempt at money-making, which is not in my line."[5] Whatever scruples prevented Furness from making money by editing Shakespeare, however, did not prevent him from collecting a $100 honorarium for each Shakespearian reading.

The public greeted Furness's Shakespearian readings with delight. When he read Hamlet at the Pennsylvania Academy of Fine

Arts in February 1894, 1500 people crowded into the hall which comfortably seated 1250, and many were turned away. After a reading of *The Merchant of Venice* at Columbia, Furness complained that "the room, the largest in the Buildings, was crammed to suffocation, and stifling hot. The aisles were filled with women who stood the whole two long hours, and they swarmed all about my feet on the platform."[6] In March 1896 and again in March 1897 Furness read in Boston, Providence, New Bedford, at Radcliffe, and, accepting the invitation of President Eliot, at Harvard. His reading of *The Winter's Tale* at Harvard he later reported to Nannie:

> Tuesday was the evening for Cambridge. I left the Parker House at precisely 7:15 in a coupé which the driver assured me would reach Sanders Theatre in half an hour. I sat quietly thinking of my opening remarks, &c., as is my wont and never thought of the flight of time—at last I aroused myself to the fact that the horse had been very balky & that we were going very slowly through Cambridgeport—I looked at my watch & to my infinite horror found that it was five minutes before eight! I was paralysed. The rest of the journey I spent with my head out of the window swearing & screaming to the driver to beat up his horse. 'Twas a nightmare! At last we reached Sanders Theatre four minutes after eight—my first experience in unpunctuality—of course I had to rush to the stage in anything but a placid mood. The Theatre was crowded and the calm came over me as it always does when I face an audience. I alluded to the death of Professor Child and asked the audience to sit still in hushed repose for a minute or two out of respect for his memory. The Reading was quite as successful, I think, as that of *Henry V* of the previous year. The song of Autolycus, 'When daffodils begin to peer,' &c I sang to the tune of 'On thy soft bosom, gentle lake,' and the applause was so prolonged that I think they wanted it repeated, but I thought it better to disregard the appeal.[7]

The *Public Ledger*, too, applauded his performance in a feature story in March 1898.

> We have no other intellectual entertainment in Philadelphia such as Dr. Furness presents on those too rare occasions when he appears upon the platform as a reader, as he used to do on winter afternoons. To hear Furness read a Shakespearian play has been many a time better than to witness it on the stage. And yet, he is not an impressive

looking man on first sight, nor one who would seem to be fitted for public reading. His spectacles, his ear trumpet, his thin voice, his slightly Pickwickian face, his seated posture in a chair with the book before him indicate a pedantic personality. It is not until you see his happy smile and catch the twinkle of his eye through the glasses, and listen to his jocose sayings—the art with which he makes the commonplace things diverting—and to his unriddling of the direst perplexities, that you begin to realize the presence of an accomplished gentleman, whose love of truth is mingled with a kindly and exquisite sense of humor. The elocution of no actor has such power to make a scene or a character in 'Macbeth' or the 'Merchant of Venice' as vivid as he can make it with his masterful intelligence, his sympathy and his keen insight into every possible phase of meaning in the text, 'I have seen Irving play "Hamlet,"' said Henry M. Hoyt, who was a good judge of acting, when the Englishman first appeared in the part at the Chestnut Street Opera House in 1883, 'and I have heard Furness read it, but Furness gave me a better idea of "Hamlet" in a quarter of an hour than Irving did in the whole evening.'[8]

By the spring of 1897, however, Furness had begun to decline invitations to read in order to drive himself doubly hard on the Variorum, finishing *The Winter's Tale* in February 1898, *Much Ado About Nothing* in November 1899, and *Twelfth Night* in October 1901, instead of taking his accustomed three years to a volume. But the attractions of reading and interpreting Shakespeare on stage proved too much to resist for long, and in July 1900 he announced to Nannie that he was ready to read again.

Speaking of Readings reminds me to say, that to my great surprise a change seems coming over me. For a year or two past, as you know, I have had an invincible repugnance to any thought of reading again in public. Working, as I now am, on this iridescent 'Twelfth Night' puts me, time and again, in such a merry pin, that I find myself wishing to share this fun with others, and the only way I can do so is by reading it aloud. O Nannie, wilt thou gang wi' me sometime on a Reading tour? And won't you read 'Lady Macbeth' with me? More will be heard than the owls scream and the crickets cry if you will. You would lift the hair of every hearer.[9]

An earlier letter on the same subject reveals the pleasure Furness derived both from reading by himself and from reading with Nannie.

Clearly you and I ought to read [Macbeth] together—the only objection would be that we should have no audience. Under the terror of
your Lady Macbeth, one half the audience would be needed to carry
out the fainting other half. Think it over, dear, and make up your mind
to try it with me some blessed hour of the future; I'll read every night
in the week, if you'll read with me. Just think what a lovely career for
two white haired old people. To enjoy themselves to the utmost limit
left to gray hairs and at the same time do good to countless charities.
There is a keen joy in reading Shakespeare and I ain't a-going to deny
it.[10]

As he resumed reading in the fall of 1900, he confined his
readings to private gatherings of friends and public readings for the
benefit of charity. Reading tours to Boston and Cambridge invariably included an informal reading before friends. When passing
through New York he often stopped over to read at the home of
Edmund Clarence Stedman, his friend from Sanitary Commission
days. In April 1904 he made a special trip to Cambridge to read
Henry V to the ailing Norton at Shady Hill; on February 15, 1906 he
provided birthday entertainment at a party for S. Weir Mitchell; and
on April 16, 1909, Furness read *Henry V* at one of the monthly Friday
dinners at the Franklin Inn in Philadelphia, a literary club on whose
board of directors he sat from 1902 to 1912.

Response on such occasions ranged from fiercely competitive
admiration to idolatry. Agnes Repplier, in her biography *Agnes Irwin*,
relates a conversation that occurred after a crowded reading in Mrs.
Wister's summer cottage at Northeast Harbor.

A Boston lady of high estate and unimpeachable lineage assured Miss
Sophy [Irwin] that she had enjoyed hearing Dr. Furness more than
had anybody else. If this had been said to Miss [Agnes] Irwin, she
would have let it pass. She had a talent so sustained that it amounted
to genius for letting things pass. Miss Sophy was, however, easily
ignited. She admitted that the lady might have had as much pleasure
as her neighbors (although she did not really think so), but she
denied with heat that she had had more.

'I dare say,' observed the lofty one, 'that you read Shakespeare.'
Sophy admitted that she did—or had.
'Well, I don't,' was the dignified rejoinder. 'So it stands to reason
that I must like better than you do to hear him read.'[11]

Of another reading attended by Agnes Irwin, Annis Wister, and Agnes Repplier, the latter writes,

> If the general public listened to Dr. Furness with delight, his sister, to whom he was a species of divinity, sat spellbound and ravished as did the Delphic priestess when the god spoke. Once, at a reading of *Hamlet*, Miss Irwin watched for some minutes the growing wonder in her eyes, the deepening rapture on her face, and then whispered warningly: 'He didn't write it, you know, Nannie. Shakespeare did.' In later years, when Dr. Furness read the plays in Boston, at Harvard, and—for her sake—at Radcliffe, she confessed to him that she had grown 'quite mixed about the authorship,' and was disposed to think that Mrs. Wister may have been right.[12]

Such readings even inspired poetry of their own. After hearing Furness read *Henry V* on January 15, 1896, Mitchell wrote his first version of "On a Boy's First Reading of the Play of 'King Henry the Fifth'" and sent it to Furness. "I wrote in my journal that never to be forgotten night these three verses and meant to send them to you, not because of their being good, but to show you how I felt the stormy splendor of it all—Read and burn them; with time which now I have not, they could be bettered into poetry—now they be verse—and no more."[13] Burn them Furness did not, and two years later Mitchell produced the final version of his poem celebrating Furness's reading of *Henry V*.

On a Boy's First Reading of the Play of "King Henry the Fifth"

> When youth was lord of my unchallenged fate,
> And time seemed but the vassal of my will,
> I entertained certain guests of state—
> The great of older days, who, faithful still,
> Have kept with me the pace my youth had made.
>
> And I remember how one galleon rare
> From the far distance of a time long dead
> Came on the wings of a fair-fortuned air,
> With sound of martial music heralded,
> In blazonry of storied shields arrayed.
>
> So, the Great Harry with high trumpetings,
> The wind of victory in her burly sails!

And all her deck with clang of armor rings:
And under-flown the Lily standard trails,
And over-flown the royal Lions ramp.

The waves she rode are strewn with silent wrecks,
Her proud sea-comrades once; but ever yet
Comes time-defying laughter from her decks,
Where stands the lion-lord Plantagenet,
Large-hearted, merry, king of court and camp.

Sail on! sail on! The fatal blasts of time,
That spared so few, shall thee with joy escort;
And with the stormy thunder of thy rhyme
Shalt thou salute full many a centuried port
With "Ho! for Harry and red Agincourt!"[14]

Nor was Mitchell the only listener that year to turn to verse to
describe Furness's Shakespearian readings. Another long-time summer resident of Northeast Harbor, William Croswell Doane, Episcopal Bishop of New York, produced this poem, later printed in *The
Critic*, after hearing Furness read *A Midsummer Night's Dream* on
June 10, 1896.

'Αριστον μὲν ὕδωρ

(To Dr. Furness, After Hearing Him Read a Play of Shakespeare)

GOD FINDETH water in most various ways,
For thirsting men in life's most desert days.
Some dig and bore, or pump with might and main;
To some a mirage o'er a dry, flat plain,
To some a green oasis in the sand,
Tells of the crystal moisture near at hand.

But the most wondrous gift is his, whose hand,
With the witch hazel in unmeant command,
Points, where no eye had seen, no search had found,
To some unmarked, unlikely piece of ground,
And strikes—as Moses' rod the Rock—the place
Where a fair Naiad hides her modest face.

This is thine art, my friend. Where ponderous pumps,
Artesian bores, deep diggers—critics called,—
Have worried Shakespeare's wonder-world, with thumps

> And throes of toil, thy magic wand, enthralled
> With the sweet witchcraft of thy thought and voice,
> Touches, now here, now there, spots bare and bald,
> And a fresh spring of beauty makes our hearts rejoice.[15]

Although Furness still occasionally read before academic audiences—Radcliffe in January 1901, Harvard in March 1901, Princeton in December 1902 at the invitation of Woodrow Wilson, Vassar in November 1903, and Yale in February 1911—he limited his readings largely to charitable causes. "In two or three weeks I'm going to Boston, to read for some Charities," he wrote to Aldis Wright on December 30, 1900. "I don't much like this public reading but if people are such fools as to be willing to give their money to hear me, I'm delighted to be able to contribute a thousand dollars to some Charity, by one evenings work. I shall read five times in six days, and expect to be that limp, when I'm through, that you can hang me over a clothesline."[16] Several times he tried to withdraw from the lecture circuit, but his generosity and perennial love for Shakespeare invariably combined to weaken his resolve. "You may remember that not long ago I told you that I had resolved to read no more in public," he wrote to Professor Allen on January 14, 1905, declining an invitation to read at Bryn Mawr.

> Since then I have weakened under the appeals that have been made to me in behalf of Charities, and have now promised to read for three or four. I do not regard it as at all proper that a man of my age should read in public, but as long as substantial sums of money can be raised for Charities by this means, it seems wrong and selfish in me to decline.[17]

And so he read *Much Ado About Nothing* and *The Winter's Tale* for the Travelers' Aid Society, *Hamlet* for the Rush Hospital, *As You Like It* for the Home for the Homeless, *Henry V* for the Catholic Women's Club, and *Julius Caesar*, at the request of Archbishop Ryan, for other Catholic charities. One such occasion in March 1905 he described to Nannie.

> On Wednesday P.M. I read 'As You Like It' in Association Hall for the College Settlement, and had a striking illustration of the effect of good management. 'Hamlet,' the most popular play by far, produced for the 'Consumers' League' a little over $400 (not as much as the Reading in

Media yielded). Dr. Horatio Wood wrote to me yesterday that 'As You Like It' will bring in over $700.—Nannie, dear, I do not think I am vainglorious when I say that I fervently thank heaven that it lies in my power to do this much for charity. It does warm my heart that at my age I possess a something for which people will give money, and that I am enabled to contribute by my own exertion over two thousand dollars to alleviate distress, in many a shape. I don't see what it is, that makes people want to hear me, any one of whom could do just the same if the trial were made! The audience in Association Hall was really delightful. The Hall was very full, many were in the topmost gallery, and yet they say, the Reading was not adequately advertised, & that many failed to get tickets. If I read again next winter, I trust the managers of the various charities will take the lesson to heart.[18]

Even at age seventy-seven he was still reading for charity. On March 2, 1911, he read *The Merchant of Venice* at the College of Physicians and Surgeons for the benefit of the Penn School for Negro children in Beaufort, South Carolina; and again on March 30 that year at the Bellevue-Stratford he read *As You Like It* to establish a scholarship fund to send Philadelphia girls to Radcliffe College.

Long before his last Shakespearian Reading, though, Furness had committed himself, again in a weak moment, to another new profession. Through his readings at Johns Hopkins in 1893 and 1894, Furness had become acquainted with Paul Haupt, philologist, theologian, and Assyriologist, for years the chief interpreter of the Gilgamesh epics. When Furness first read in Baltimore, Haupt, formerly a tutor at the University of Göttingen, had been teaching for ten years as Professor of Semitic Languages at Johns Hopkins and had written an Assyrian grammar as well as numerous books and articles on the Old Testament. Although an intense, scholarly man, author of some 522 titles during his career, he did not lack a sense of humor, having once sent Furness a birthday greeting written in cuneiform. Perhaps his most ambitious project was a new edition of the Old Testament called *The Sacred Books of the Old and New Testaments: A New English Translation with Explanatory Notes and Pictorial Illustrations. Prepared by Eminent Biblical Scholars of Europe and of America and Edited with the Assistance of Horace Howard Furness* (1898-1899). Popularly known as the Rainbow Bible or the Polychrome Bible, the edition consisted of two parallel series—one in Hebrew and the other in Modern English—printed on a background of different colors showing the various sources or documents used to compile the Hebrew manuscripts. In Isaiah, for example, the prophetic passages were printed on light red, the poems on purple, and links connecting the songs with the prophecies on dark blue. Haupt had gathered around him over thirty of the best Old Testament scholars of his day—including S.R. Driver, H.A. White, and T.K. Cheyne from Oxford; W.H. Bennett from New College, London, G.F. Moore from Andover Theological Seminary, C.H. Toy from Harvard, J. Wellhausen from Göttingen—and in 1894 he recruited Furness to edit the English translation series.

For the next six years with mixed feelings Furness worked diligently, although never enthusiastically, on his part of the project. He was annoyed at the loss of time; he chafed under Haupt's editorial guidelines, he swore at the inept translators as he patched up their work. Nevertheless, he liked Haupt, entertained him at the Penn Club, and read proofsheets with him until three o'clock in the morning. Haupt's request had come at just the right time. While finishing *A Midsummer Night's Dream* during the summer of 1893 Furness had grown weary of the daily train ride from Wallingford into town where he would work in solitude in his library from ten o'clock until five. Furthermore, the family home at 222 West Washington Square no longer belonged to him. According to the will of Evans Rogers the house had passed to Kate as long as she lived and then to Walter. With Kate's early death in 1883, Furness felt obliged to pay rent to his son. When Walter married Helen Bullitt in 1886, the couple at first took up residence at Wallingford; and Furness remained in town with the other three children during the winter social season, joining Walter and Helen at Wallingford in the summers. After Horrie's marriage to Louise Winsor in 1890 and Caroline's marriage to Horace Jayne in 1894, Furness decided to leave Washington Square to Walter, build a fireproof library at Wallingford, and live in the country the year around. Just at this time came Haupt's invitation to trade Shakespeare for Scripture. Proofs of *A Midsummer Night's Dream* would all be corrected in early 1895, the Shakespeare books would have to be packed away awaiting the move, and Wallingford would be reduced to chaos with the new library under construction. He would need something to occupy his time, and in an "evil moment," as he later termed it, he agreed.

Long before *A Midsummer Night's Dream* reached the press,

however, Furness had already read the translation of Leviticus and on October 31, 1894, found himself explaining Haupt's project to Wright, who for fifteen years had helped edit the English Revised Version of 1885.

> As I understood him, he wished his translation to be unBiblical in phraseology and absolutely clear. All my share in the matter was to see to it that this end was attained. Whether or not this end be a good one, is a separate question, and grave doubts may be entertained of its propriety. But this question was not, in legal slang 'coram judice.' All I had to do was to make it certain that the elaborate sacrificial formulas were so clear that no one could go astray, and to quite disregard Jacobean English.[19]

Things did not remain quite so simple when Furness turned to Psalms and Kings. In disgust he returned the translation of Kings to Duncan McDonald, Haupt's Associate Editor, on July 7, 1895. "Brünnow has taken printed pages of a Bible & pasted them on sheets of paper, written the changes and corrections in the margin, so that it presents the appearance of an intricate proof sheet—an enormous spilth of time and eke of money—no printer, I am sure, would accept it as copy without extra remuneration."[20] His own manuscripts neatly written with text spaced three lines apart, Furness had little patience for sloppy copy. Nor could he abide sloppy scholarship. On July 18 he again appealed to McDonald. "I am embarrassed in regard to the 'Psalms' & if you'll allow me, I'll make you my ghostly confessor:—I cannot use the trans. which Haupt has sent me, made by a Mr. Taylor in England. In general 'tis literal enough (albeit I do not like such translations as 'tabernacle' for *Zelte*) but it is humdrum to the last degree."[21] Ten days later he wrote to announce that he had launched his own translation of the Psalms.

> I have discarded Taylor's trans. of Wellhausen utterly. Mark you, he translates *Strauch*=briar; *besinnung*=art, *Schwinden*=faint, *Mauer*=fence, *Freunde*=beloved ones etc. etc. In German grammar he is perfect, but his English vocabulary is small, and not of Elizabethan best. It is Taylor's knowledge of Hebrew which hurts him and it is my ignorance of it which ought to help me, as a translator of the German. It is one of my prime qualifications that I am absolutely ignorant of the Hebrew original.[22]

As he labored over the Psalms through the hot and humid Philadelphia summer, the Polychrome Bible dissolved into a kaleidoscopic wonderland of many colors. J. Wellhausen, Professor at the University of Göttingen, had translated the Hebrew Psalms into German; the Englishmen John Taylor had translated Wellhausen's German into English; and now he, Furness, having retraced Taylor's tracks to the German and discarded his translation, had embarked on his own translation of Wellhausen's German. Over the notes, translated from German by Taylor, and the appendix, translated by one J.A. Paterson, Furness was to have no responsibility. "Indeed Haupt's Bible is an indigesta moles to me, curiously wrought and very fearfully and wonderfully to be made," he wrote to McDonald in July, "and I regard it as Thackeray's Pliceman regarded the Duke of Wellington: 'with hor.'"[23] Again he complained to McDonald in another letter, borrowing a favorite word from *The Winter's Tale*: "Were it not that the work really interests me and that this is a season of enforced idleness, away from my library, I'd landdamn Haupt for leading me into the mess. (I don't know what 'landdamn' is nor does anybody else but it sounds just right for my feelings.)"[24]

Nevertheless, amid the chaos of carpenters and masons and boxes of books Furness persevered through the Psalms, and by October, when he laid aside the Bible and took up *The Winter's Tale* for the winter, he had finished not only his translation of the Psalms, but also the first reading of Ezekiel, Samuel, Daniel, Hosea, and Deuteronomy. On September 8, he wrote to McDonald, rather pleased with his finished product.

> The Psalms have greatly interested me. Some of course would not lend themselves to any sort of a rhythmical treatment, but in a large majority there were lines here and there which would fall into cadence—enough to give the impression that the original was rhythmical poetry—which I take it is all-sufficient. If they were too rhythmical, the fidelity of the translation would be questioned. I have a mind to copy off for you part of the 77th which quite charmed me last eveg. when I was looking them over. It is exceedingly faithful to Wellhausen's German, not a word is added. Pray compare it with the Authorized Version, and let me know what you think of it—whether the public will stand such a version.[25]

Psalm 77
1. With my voice I cried unto God—
   With my voice unto God—I hoped He would hear me!
2. In the hour of my need I turned to the Lord:
   My hand was stretched out in the night without ceasing.
   But my soul would allow itself no consolation.
3. I cried unto God, and I wailed,
   I prayed, but my soul was wrapped in gloom.
4. My eyelids Thou heldest fast closed,
   I was filled with unrest, and nought could I speak.
5. I pictured the days of old,
   The years of ancient times.
6. I remembered my harp in the night,
   And I prayed from my heart:
   But my soul suffered anguish.
7. Will then the Lord be for ever rejecting,
   And never again show Himself pleased?
8. Is then His goodness ended for ever?
   And His faithfulness,—is it clean gone for all time to come?
9. Has God forgotten again to be gracious?
   Has He withdrawn his pity, in wrath?
10. And I said: 'Lo! this is my anguish:
    The right hand of the Highest is no longer the same.'[26]

After this initial burst of work, Furness's enthusiasm for biblical translation dwindled to duty as Shakespeare vied with Scripture in his newly constructed Shakespearian library. In March 1896, amid Shakespearian readings and collation of *The Winter's Tale*, Furness sent proofsheets of the Psalms to Norton, Child, and Wright. From the last came both corrections and commiseration. "Oh my dear Furness, what have you done that you should be set to this task? I wish you were well through it,"[27] a wish that Furness himself echoed to Rolfe as he prepared to read the last revision of the Psalms in November. "I am not at work on 'Julius Caesar,' but 'The Winter's Tale,' and advance very slowly. This wretched new translation of the Bible has consumed an enormous amount of my time; I say 'wretched' only because it keeps me from Shakespeare—it is in itself extremely interesting."[28] The disclaimer notwithstanding, Haupt's Bible did consume an enormous amount of time; and when Haupt came to town, not even a Shakespearian Reading could stop him.

After reading proofsheets of *Judges* with Haupt, Furness sent Nannie the following report in January 1897.

> Thursday night I returned at midnight with Haupt, who had been to the Oriental Club and then we fell to work on *Judges*. I was drug out by the Reading, refreshed by the Penn Club, and tired out when I reached home.—Nathless, I worked away with Haupt and got to bed at twenty five minutes of four A.M. A pretty good day's work for an old man of 64.[29]

By May 1897 the Psalms, Isaiah, and Judges had been electrotyped; Leviticus, Ezekiel, and Deuteronomy were in the hands of the printers; and Furness was trying to bow out of the project. "My work on The Psalms is over," he wrote to Wright on May 12.

> I have been faithful to every line, and have not neglected a single syllable. Having thus devoted to them the full measure of my limited ability, my sense of duty fulfilled is complete and I dismiss them with 'frigid tranquillity.' If I am anathematized for my work on them, I'll open my ears to the charm of A Winter's Tale and hear no other sound.[30]

But extricating himself from Haupt did not prove so easy. Final proofsheets stretched into 1898, Joshua was already in the works, and in May 1899, in spite of himself, he was working on Proverbs. In January 1898, when he sent to Wright a copy of the Psalms,—"a translation in which I take no jot of pride or pleasure"—he again sounded the complaint.

> Woe worth the day when I weakly consented to do no more than what I supposed to be the reading of proofsheets! I am hampered at every turn until I'd fain cry 'And so come Death!' Drop me a tear of pity, an thou lovest me. . . . Of course 'twill not fall in your way to mention to any one this torture of mine, but none the less I beg you'll not do it. I must dree my weird, until I can wriggle out."[31]

And in December almost a year later he was still trying to wriggle out. "Whew! how I have struggled and am still struggling to emancipate myself from that 'Polychrome' Bible," he again wrote to Wright.

(What a hideous title! like the 'chromos' that are given at groceries with a pound of tea!) I am disappointed in the book in many ways. It is too scholarly for common folk, and it is too common for scholars. It has pictures that can please no one but 'consecrated cobblers,' and its spelling is that of the newspaper. But I can blame no one but myself. I weakly yielded to downright tears. Of course I do not receive a doit of remuneration, perhaps, if I did, I'd show more valour. But, ohe! jam satis.[32]

Wright echoed Furness's disillusionment and urged him to return to Shakespeare. "Don't tell me of Polychrome," he wrote in March 1899, "motley's the only wear! The thing seems to have stopped; at any rate I have heard nothing of it for some time. It seems to me that the editors profess to know too much."[33]

In the end not frustration with Haupt, but the financial failure of the Polychrome Bible, brought Furness his emancipation. Between 1883 and 1904 sixteen books were published in the Hebrew series, but only six books appeared in the English series: Leviticus, Judges, Isaiah, and the Psalms in 1898 followed by Joshua and Ezekiel in 1899. Although the *Expositor* for April 1898 favorably reviewed the English translations, neither series was completed owing to cost. Samuel, Daniel, Hosea, Deuteronomy, and Proverbs—all prepared for the press by Furness—never saw printer's ink. The last word on the Polychrome Bible came during the summer of 1900.

"I had a most queer and characteristic note from Haupt," he wrote to Nannie on July 15, "wherein he told me that the publishers of the new translation of the Bible had 'grown impatient' over the lack of success financially of the venture and he had 'therefore' (!) brought suit against them! Surely, one ought not to miss out of the world such a character as Haupt's—he's a subject of never-failing interest to me."[34]

"How he stared at me in mute surprise," Furness had written on an earlier occasion, "when I told him that the world I lived in cared six times more for Shakespeare than it did for the Bible. The latter it reads one day in seven, Shakespeare it reads six days in seven. And it's true. The world which will accept or even appreciate a new translation of the Bible is not as large as the Shakespearean world."[35] And so, in 1900 after six years of editing the Bible, Furness returned with relief to the Shakespearian world of *Twelfth Night* and Shakespearian readings.

Yet even as Furness disentangled himself from the web of Haupt's Polychrome Bible, the demands of a third profession— public speaking—grew tighter around him. Having distinguished himself as a public orator at the groundbreaking for the University of Pennsylvania Library and again at its dedication, Furness increasingly found himself speaking for the Trustees on formal occasions. When provost William Pepper announced his resignation on April 23, 1894, the Trustees appointed Furness to make an address in honor of Pepper at the next commencement. Thus, on the morning of June 7, address tucked under his doctoral gown, Furness walked in procession with Pennsylvania Governor Pattison, escorted by the First City Troop, Mayor Stuart, and other Philadelphia officials, the Provost, Trustees, Faculty, and students from the University to the Academy of Music for the 138th commencement of the University. Furness's praise for Pepper was both personal and professional. Recalling the search for a provost in 1880 and his own unsuccessful journey to Boston, deputized by the Trustees to persuade Phillips Brooks to accept the position, Furness enumerated the qualities of the Provost who had since become his friend:

> Our ideal Provost had to be a man of marked individuality (a quality predestined to hostile criticism); a man of administrative ability (which is sure to collide with indolent inertia—the besetting sin of students); a man of firm will; able to read the future in the instant; of consummate tact; and above all he must be vigilant to discern in the educational heavens the signs of the time. Lastly, our ideal Provost, while he need not of necessity be an anatomist, must, nevertheless know, to the extremest nicety, the exact location in every rich man's body of the *pocketbook* nerve—that nerve of the keenest sensibility in the whole system, and our ideal Provost must know when, and where, and how to touch this nerve so as to excite the largest reflex action.[36]

No doubt thinking of Pepper's unflagging fund-raising for the University Library and his support for Furness's reorganization of the Department of Arts, Furness went on to catalogue the growth of the University—new buildings, new courses of study, and new faculty— during the thirteen years that Pepper had served as Provost. At the end of his address Furness unveiled the clay cast of a bust of Pepper, part of a statue of the Provost by Karl Bitter, to be cast in bronze and placed in the University Library.

Four years later at the death of Pepper, Furness attended a memorial meeting at the University of Pennsylvania Chapel, and again on April 12, 1901, he delivered a eulogy for Pepper at memorial observances held by the American Philosophical Society and on behalf of the donors presented to the Society a portrait of Pepper. "The one thought that possesses me, is the loss of Pepper—a great power is vanished from the city, and there is none to supply his place," he wrote to Nannie upon receiving the news of Pepper's death in July 1898. "People will now perceive that with no trace of self-seeking he was one of the prime movers in whatsoever made for the intellectual and commercial life of the community. . . . If only a little of the praise now lavished on him had been bestowed while he could hear it, how much more lightly would his heavy burdens have been borne."[37]

Other University occasions, less personal and more official, also called forth his oratorical skills. In December 1892, when the University formally opened its Canine Infirmary in the Veterinary Building, Furness gave the address and accepted the keys on behalf of the Trustees. On December 27, 1894, on behalf of the Trustees, he welcomed to the University of Pennsylvania a joint convention of the American Oriental Society, the American Philological Association, the Society of Biblical Literature and Exegesis, the Modern Language Association, the American Dialect Society, the Spelling Reform Association, and the Archaeological Institute of America. On December 27, 1900, he welcomed the National Federation of Graduate Clubs, meeting for their sixth annual convention at the University. Commenting on the 1894 Philological Conference, *The Critic* noted the "graceful address from Dr. H.H. Furness, whose amazing erudition as a Shakespearian cloaks the fact that, as a speaker on any occasion of ceremony, he ranks among the best three or four in the country."[38]

Twice in 1902 and again in 1903, he served as Public Orator for University Day, the annual academic convocation held on Washington's Birthday. Dressed in his red silk Cambridge gown ("I like to wear it," he once confessed to Charles Norton; "it distracts attention from the twaddle I utter."[39]) he presented the candidates for honorary degrees, among them in 1902 his friends Bishop William Croswell Doane—"His God-given intellect has been devoted to the service of God, and he has made it the star to many a wandering bark; drifting in sad perplexity"[40] —and Agnes Repplier—"because she has revived the art, well-nigh lost in these days, of the Essayist."[41] *The Philadelphia Press* captures the flavor of these occasions in its description of the 1903 convocation, presided over by Pennsylvania Governor Pennypacker and addressed by S. Weir Mitchell.[42]

Seldom in the history of the University of Pennsylvania has a University Day been so brilliant. True, leaden skies and a thaw which converted the streets into muddy streams of slush rendered impossible the parade of the student body from the campus to the Academy, a feature of the exercises that has always been unique.

But within the Academy's walls the picture was a thing long to be remembered. On the stage, side by side in twin chairs, presiding over the ceremonies sat the Governor of the State and the Provost of the University. To one side were ranged three college presidents, a famous painter and a gallant general and statesman, the five distinguished guests whom the corporation had decided to honor with honorary degrees. On the other side sat the orators of the day, two of the University's most celebrated sons.

Stretched across the first row from the footlights they formed an impressive line. In the center, in modest attire, on their raised chairs the provost and the Governor; to the right, President Woodrow Wilson, of Princeton; President Humphreys, of Stevens, and President Peterson, of McGill University, all in their gowns and varied colored hoods; beside them, plainly clad, America's greatest portrait painter, John S. Sargent, and next the uniformed martial figure of General Leonard Wood, who so ably guided the first steps of Cuba into the area of independent nations.

To the left were Dr. Horace Howard Furness and Dr. S. Weir Mitchell, both members of the Board of Trustees of the University. These two men, the one of whom has shed the light of a brilliant mind on the text of immortal Shakespeare, the other made Philadelphia again the home of American literature, were both gowned and hooded in the scarlet hue which proclaimed their degrees, one from Cambridge and the other from the University of Edinburgh.

Behind them, row on row, the faculty and trustees of the University filled the stage. In front the 2000 students of Pennsylvania sat capped and gowned, a solid mass of black, broken only by the red and blue pennants that rose at various points to tell the class and its department.

For his subject this time Furness chose "Culture."[43] Defining culture as the development and cultivation of one's natural talents and abilities gained through "reading, reading, reading," Furness argued that culture "widens our horizon, opens new avenues of thought, quickens our perception, matures our judgement, and inspires that calm composure wherein lies the mastery of an untoward situation." Unlike one's profession, culture is extensive, not intensive, and one need not attempt

> to acquire a thorough knowledge of all human learning. . . Culture, in this year of grace, is superficiality. The generally cultured man is a superficial man. And why should we find anything appalling therein? Can we not be superficial and happy? Because we cannot distinguish all the varieties of *Solidago* must we forego the charm of recognizing Golden Rod when it transforms an autumn meadow into a field of the cloth of gold? Because we cannot expound the theories of the binary stars, are we to forebear to name the constellations of the midnight sky? Shall we close our Homer because we cannot name the ships that went to Troy? A little knowledge is *not* a dangerous thing. If I cannot, for lack of time, drink deep of the Pierian spring, let me, in heaven's name, at least take a sip.

Then, alluding to Goethe's rule that we should every day listen to some good music, gaze upon some good picture, and read some poetry, Furness went on to prescribe his list for lifetime reading: Horace, Catullus, Ovid, Propertius, Martial, Aeschylus, Sophocles, Euripides, Aristophanes, Shakespeare, Milton, Charles Lamb, Wordsworth, Emerson, Carlyle. And what profit acrues from such devotion to culture?

> It is a pearl of great price, and worth many a sacrifice to obtain. By living in daily communion with great writers, by weighing their words, by tracing their meaning, by analyzing their thoughts, it will follow, as the night the day, that we shall ourselves become more accurate in language, more fastidious in the use of words, nicer in the turns of expression. Whatsoever is loose, or slovenly, or vulgar on a

printed page will jar and grate the nerves like the filing of a saw. When our nerves become thus sensitive in reading, be very sure that the day of our own reformation in speaking and writing is dawning.

The oration caused some stir beyond Philadelphia. William Thayer reprinted excerpts in the *Harvard Graduates' Magazine*, and other universities began to solicit Furness's oratory. Ira Remsen, President of Johns Hopkins University, requested Furness to deliver a similar address at the University's Commemoration Day in February 1904. On June 3, 1903, just two weeks before the Pennsylvania Commencement address, Furness had delivered a speech at the Commencement exercises of Bryn Mawr College, marking the laying of the cornerstone of the new library. Four years later on May 16, 1907, in the finished cloister of the Bryn Mawr College Library, he again spoke at the dedication of a tablet commemorating a scholarship in honor of Elizabeth Duane Gillespie, founder of the National Society of the Colonial Dames of America; and on October 22, 1910, surrounded by the presidents of Vassar, Wellesley, Smith, Mount Holyoke, Johns Hopkins, and Harvard, Furness delivered the principal address at the twenty-fifth anniversary convocation of Bryn Mawr College.

Nor did his alma mater overlook his rhetorical skills. The Harvard Club of Philadelphia heard Furness speak at its annual dinner on January 16, 1904. His topic, reminiscenses of Harvard fifty years before when he had received his degree, earned him the dubious honor of election to the office of President of the Harvard Club of Philadelphia, dubious since it required an additional speech at each of the three annual dinners over which he presided during his term. The first of these three speeches, "The Joys of Old Age," delivered in January 1905 and printed in the *Harvard Graduates' Magazine*, proved so popular that it was reprinted in *The Philadelphia Press* and in *The Liverpool Daily Post and Mercury*. When the Associated Harvard Clubs held their twelfth annual meeting in Philadelphia in May 1908, Furness again sat at the speakers' table in the banquet hall of the Bellevue-Stratford, surrounded by close to five hundred Harvard men arrayed by classes in front of him.

His final and most significant Harvard speech came in Sanders Theatre on June 25, 1908, at the annual meeting of the Harvard Chapter of the Phi Beta Kappa Society. Here Furness returned to his favorite subject: Shakespeare. When he received early in 1908 the invitation from Norton to speak, he had debated his answer. "There are certain things about Shakespeare and his plays which I should like to utter as my last, dying speech before 'shuffling off this mortal coil;' but I mistrust my power of concentration and persistence in setting them forth; and, above all, whether I could so set them forth, that any human being would care to listen to them."[44] Yet, in spite of his insistence that he was "no orator, but merely a humble student" and that his speech might better be called "the maunderings of an old man," the oration, entitled "On Shakespeare, or, What You Will,"[45] recapitulates succinctly many of the themes developed at greater length and scattered in diverse nooks and notes throughout the Variorum. Again he argued the futility of discovering the genius of Shakespeare in mundane facts, the historical sifting of Halliwell-Phillipps and Charles Wallace notwithstanding.

> Can no Act of Parliament be passed forbidding, under pain of death, without benefit of clergy, all further research into Shakespeare's life? Can we not all fervently reecho: 'Good friend, for Jesus' sake forbear, To touch the dust enclosed here!' If the mundane facts of his life were tenfold as numerous as they are, what conception from them would be gained of the Creator of that splendid procession of characters that crosses his stage, more august, more brilliant, more varied than any single page of history can show?

Then modulating easily to a related key he struck another familiar chord: the misguided subjective search for Shakespeare's life in the plays.

> When we seek to find in his dramas his lesser, distinctive, purely personal traits, we cannot find him, he is not there, and it is because he is *not* there, that his plays are so heaven-high above the plays of other dramatists, Lear is Lear; Shylock is Shylock. They are not William Shakespeare behind a mask. Can we at any instant detect a gleam of Shakespeare's eye behind that mask, at that instant there is revealed a flaw. The character is not perfect, it is not true to itself. I must not speak in terms of exaggeration. There are unquestionably, here and there, such flaws as local, or temporary, or even personal allusions to be detected in his plays. But I do not deem it exaggeration to say that they are neither so numerous nor so pronounced that we can draw from them any conclusions as to Shakespeare's personal

character. His genius, his intellect, his sympathy are everywhere, in all ᴧnd through all, from the first scene to the last. But he, the man, the son of John Shakespeare and Mary Arden, is nowhere.

Skillfully weaving his familiar strands of melody into the finale, Furness quickly moved from theme to theme: Shakespeare's unfailing knowledge of human nature, dramatic time in Shakespeare and Aeschylus, the failure of German critics to pass beyond "microscopic examination of Shakespeare's text and grammar" to "enlightened comprehension," the superior textual criticism of Theobald and Capell, the brilliant aesthetic criticism of Coleridge, Hazlitt, Campbell, North, Mrs. Jameson, Mrs. Kemble, Hudson, Swinburne, Lowell, Lady Martin, and A.C. Bradley. Then came the crashing chords of the final bars.

Lastly, let me entreat, and beseech, and adjure, and implore you not to write an essay on Hamlet. In the catalogue of a library which is very dear to me, there are about four hundred titles of separate editions, essays, commentaries, lectures, and criticisms on this sole tragedy, and I know that this is only the vanguard of the coming years. To modify the words, on another subject, of my ever dear and revered Master, the late Professor Child, I am convinced that were I told that my closest friend was lying at the point of death, and that his life could be saved by permitting him to divulge his theory of Hamlet, I would instantly say, 'Let him die! let him die! let him die!

Thus concluded his Phi Beta Kappa oration—with a coda quoting from Sonnet 55 "not Marble, nor the gilded monuments / Of princes, shall outlive this powerful rhyme,"—a distillation of Shakespearian wisdom of a lifetime that Furness with characteristic modesty dismissed as "twaddle." "Please do not call the Phi Beta thing an oration," Furness had written three months before to William Thayer, editor of the *Harvard Graduates' Magazine,*

The word had frightened me off when they asked me, two or three years ago, to deliver it. I think, on the present occasion, 'gossip' would be the more appropriate term. I shall make it absolutely informal, and ramble on as I please. If, after hearing my twaddle, you think it fit to go into the Harvard Magazine, it is freely yours. I am very sure I shall never want to see it again.[46]

"Twaddle" again it was, to use Furness's phrase, on February 23, 1905, when he addressed nearly three hundred distinguished guests assembled for the centenary banquet of the Pennsylvania Academy of Fine Arts. In the building designed by his brother Frank, standing where his father had stood to deliver the dedicatory address twenty-nine years before, Furness defined for his audience the meaning of "academy" and the meaning of "fine arts," both "dedicated to the worship of Beauty," a purpose that distinguishes them from the mechanical arts dedicated to utility.

> Utility is transient. Beauty is permanent. Utility is local. Beauty is universal. What is useful today, may be useless tomorrow. What was beautiful when the morning stars sang together, will be beautiful when the heavens are rolled together as a scroll. What is useful in one zone is useless in another. But it is the same love of Beauty which prompts the carving on a South Sea paddle and on the bone implement of the Arctic circle. Utility comes to pass; Beauty comes to stay, and to be a 'joy for ever.'[47]

The speech, interrupted several times by applause, earned its reward. The Academy, for its own portrait gallery, commissioned from artist Joseph de Camp a portrait of Furness in his scarlet Cambridge gown. Completed in time for the one hundred and second Annual Exhibition in January 1907, the portrait still hangs in the Academy's permanent collection.

In spite of the honor, the occasion well illustrates the difficulties of a septuagenarian (or "septuageranium" to use his own phrase) cultivating three professions at one time. After consenting to speak at the Academy dinner, he recalled that he had agreed to read *Hamlet* for the Rush Hospital on the same afternoon. All attempts to bow out from either engagement proved futile. "How woefully I need you here, to protect me from appeals for charity and courtesy, by your stern uncompromising 'no!'" he complained to Nannie, who was spending the winter on the Continent. "I cannot say it."[48] His own account to Nannie, the following Sunday, reveals the whirlwind beneath the placid smile and carefully balanced phrases.

> I think I told you that I was to read for the Rush Hospital, and also to speak at a great dinner at the Academy of Fine Arts. But I hardly realised until the day drew near the full enormity of the task. Of all

plays, the play was to be "Hamlet," and in the afternoon; and the speech was to follow it in the evening. A tour de force rather pleases, but this tour pleased me most too much. . . . At the Reading, I greeted the Ghost in clear tones, and did not cough in his face as I had feared I should. The audience was sympathetic, and the New Century Drawing Room, Gallery and all, was filled. After the Reading I was reduced to a pulp, and I hied me to Caroline's to pass the hour and a half before I had to go to the Academy. The dear blessed girl anticipated her dinner hour, and I had time for a refreshing bite and sup. Thus fortified I went at seven o'clock to the Academy dinner, with the most lamentable string of commonplaces in my pocket, by way of a speech, that you can imagine. I am growing, indeed have grown, extremely philosophic. Failures possess no terrors for me. I take things as they come and as they go, Lord forbid. 'Twas a brilliant scene at the Academy. The tables were set in the main gallery, flowers and green-ery were everywhere, the lights were brilliant, pictures covered the walls; the guests numbered, I believe, about three hundred. I sat alongside of the President, Edward Coates, with Weir on my right. Rag that I was, the sight of my companions inspired me. The dinner itself, like all public dinners, was detestable, albeit there were lashin's of terrapin and champagne, and I was glad of my damper at Caroline's. The speech?—well, when Coates had asked me by what title it should be called on the printed Bill of Fare I had replied "Twaddle" and twaddle it was. It makes me blush to think how it was received. I will tell you an unvarnished tale and in your secret ear confess I was never in my life, in such matters, more surprised. Two or three times I was interrupted by applause, and at the close, when I sat down, such a clapping and clattering, and, even calling, arose, and continued, that Coates said to me, "You must get up and make a bow," which I had to do, grinning the while like a chessy cat. I finished at 10.10 and, as I had to catch the 10.32 train, had to scuttle. When I reached my library, utterly "tuckered-eout" as I was, I knew 'twould be folly to go to bed and lie broad awake, so I sat down to my regular work and pegged away till half-past two, awoke the next morning with our Father's Monday-feeling over me in fullest force; for the rest of the day I dawdled over the English Magazines. By Saturday I was as brisk as a septuageranium can be and accomplished a brave day's work, over *Anthony & Cleopatra* which as I advance interests me far more than *L.L.L.* or even Twelfth Night. An interpretation of the play has dawned on me which, if I find holds good to the end, I'll tell you all about it.[49]

Philadelphia's highest tribute to the oratorical skill of Furness came during the bicentennial of its first citizen: Benjamin Franklin.

From Tuesday evening, April 17, to Friday, April 20, 1906, cultural and scientific Philadelphia, joined by representatives from England, Germany, and France, gathered to celebrate the two hundreth anniversary of Franklin's birth. Scientific papers, glittering receptions at the Bellevue-Stratford, academic convocations at the University of Pennsylvania and the American Philosophical Society, a parade from City Hall to Christ Church, and a wreath-laying ceremony at the Christ Church Burying Ground culminated in a public convocation at the Academy of Music on Friday morning. Harvard's President Charles William Eliot spoke on "Franklin as Printer and Philosopher," Joseph Choate, former American Ambassador to Great Britain, spoke on "Franklin as Statesman and Diplomatist," and Furness spoke on "Franklin as Citizen and Philanthropist." At the conclusion of the speeches Elihu Root, Secretary of State, stepped forward to present to the French Ambassador J.J. Jusserand the Franklin Medal struck in gold according to an Act of Congress to commemorate the contribution of France to the American Revolution. A doubly significant occasion for Furness and Jusserand, himself an accomplished amateur Shakespearian, the convocation marked the renewing of a friendship that stretched over the final years of the Variorum.

As he neared his seventy-fifth birthday in 1908, Furness moved to conclude his public speaking career. During the first half of the year he had delivered four major speeches: an historical address at the installation of the Reverend Charles E. St. John as minister of the First Unitarian Church on January 12, another speech on Franklin at an American Philosophical Society dinner on April 25, the welcome to the Associated Harvard Clubs on May 9, and the Phi Beta Kappa speech at Harvard on June 25. In the years that followed, with the exception of his address at the twenty-fifth anniversary of Bryn Mawr College in 1910, he confined himself to the increasingly frequent eulogies at memorial services for his friends. In March 1897, he had delivered a memorial address at the dedication of the Alice Lippincott School, and in 1901 he had spoken for Pepper; now on February 8, 1910, in the main gallery of the Pennsylvania Academy of the Fine Arts he presided over a memorial meeting for Richard Watson Gilder, for many years the editor of *The Century Magazine*; and on January 20, 1911, representing the Library Company of Philadelphia, he paid tribute to Henry Charles Lea at memorial services held at the Hall of the College of Physicians. Later that year, when Isaac Clothier invited him to address the Founders Day Convocation at Swarthmore College, he refused. "My answer must be given, however, not in accordance with my wishes, but by a handicap of seventy-eight years, which lies very heavily on my shoulders. The last time that I spoke in public, though but for a few minutes, at the memorial service for my very dear friend, Henry C. Lea, I was convinced thereafter, that I had uttered my final work, and that in the future, I must, 'Trim myself to the storm of time,' and 'reef the sail.' "[50]

THE FINAL VARIORUMS
(1904–1912)

Here is my journey's end, here is my butt,
And very seamark of my utmost sail.
—*Othello* 5.2.268-69

Amid the demands of speaking and reading, the delights of grand-children and gardening, and the death of family members and friends, progress on the Variorum slowed from the frenzied tempo of *The Winter's Tale* (1898), *Much Ado About Nothing* (1899), and *Twelfth Night* (1901) to the more leisurely pace of *Love's Labour's Lost* (1904), *Antony and Cleopatra* (1907), and *Cymbeline* (1913). Work proceeded at irregular intervals interrupted by long periods of inactivity.

Long before the first copy of *Twelfth Night* reached Wallingford in October 1901, Furness had been thinking about *Love's Labour's Lost.* "I am going to try a two-horse act, and work at a couple of plays

225

at the same time," he wrote to Rolfe on Christmas Eve 1900. "My choice will fall on two of the following three:—Love's Lab. Lost; Julius Caes. and Ant. and Cleop. At present I incline to the first and the last. The last has always been one of my greatest favourites. I think I turn to it oftener than to any of the others."[1] Yet in the next year and a half, devoted to seeing *Twelfth Night* through the press, fishing for tarpon in Florida, and reading Shakespeare for charity, he had come no nearer his goal than to order the necessary books for *Love's Labour's Lost.* "The winter is passing for me in absolute laziness," he reported to Wright in January 1902. "I have been cataloguing my library, sending books to be bound and ordering new ones. An intolerable aversion to any respectable work has clawed me in its clutch, and I haven't even cleared off the duties which I said should stand between me and Clarissa Harlowe. I am just longing for that abandoned flood of tears over her death."[2] Not until midsummer 1902 did he begin in earnest on the collation. To Nannie, who was spending the season in France, he wrote the following letter on July 20:

My dear, I have actually begun to work again, after the longest season of inaction (and its consequent depression) these fifteen years. Whatever the cause, be it the reaction accumulated during a lifetime, or be it old age, certain it is that ever since you went away I have had an aversion, amounting to nausea, to all qualities of the work to which my life has been devoted. I didn't want to read Shakespeare, or about him, or to hear a drama mentioned. I didn't want to read, or to look, or to think, or to be. I didn't want to eat, or to sleep, or to go to bed, or to get up. I wanted merely to scramble through the days and to be able to check them off. My life was over and it had been a failure. Although this latter opinion I have not shaken off and never shall shake off, yet I know that to sit with folded hands would not tend to improve it, and that it would infallibly lead to repulsive senility. So about ten days ago, I arranged all my books for the work of collation, drew my breath, set my nostrils wide, and bent up every power to its full height, and actually collated the first few lines of *Love's Labour's Lost.* The exertion was so severe that I had to rest for two or three days—Then another heave-yeo and I snapt the spell that bound me. For the last four or five days I have worked with all the old ardour,— should I not say, young ardour?—and really surprising myself with a capacity to carry sixty lines of text through thirty editions and detect the variation of a comma, or a letter in any one of them. The old truism that nothing succeeds like success may be modified into nothing encourages like encouragement; so I am now working away and shall so continue while the fit is on.[3]

That autumn he reported to Rolfe, that "Love's Labours Lost' is advancing as fast as many distractions will permit,"[4] and work continued sporadically through 1903 with time out to serve as Public Orator at University Day in February, to give commencement addresses at Bryn Mawr and the University of Pennsylvania, and to accept the inevitable invitations to read Shakespeare before the public. Finally the printing began in April 1904. "Just at this present, "he wrote to Rolfe on June 22,

> I am working night and day to finish *L.L.L.* before I take my vacation which has been postponed and postponed from the middle of June to the 5th of July, on which date I *must* leave for Texas. This year I take my son and grandson with me. I want to see three generations, all fishing for tarpon at the same time on the dancing waters of the Gulf of Mexico. . . . 'L.L.L.' has given me no end of trouble, partly because old age has clawed me in its clutch, and the drudgery wearies me inexpressibly.[5]

Nor did the drudgery lessen during the autumn of 1904 as he turned from the congratulatory letters for *Love's Labour's Lost* to the collation of *Antony and Cleopatra*. The play stretched forever in front of him, threatening like *Hamlet* to turn into two volumes, and in December 1904 searching for escape he began to plan a European trip for the summer. Nannie, increasingly crippled by rheumatic gout, had traveled to the Continent to escape the damp Philadelphia winter in the warmer climate of southern France and Italy, and Furness planned to sail to England in May, meet Nannie in Paris and leisurely return to London to visit his English friends by August, and then sail for home.

With eerie similarity to his European trip with Kate in 1880, however, sickness twisted pleasant plans into wretched nightmares. Forgoing until August visits with Wright and Gosse, Furnivall and Garnett, who in 1903 had dedicated to Furness his latest book *The Twilight of the Gods and Other Tales*, Furness left London almost immediately for Paris where he found Nannie so convulsed with pain that immediate return to Philadelphia seemed advisable. From Paris he wrote on July 13,

The main purpose, my dear Wright, which brought me across the vast of ocean was to bring home my sister, who had an escort only as far as England. The second purpose was inspired by the confident hope of seeing you. And when I missed you in June I did not despair; August was in reserve. But now this hope has faded. My sister's rheumatism is become so outrageous and rampant, and she, in consequence, so helpless, that my only safest course seems to be to get her away as soon as possible from this hampered and dolorous life in hotels to my home, where, with every possible creature-comfort supplied, she can have some chance to recuperate in an atmosphere of complete rest and peace. Accordingly, we shall sail in the Steamer which leaves on the 22nd of this month. We shall leave here on Saturday in my boy's automobile, travel by easy stages, and reach 'The Brunswick Hotel,' in Jermyn St. on Monday or Tuesday. This gives us three or four days before we sail. If I can by any possibility eke out the time I'll still make a frantic struggle to rush to Cambridge to see you, my earliest and dearest friend in England. But if I fail, I'll look forward to another chance before I become sans eyes, sans taste, sans everything.[6]

Wright arranged to meet Furness at the Brunswick Hotel, but even that promise fell prey to Nannie's painful suffering. On August 8, once again at Wallingford, he wrote to Nannie's sister-in-law Sarah Wister.

Our dear sister is at last at home, safe, and I wish I could add, sound. We had a wretched voyage, horrors on horror's head accumulated— bad weather, bad food, bad maid. At times the poor invalid was one unbroken ache from head to foot. Sleep by day or by night was impossible, the boding scream of the fog-horn was never silent for twenty four hours. It would be hard to imagine a 'Thank God!' more fervent than mine when at last Nannie was set down, in her portable chair, in her own peaceful room here. She has not left her bed since then.[7]

With Nannie's health foremost in his mind, the editions of *Antony and Cleopatra* lay in the library untouched. Slowly she gained strength, until by December she could be carried downstairs in the afternoons. "Much of my time has been taken up with looking after my sister, whose recovery is very, very slow—but 'tis certain she is not going backward," he reported to Wright in March 1906.

> I have what you call a 'lift' and we an 'elevator,' so that she descends without difficulty every day at about noon and stays to dine with me in the eveg. and then I read an hour to her before she goes to bed. 'Und so fliegen meine Tage.' Spring, I am sure, will revive her interest in flowers. I have set apart a plot of ground wherein she reigns supreme, and whereon the heavens rain when they feel like it.[8]

As the danger gradually passed, Furness resumed work on *Antony and Cleopatra*, and by October he had finished the collation and the commentary and was working on the appendix. After an altercation over royalties and a brief flirtation with a New York publisher, Furness authorized the printing and Lippincott's began to advertise the new volume in December 1906. When he finished reading proofs in June 1907, he declared to Wright,

> 'The long day's task is done,' or will be by the time you get this, and I shall have finished with 'Anthony & Cleopatra' for ever—possibly with editing any more plays. I think I've done enough and I'm tired. The present is a turr'ble big book—over 600 pages; I think the public will cry, 'hold, enough!' Mind, I don't wish you any harm, but I shall be exceeding glad when a copy is on its way to you.[9]

Still the public approved, and by October he was busy making changes and corrections for the second edition.

The potent attraction of Shakespeare, as usual, overruled all resolutions about "last plays." After a winter devoted to public speaking, Furness again felt the old fire as he prepared his Phi Beta Kappa speech on Shakespeare. "The widely spread devotion to Shakespeare, is to me a source of constant surprise and pleasure," he confided to Norton in June 1908.

> This surprise led me not long ago to ask Lippincott for the number of editions thus far issued of the New Variorum. . . . That *Ant. & Cleop.* should be already in its 2nd edition does surprise me. Old man Lippincott told me, thirty years ago, that if I would only complete all the plays I needn't wish to leave to my children a 'handsomer fortune.'[10]

The Phi Beta Kappa oration having been delivered on June 25, Furness could resist temptation no longer, and on July 6 he wrote again to Norton, "It is my season for work. I have consequently began, what I thought I never would begin again, a new play, and am making out a list of works on 'Cymbeline' which I shall at once import from England and Germany."[11] The flame burned bravely, flickered, and went out. In October he wrote yet again to Norton,

> I have gathered about me ever so many books on 'Cymbeline,' and am fully prepared to start at once. But a strange distaste of them all comes over me and overcomes me. I even started with the Four Folios before me, and collated more than fifty lines and there I halted. I could not go on. The fire was cold and dead. I longed to read Faust, I pined for Horace, and I yearned for Milton. I closed the books and restored them to their shelves. This was a week ago; I haven't opened them since. I must await the spirit.[12]

Again family tragedy had quenched the spirit. Even as Furness began the collation of *Cymbeline* that October, Nannie became critically ill, and on November 2, Furness wrote to Gosse, "the air seems full of farewells."[13] The inescapable comparison to Kate deepened his despair. Since their father's death in 1896, she had been his closest companion; they had read Shakespeare together; he had tenderly nursed her, an invalid in his house for the past five years. Side by side they had worked in his library—he reading proofs of *Antony and Cleopatra*, she reading proofs on her fortieth translation for J.B. Lippincott of current German novels. Now she, too, was going. On November 15, 1908, almost twenty-five years to the day after Kate's death, Nannie died from Bright's disease, and again an impassioned plea crossed the Atlantic to his oldest Shakespearian friend.

> Dearest, dearest Wright, For a second time a great light is gone out of my life. The dear and gracious Lady whom you admired (but not one whit more than she admired you) slipped from my arms in the early hours of this morning and has left me stumbling in disastrous night. I would give much at this moment for a silent grasp of your hand and a look of sympathy from your dear kind eyes.[14]

Hardly had he answered the flood of sympathy notes and fulfilled his legal duties as executor of her will, however, when tragedy struck again. In June 1909, his only daughter, Caroline, contracted typhoid, and, in spite of blood transfusions from Willie, died on June 27, 1909, leaving behind her husband Horace Jayne, two children, and a dazed and broken-hearted father. Again he turned for comfort to Wright, who replied,

> Oh my dear dear Friend, What can I say to you, how can I comfort you in this sorrow upon sorrow, now that for the third time a chasm has been made in your heart's affections and the tenderest of family ties has been rent. . . .God bless you, my dear Furness, I commend you in this sore trouble to the healing influence of memory and hope.[15]

But Furness had little hope for his consolation. "This weary, weary life! I long to be done with it. But 'tis no use in rebelling; 'tis merely biting on a file," he had complained to Corson a few years before.

> I wish I could believe in a Hereafter with the assurance that you happily own. I should then hope for the chance to give somebody or something a piece of my mind and have a most satisfactory time in denouncing the mean, dirty trick that is played on us here in this life by the misery and agony of a Farewell. But, confound it all, at the time when this happy moment should be mine, my mouth will be crammed with dust, and dumbness and eternal silence shroud me.[16]

He drew what bleak comfort he could from the knowledge that his sister and his daughter had been spared the anguish of separation and that his own death would come soon, yet the sight of Horace Jayne and his two young children only intensified his own loss. Six months after Caroline's funeral he wrote to Walter, "Horace Jayne is still brooding, as is most natural, over his shattered life. Time will bring, not comfort,—a silly idea which those express who never felt real sorrow,—but acquiescence, and capacity to hide the agony."[17]

Again Furness took refuge in the routine and in Shakespeare. After a European trip in July and August 1909, he settled back into his work on *Cymbeline*; by the middle of April he had finished the collation of the four folios and, by the end of June 1910, the rest of the texts. Through the remainder of that year and the next two, Furness worked in desultory fashion, often expressing his conviction that he would never finish the play. On August 12, 1911, for example, he wrote to Horace Jayne, "At last, I've got to work again, but 'tis terribly mechanical. . . . I have no thought that I shall ever finish this play of 'Cymbeline,' yet I'll 'peg away to the end.'"[18] A year later, just before his death, he had finished the commentary, the preface, and articles on the source of the plot and the date of composition for the appendix. "If all goes well," he had written to Samuel Chew four days before the end, "I hope to deliver 'Cymbeline' to the mercies of the printers in a month or two. And then I shall rest and patch up my old body for heaven."[19] The volume, published posthumously in 1913, appeared without correction just as he had left it.

Thus ended the final period of the Variorum—three volumes spread over twelve years and published at irregular intervals. Taken as a group, *Love's Labour's Lost*, *Antony and Cleopatra*, and *Cymbeline* offer few surprises in content or method. Furness's textual conservatism during the middle years of the Variorum solidified as he reproduced the First Folio, misprints, mispunctuation, and all, baiting the critics who struggled to explain obscure passages and defending disputed First Folio readings against emendation even in cases where every editor since Theobald had agreed on a change of a corrupt passage. Where the First Folio, the sole source of *Antony and Cleopatra*, says that Antony "soberly did mount an Arme-gaunt Steede (1.5.56), for example, the commentary filled three pages of the Variorum, ending with a typical jab from the editor at the commentators: "In view of the formidable, not to say appalling combination of equine qualities and armourer's art which has been detected in this adjective, Anthony would have been more than mortal had he not approached his steed with extreme caution and mounted it 'soberly.'—ED."[20] If sense could be made out of disputed readings, Furness predictably argued against emendations, sometimes even against those of Theobald, the textual critic he most admired. In Act V of *Antony and Cleopatra*, Cleopatra's eulogy for her dead lover reads in part, "For his Bounty, / There was no winter in't. An *Anthony* it was, / That grew the more by reaping." Every editor since Theobald, except Furness, and most since Furness have regarded the word "*Anthony*" as a misprint for "autumn," producing the metaphor of a farmer repeatedly reaping the ripe grain of autumn and finding the field more bountiful with every repetition. Furness, however, regarded "*Anthony*" as an antonomasia—a substitution of a proper name for a quality associated with the name—

and argued that for Cleopatra the name "Anthony" equaled the limitless bounty of a magically recurring harvest. Still arguing his case before Norton six months after *Antony and Cleopatra* appeared, Furness wrote,

> I still adhere to 'Antony' in preference to *autumn*. To Cleopatra that name was the exponent of every thing generous, bountiful, lavish in nature. Suppose I were describing a character overflowing with generosity and with iterated lavish kindness, would it not be understood were I to say that his bounty had no winter chill, 'twas always warm and glowing,—it was a very Charles Norton that grew by giving, and that throve by wasting?—Tell me that and unyoke. If you don't assent to this, I'll only resign myself to God and say, with Punch, none so blind as those who can't see.[21]

Such points, of course, admit differences of interpretation; nevertheless, they aptly illustrate Furness's consistent editorial conservatism.

Critical opinion varied on his editorial success. *The New York Times* reviewer of *Antony and Cleopatra* noted with wry approval, "Dr. Furness is so far from frolicking in conjecture that we have not observed in the present goodly volume a single original emendation;"[22] and the *Boston Evening Transcript* commented about his scorn for ingenious expositors, "For a problem that cannot be solved, Dr. Furness's method of humorous non-solution may be commended to the many over-serious editors who consider the correct reading of disputed Shakspearean passages as the chief end of human existence."[23] Nevertheless, other reviewers objected both to his adherence to the First Folio and his increasingly cavalier attitude toward textual critics. Citing numerous examples of successful emendations in *Antony and Cleopatra* turned down by Furness in favor of less happy First Folio readings, *The Atlantic Monthly* issued its judgement:

> Dr. Furness is now the leader of the wholesome reaction against reckless emendation,—a reaction which itself tends towards an opposite extreme, that of a superstitious veneration for the authority of the First Folio. It comes to be a foregone conclusion that, where any defense in any degree rational can be made for a Folio reading, Dr. Furness will be found on the conservative side. Of the two extremes

this is undoubtedly the safer; yet surely there is a more excellent way.[24]

Both Samuel Tannenbaum and Joseph Quincy Adams, when reviewing the posthumous *Cymbeline*, objected not only to the conservative textual readings, but also in places to Furness's attempted humor. In *The Dial* for March 1, 1914, Tannenbaum pointed out several "exquisite flashes of humor" scattered throughout the volume, but continued,

> Unfortunately his pleasantries have not always this charm and affability; sometimes they are quite puerile, and even of a nature to cause pain to his victims—if the latter were alive. Walker's statment that occasionally words like *blowing* are to be pronounced as monosyllables calls forth this burlesquing comment: 'Ha'ng laid down this jew'l of a rule he is able to regard some po'ms written by po'ts as undy'ny po'try.' . . . To be sure, this is humor of a certain sort; but is it literary criticism?[25]

When reviewing the same play for the *Journal of English and Germanic Philology*, Adams, too, noted that "perhaps at times the temptation to be humorous led Dr. Furness too far."[26]

His increasing outspokenness both in the commentary and in the preface of the final Variorums caused *The Nation*, when reviewing *Antony and Cleopatra*, to comment: "It has been often observed that in the later volumes of this edition the comments of the editor appear with greater fulness and frequency than in the earlier. This tendency has now reached such proportions that the new volume contains more of Dr. Furness than of any other one critic. We thus have a new as well as a variorum edition."[27] The most striking comments, not all of which have been upheld by later scholars, Furness reserved for his prefaces. In *Love's Labour's Lost*, for example, he attacked the prevailing opinion that in the 1580s the highly ornate and exaggerated speech of John Lyly's novel *Euphues* had influenced the speech of Elizabeth's court and that in the speech of certain characters, most notably Armado, Holofernes, Moth, and Costard, Shakespeare had both successfully imitated Lyly's style and ridiculed its excesses. In *Cymbeline*, too, he argued a position, not subsequently upheld, of extensive collaboration in the play. "I am astounded at the proofs which meet me on every

page (hardly an exaggeration) of another hand than Shakespeare's"
he had written to Owen Wister after collating the folios. "I don't refer
to the trash of Posthumus's dream, which no-one, since Pope's time,
has ever supposed to have been Shakespeare's; but there are expressions here and there which, if Shakespeare rose from the dead
and told me that he wrote, I should reply, with reverence and
firmness: 'You lie.'"[28] This sentiment, repeated again and again in
Furness's letters written while he worked on *Cymbeline*, issued in a
lengthy discussion of his theory in his preface to the play.

> Regarded broadly, I believe that the Imogen love story and all that
> immediately touched it interested Shakespeare deeply; the Cymbe-
> line portion was turned over to the assistant, who at times grew
> vainglorious and inserted here and there, even on the ground sacred
> to Imogen, lines and sentiments that shine by their dulness. Nay, one
> whole character was, I think, confided to him. It is Belarius—who
> bored Shakespeare. To rehabilitate that hoary scoundrel was not (I
> may not say) too great a task for Shakespeare, but one that would
> divert him from fairer and more entrancing subjects.[29]

Critics since Furness have generally attributed the inconsisten-
cies of the play to Shakespeare's experiments in tragicomic romance, experiments subsequently perfected in *The Winter's Tale*
and *The Tempest*. Furness should have recalled his own advice,
given years earlier to Horrie, about a college theme on the collaboration of Beaumont and Fletcher.

> You can separate his work from Fletcher's only by the closest analy-
> sis of style and metre—and even then your grounds are shifting and
> uncertain—and someone else can say 'tisn't' after you've said 'tis.'
> You have got to assume (which I think is a folly) that a man always
> writes exactly the same—and that no one has ever imitated him—not
> even his fellow labourer who works in the composition of the same
> drama with him. To me such questions, with their long laborious
> solutions of tables and lists, are waste time. Very little thought is
> required, it's mainly a ponderous mechanical labour. You've got to
> lay down certain rules, & they're simple enough for a child to devise,
> and then go through the plays and tabulate. Ugh! You must count
> up how many feminine endings there are in each play, and how
> many lines run on—and when your long heavy work is done,

you've done no good to God or man—and anyone with a different crotchet in his head will upset and deny your every conclusion.[30]

His finest critical argument in these volumes was his defense of Cleopatra. Insisting that her "love for Anthony burned with the unflickering flame of wifely devotion," Furness argued that never during the play did Cleopatra play false to Antony. As evidence he cited the difference between Shakespeare's Cleopatra and Plutarch's Cleopatra.

Never does Cleopatra waver in her wild and passionate love for Anthony. Even in the Scene with Caesar's ambassador, Thidias, who comes to Cleopatra with overtures of peace and favour on condition that she will give up Anthony, we knowing ones, crammed with history as pigeons are with peas, tip each other the wink and lay our fingers on our shrewd noses at Cleopatra's evident treachery when she sends word that she kisses Caesar's conquering hand, and kneels, with her crown, at his feet, but those who read the Queen only by the light thrown by SHAKESPEARE, see clearly enough that at this lowest ebb of Anthony's fortunes this was the only course she could prudently take; to gain time for him she must temporise with Caesar. And when Anthony surprises Thidias kissing her hand and rages 'like a thousand hurricanes,' she patiently waits until the tumult of the earth and skies abates, and then calmly asks, 'Not know me yet?' Are we blind that we do not see that SHAKESPEARE here means to show that Cleopatra has been throughout as true as steel to Anthony, 'her mailed Captain,' and that her protest that, if she be cold-hearted toward him, let heaven 'the *next* Caesarion smite,' is as sincere as it is tender and pathetic. From this deep, enduring, passionate love she never swerves, and in the very last moments of life she calls to Anthony, '*Husband*, I come,' thus sanctifying her love by the holiest of bonds. In accepting her right to claim this relationship our hearts bow down before SHAKE-SPEARE, not Plutarch.[31]

Moreover, in the final scene, Furness argued, Cleopatra firmly intended to join Antony in death and deliberately arranged for Caesar to discover the treasure that she had withheld from her inventory in order to deceive him about her intention to commit suicide.

Be it remembered that Cleopatra's last words, as Anthony's dead body is borne away, are 'Ah, women, women! Come we have no friend

/ But resolution, and the briefest end!' And from this resolution to compass the briefest end, she never for one minute departs. Before she could even begin her plans she was taken prisoner, and her scheme for procuring an asp demanded the closest secrecy. What she had most to fear was that Caesar should get some inkling of her design. It was, therefore, of the very highest importance that Caesar's mind should be utterly disabused of any suspicion of her suicidal intent, and that, instead thereof, he should be firmly convinced, not only that she intended to live, but that she was becoming reconciled to the thought of going to Rome. To give Caesar a list of her possessions was obligatory; but what proof that she intended to live could Caesar have greater than the withholding, from her list, treasure sufficient to maintain her hereafter in regal state? This whole Scene, then, with Seleucus was pre-arranged in order to deceive Caesar. The rage, the fury, the virago were all assumed. One exquisite touch there is which must have extinguished, in Caesar's mind, the last spark of suspicion that she intended to destroy herself. In pleading her excuse for thus retaining some of her treasure, she slights to the uttermost its value, calling it 'immoment toys,' 'lady trifles,' etc., and then with infinite cunning she refers to 'some nobler token' which she had kept apart 'for Livia and Octavia' as a friendly greeting,—in Rome, of course. In this last of all her encounters Cleopatra triumphed, and Caesar was the ass unpolicied.[32]

The reviewers received Furness's foray into literary criticism with mixed response. *The Atlantic Monthly* sharply objected, accusing Furness of ignoring half of the evidence.

What Dr. Furness has done in this attempt to ennoble Octavius and whitewash Cleopatra is to select, under the obsession of an idea, one set of passages, all of which have their due significance, and from these to derive portraits of a man and a woman lacking precisely that subtlety and that delicate balancing of opposing tendencies which are essential elements of some of the most superb characterizations in all literature. The critic's laurels are not always to be awarded to the scholar.[33]

Most other reviewers, however, applauded. The *New York Herald* summarized his defense of Cleopatra with approval; the *Liverpool Daily Post & Mercury* concluded, "This is an interesting discussion to whet a new perusal of the great play",[34] and the *Boston Evening Transcript* added, "Furthermore, the brief preface that introduces the present volume displays Dr. Furness in the equally sensible guise of appreciative critic," and, after quoting excerpts from his argument, continued, "This and other passages from Dr. Furness's preface plainly show that a keen critic was lost in the making of a scholarly editor and commentator."[35] The most unstinting praise came from *The Outlook* and indicates, in spite of the occasional disagreement over emendations and interpretations, the high regard with which Furness was viewed by his contemporaries.

> No one can read the Preface to the 'Tragedie of Anthonie and Cleopatra' in the New Variorum Edition without recognizing that Dr. Furness brought to his great undertaking a rare insight of heart as well as keen intelligence and a scholarship which rests securely on all the sources of Shakespearean knowledge. . . . For thirty years Dr. Furness has lived in the atmosphere of the great mind whose creations he has been studying; and if those who know and love him felt at liberty to speak, they would agree in saying that in the temper of his thought and the atmosphere of his life there is a disclosure of the dramatist in harmony with the loftiest spirit of the plays and with the traditions of the poet's personal sweetness and charm. . . . When Dr. Furness affirms his belief that in Shakespeare's view Caesar's love for Anthony was sincere and deep-seated, and that in Cleopatra's deep, enduring, and passionate love for Anthony, from which see never swerves, he finds the loftiest note of the tragedy, he discloses that insight born of profound human feeling which must always penetrate and suffuse scholarship if scholarship is to deal vitally and not superficially with great works of art. To exactness and fullness of knowledge the editor of the Variorum Edition has added the wisdom which is born of a great love.[36]

Such devotion to the man who had devoted himself to Shakespeare prompted further honors during his last decade. On November 19, 1909, fifty years after his admission to the Philadelphia bar, the legal profession paused to pay tribute to Furness. In Quarter Sessions Court Judge William H. Staake read the following appreciation:

> Dr. Horace Howard Furness was admitted to the bar November 19, 1859, so that today is the golden anniversary of his admission. While not an active practitioner at the bar of Philadelphia and Pennsylvania, the members of the bar rejoice to have his distinguished name upon

their roll of membership and recognize the debt they owe to him for his ripe scholarship, great learning and valuable contributions to the literature of America. His genial presence, forceful personality and great gifts have been a helpful inspiration to the members of the bar, who have known him personally, have listened to his readings of the great Shakespearean dramas or have profited by his learned literary productions.[37]

Less than a month later, on December 11, 1909, Furness travelled to New York for the eleventh annual dinner of the Pennsylvania Society of New York. There, surrounded by Governor Stuart, Senators Penrose and Oliver, three members of President Taft's Cabinet, and other distinguished Pennsylvanians in commerce and industry, Furness received from Andrew Carnegie, President of the Society, the first gold medal awarded by the Society for distinguished achievement. "There will be a unanimous acquiescence in the selection of the distinguished gentleman who is to receive your first Medal," said Carnegie in his presentation.

He is the Editor of the Variorum Shakespeare, Dr. Horace Howard Furness, of Philadelphia, Pennsylvania, not only the greatest Shakespearian scholar of his day, but the greatest who has ever lived. 'We are all subjects of King Shakespeare,' says Carlyle. The Pennsylvanian is the Master Interpreter of the Master. The honour we confer to-night will be applauded wherever the English tongue is spoken.[38]

The newspapers did applaud the tribute from the worlds of industry and finance to American scholarship, and Furness, in turn, in his graceful acceptance speech noted the primacy of Pennsylvania in finance, philanthropy, and applied science.

The greatest honor to Furness during the decade came in March 1905: his election to the newly established American Academy of Arts and Letters. Among the original twenty sculptors, painters, musicians, architects, and men of letters elected to the Academy by the National Institute of Arts and Letters for their "notable achievement in art, music, and literature," Furness joined William Dean Howells, Augustus Saint-Gaudens, Edmund Clarence Stedman, John La Farge, Samuel Clemens, John Hay, Edward MacDowell, Henry James, Henry Adams, Charles Eliot Norton, Theodore Roosevelt, Charles McKim, J.Q.A. Ward, T.R. Lounsbury, Thomas

Bailey Aldrich, Joseph Jefferson, John Singer Sargent, R.W. Gilder, and John Bigelow.[39] Although Furness declined Howell's request to read a paper at the Academy's first public meeting in Washington in December 1909, the following year in New York he did consent to read *Henry V*. At the close of the reading, William Dean Howells, President of the Academy, picked up Furness's ear trumpet and announced to the audience, "I am going to speak to Mr. Furness through this trumpet and tell him that he has made his gloss so much a part of the poetry of Shakespeare that we shall never be able to tell hereafter the gloss from the text."[40] To this tribute the *Public Leger* later added, "It is safe to say that no name is more honored among the American Immortals than that of the learned author and editor of the monumental 'Variorum.'"[41]

In spite of the public praise, the popularity of his Shakespeare reading and public speaking, and the publicity attending each new Variorum volume, fanned by the occasional feature story on his library and the annual interview on his birthday, Furness increasingly withdrew during the last decade to his gardens, his library, and his family at Wallingford. His short, stocky figure, clad in black suit and buckled shoes, genial face framed by white hair and moustache, green trumpet bag in hand, could still be seen on the streets of Philadelphia, yet Furness appeared less and less often in the city's board rooms and gentlemen's clubs. He had removed his name from *Boyd's Blue Book* in 1898, and then with *The Winter's Tale, Much Ado About Nothing, Twelfth Night*, and *Love's Labour's Lost*, to say nothing of the Polychrome Bible, demanding most of his time at the turn of the century, he had lost interest in the day to day affairs of the University of Pennsylvania. Aside from his duties as Public Orator and commencement speaker in 1902 and 1903, Furness attended only one meeting of the Board of Trustees after October 1898, and on October 4, 1904, after twenty-five years of service, submitted his resignation. The following month he also submitted his resignation to the Board of Directors of the Library Company, and in 1905, after thirty years as a club director, ten of which he had served as president, he resigned from the Board of Directors of The Penn Club. "I am reefing sails," he explained to Stedman in January 1905, "my butt and sea-mark cannot be far off."[42] In 1902, at the urging of Weir Mitchell, he had agreed to serve as a founding director of The Franklin Inn Club, formed "to promote social intercourse and friendship among authors, illustrators, editors and publishers,"[43] and continued on its Board of Directors until 1912; yet he took little active interest in the club beyond once reading *Henry V* at a club dinner commemorating the birthday of Franklin. Even the brothers of the Shakspere Society saw Furness only at the Annual Dinner on April 23.

Instead, the Shakespearian shrine at Lindenshade, now the focus of Furness family and social life, attracted a constant pilgrimage of literary and Shakespearian friends. The house itself stood at the end of a long avenue of trees, almost hidden behind three tall lindens, and the lawn, dotted with shrubs, white birches, and fir trees, sloped away to the south. Next to the house stretched a series of flower-filled terraces, lined with box hedges and decorated by statues, a sundial, and an English box maze patterned after the Hampden Court maze. To the immediate right of the house in the Japanese garden, a shallow waterway filled with goldfish encircled several small islands connected by stone bridges. In the center of the garden on the largest island grew a bamboo teahouse with its thatched roof. Japanese waterlilies, irises, dwarf maples, and stone lanterns completed the picturesque view. Whether carefully tending cuttings of English heath and seeds from Anne Hathaway's Cottage in the greenhouse or supervising the planting of sweet potatoes and watermelons in the vegetable patch, Furness delighted in the gardens of his country estate.

Inside the glass-enclosed porch filled with tropical plants and Chinese bamboo chairs at the front of the red frame house, through the entrance hall with its wide brick fireplace and tall brass-dialed mahogany clock, and up the broad stairway between photographs of actors interspersed among Japanese swords, heads of pagan gods, and other trophies from Willie's travels in the Far East, lay the center of this Shakespearian shrine: the library. After spending the winter of 1894 at Lindenshade, Furness had decided to remain there the year around and had begun during the next summer the construction of a fireproof addition to the house for his library, then numbering between seven and eight thousand books. Constructed of brick and iron, with a cement floor and an asbestos ceiling two feet thick, the new rectangular wing stood along the north side or rear of the house. A music room lined with paintings and with portraits by William Henry Furness, Jr. occupied the first floor, and the library filled the second. Access from the house to the library came through a wide, rectangular opening guarded by an iron sliding door that closed automatically in case of fire. Even the heat from a single burning match would have melted the wire restraining the heavy door. An iron gallery extended around three sides of the room with wrought iron staircases descending on either side. On the fourth side stood a huge fireplace guarded by a brick hood. Persian rugs covered the cement floor. Along the walls, except where six large windows poured their light on the desk in the center of the room, the black walnut cases of books rose from floor to gallery and gallery to ceiling. After fifteen years amid the treasures of this Shakespearian shrine, at the further urging of his insurance agents, Furness constructed in 1910 an additional fireproof room adjoining the library. About fifteen feet square, without windows, and constructed entirely of brick and reinforced cement, save for an iron door, the chamber housed about two thousand irreplaceable books. "In it are to be such of my books and treasures, whereof the loss would be irreparable in case of fire," he explained to Kate Bartol. "I do it for Horrie's sake—not my own. I shall need them but a very little time longer."[44]

Everywhere along the stairway and gallery railings hung photographs of his Shakespearian friends and portraits of his family, and scattered throughout the room in glass cases and atop bookcases and tables were his Shakespearian relics, including Shakespeare's gloves, the piece of the mulberry tree planted by Shakespeare in 1609, a cane used by David Garrick, the red baize-covered table used by Fanny Kemble in her Shakespearian readings, a section of Herne's oak in the royal forest of Windsor where Falstaff kept his tryst in *The Merry Wives of Windsor*, and the skull used in performances of *Hamlet* at the Walnut Street Theatre in Philadelphia and autographed by Kean, Macready, the elder Booth, Edwin Booth, Irving, and Beerbohm Tree. Although Furness disclaimed collecting such relics, he did confess to Norton having offered in 1905 a thousand pounds for the Great Bed of Ware only to be prevented by legal complications. That famous bed, over ten feet wide, located then at Rye House in Ware, Hertfordshire, and now at the Victoria and Albert Museum, is mentioned by Sir Toby Belch in *Twelfth Night*: "If thou thou'st him some thrice, it shall not be amiss; and as many lies as will lie in thy sheet of paper, although the sheet were big enough for the bed of Ware in England, set 'em down"(3.2.39-42). Archbishop Ryan, a frequent houseguest, once commented to Furness, "I don't see what objection you could have to relics, for your house is full of them."[45]

When Furness wished to "unbend his mind" from collating texts and reading proofsheets, he turned most often to the leather-bound volumes of his general library. His literary tastes reflected his Victorian age. He admired Tennyson and Charlotte Brontë, but he disliked the "occasional coarseness" of John Donne until persuaded by Norton's *The Love Poems of John Donne* (1905) to reconsider his prejudice; he tolerated Ibsen only for Gosse's sake; and he grew increasingly disenchanted with Browning.

> There is in my veins only one small drop of Browning blood which responds to the Toccata of Gallupi, and there an end. I never wish to spend snother minute of my remnant of days in his company. His world is doubtless a genuine world, but 'tis one I never wish to enter. I do not like the lower passions at fever heat, any more than when they are subdued under a theatrical composure, or are analysed with a pseudo-philosophy throughout all their vulgar filaments. All this written in a harsh, discordant, metallic clash without a line of pure, sweet, musical poetry. I should like to examine the bumps of a man who can say that he rises from Browning with aspirations for a loftier ideal in life.[46]

Among the American poets, of course, Furness preferred Emerson. When Stedman sent him a copy of *An American Anthology, 1787-1900: Selections Illustrating the Editor's Critical Review of American Poetry in the Nineteenth Century* (1900), Furness wrote in reply,

> No American can look through your pages without pride. Throughout the whole domain where English is spoken, has the Nineteenth Century produced a poet whose words have sunk deeper into the heart than Emerson? Tennyson's music will thrill the hearts of angels, but Emerson's magic lines will echo and re-echo in the soul of man. But, O man of taste severe and pure, could you not withstand the pressure, doubtless put on you, to include the bawbling idiotcy [sic] of Emily Dickinson? I have never seen so many of her-her-(I don't know what to call 'em, verses they are not) her *words* gathered together and I thought I was reading a back number of 'The Opal' published by

the inmates of the Bloomingdale Lunatic Asylum. I screamed with laughter over them, and then heaved a bitter sigh that within the covers which held Emerson, Bryant, and Lowell there should be bound up such (pardon the word) ROT. But I know it was not your fault. You couldn't help it. Heaven alone can pardon those who first put such drivelling into print,—man cannot or at least this man cannot.[47]

To which sentiment he appended this comment at the end of the letter—"'I'm almost afraid to think on what I've done / Look on't again I dare not.'—about the Dickinson. But this letter is meant for your eyes alone."

Perhaps his greatest literary love outside of Shakespeare he reserved for the Latin poet Horace. He had read Horace with Caroline and had once set her the task of translating his favorite ode "To Sestius," a translation published in *Lippincott's Magazine* for June 1891 and so admired by Thomas Chase, President of Haverford College, that he dedicated to Furness his school edition, *Selections from Horace* (1892). While teaching Latin to Caroline, he had begun to collect the poetry of his namesake, and after her death in 1909, he established the collection as a memorial to his daughter. The bookplate, a reproduction of the memorial window in the Unitarian Church designed by the English artist Holiday, read "Bibliotheca Horatiana instituta in memoriam Caroline Furness Jayne," and above her portrait carried the legend "Neither present time nor years unborn / Can to my sight that heavenly face restore." Henry and Emily Folger contributed several volumes, including two sixteenth-century Venetian editions; and Sir Theodore Martin, John Sargent, and John Carew Rolfe sent copies of their own editions and translations. By 1912, the memorial collection numbered close to 300 texts, translations, selections, and commentaries, beginning with three incunabula: Mesconius's Florentine edition in 1482 and two Venetian editions of 1486 and 1492.[48]

Lindenshade with its two libraries—one Shakespearian and the other well stocked with general literature—had always been a literary house, and the Furnesses had always been a literary family. Horrie, before following in his father's Shakespearian footsteps, had written a textbook *Problems in Elementary Physics, With Notes and Formulas for their Solution* (1900). Caroline's husband Horace Jayne, Dean of the Faculty of Arts and Sciences at the University of Pennsylvania, had published his textbook *Anatomy of the Cat* in 1898; and Caroline herself had turned a children's game into a fascinating study of folklore *String Figures: A Study of the Cat's Cradle* (1905)— causing Willie to quip that Horace and Caroline were studying the cat from the cradle to the grave. Willie's explorations, resulting in his election to the American Philosophical Society on February 19, 1897, led to his own string of publications: *Folk-lore in Borneo: A Sketch* (1899), *Life in the Luchu Islands* (1899), *The Home Life of Borneo Headhunters* (1902), and *The Island of Stone Money: Uap of the Carolines* (1910).

One night in May 1897 the conversation at dinner had turned to the ease with which contemporary fiction was produced, and Furness suggested, to the great acclaim of the children, that the family should write a novel. The resulting love story, *Grace Auchester*, privately printed in eight copies, Furness described in a letter to Nannie.

> Again there have been laughter and merry talk all around the table and Walter, Willie, & Carrie have been children again They are now passing through a season of great fun and excitement, and gabbling the whole time over a novel which we are all writing together. They said that if I would only write the first Chapter each would follow in turn. Accordingly the other evening, I scratched one off. Walter wrote the second, Willie wrote the third, and Horace Jayne is today writing the fourth, which we are to have this evening after tea. Carrie writes hers tomorrow, & Horrie, on Monday, writes his. We are each of us to do two chapters and then draw lots who shall finish it. And I have laughed fit to split over it. My plot (of course unknown to the rest) has been most horribly distorted & how I can ever carry it out I do not see. Reduced to its simplest forms it is:—a girl is brought up in a family from her earliest infancy, as one of the children,—that she is not, none knows but the father & mother—she has some half brothers (unknown as such to her) one of whom (the villain of the story) falls in love with her & is about to carry her off by force when she is rescued by her brother (as she supposes) who loves her devotedly— but always as a brother—the secret of her birth is discovered & the change from a brother into a lawful lover completes the story. I think the plot is original and, though commonplace, capable of elaboration. But what does Walter do but convert the three step brothers, the youngest of whom he christened Gaborieau and made hump backed, into the "Pests of the County"—and Willie has introduced a hypo-

chondriac and laid the scene partly in Peru, where one of the chief characters elopes into the bush with a half-breed; of course we each of us keep our plots as dead secrets from each other. Horace Jayne, who is at his chapter, asked me at lunch if I had any objection to his making the old grandfather have a fit on the dining-room table! The novel is called "Grace Auchester" and I had intended the grand-parents to be dear old people—but Walter christened them "Pantile" and turned them into horrible old snuff-taking creations, and his hero is Gaborieau Pantile. But I'll have news to tell you about it next Sunday. . . . Horrie and Lou spent the night here, and they were engulfed in the excitement; both are to write chapters; the book then comes back to me—with my plot utterly spoiled. Horace Jayne took up the Auchester girls, married off one of them and brought Grace up to her seventeenth year. Walter had taken it on him to say that she was to receive her enormous fortune of 2,000,000 pounds on her eighteenth birthday, and it was to be paid over in gold (evidently his plot was to make the Pantile boys steal it). Carrie reforms the Pantile boys, sends the eldest to India & makes Morris fall in love with Grace, and greatly softens Gaborieau. Horrie's Chapter is finished and he is to come out tomorrow evening to read it. The only one I really dread is Willy. In my opening chapter Robert Adair says to Charles Auches-ter: 'After the birth of our last little boy, my wife left me'—meaning of course that she died;—Willie chose to interpret it that she eloped, which he had a right to do, and it is now uncertain whether or not Charles Auchester's second marriage was legal—His first wife may be still alive, & Grace be illegitimate. That will dish me and the rest too. And I can't help myself. Before we started we adopted a rule that we should not kill beyond hope of recovery any characters but our own. We can do with our own what we please, and so also we can treat our co-labourers' characters, in every way short of extermination. It is really an amusing puzzle.[49]

The rule against killing a character Furness violated in the end as he killed off almost everyone in order to unravel the snarled plot and bring it to a happy conclusion.

Surrounded by his books at the center of his literary family, Furness also entertained Philadelphia's wider literary circle. Al-though isolated by his deafness and his distance from Rittenhouse Square, he coaxed and cajoled his friends to Lindenshade, and they in turn lured him to Nannie's summer cottage at Northeast Harbor where Bishop Doane and the Mitchells and the Eliots and the Irwin sisters would listen to him read Shakespeare. Years later Harrison Morris remembered "the pewter plates and ale mugs of his hospitable table, with their Shakesperean mottoes,"[50] and Owen Wister recalled how, in spite of his deafness, Furness delighted in conversation.

At his own table (where tiresome words were uttered by none, unless by some unusual visitor) it was plain how often he wanted to catch the back and forth of the talk, and when the not rare hilarity burst out to him visibly, he would begin to laugh too and often demand, 'What is it? What on earth is it?' And when the joke or the story was told through the ear-trumpet—how he joined then! Some people do not laugh well, there is in their make-up something askew, and their performance is harsh, thin, or false; Dr. Furness laughed with a whole soul, musically and contagiously; I am sure that this cheered him often in his struggle through dark days. He would tell anecdotes at his own expense until he and the listener would be rocking helplessly, tears of mirth coursing down their cheeks.[51]

Nannie had a wide circle of literary friends both at home and abroad, including Thackeray, Dickens, Swinburne, and Tennyson; thus, when she moved to Wallingford, Furness turned over the parlor to her, and the spare bedrooms of Lindenshade were almost always occupied by houseparty guests. Her nephew Owen Wister, author of *The Virginian*, was a frequent visitor and brought with him Henry James. Henry and Emily Folger often came down from New York, and Agnes Irwin, long time Philadelphia schoolmistress before becoming Dean of Radcliffe College, brought her sister Sophie and Emerson's daughter Lizzie Homans from Boston. Furness's scholarly friends the Leas and the Schellings were frequent dinner guests, as was his long time friend, doctor, novelist, and acknowledged leader of Philadelphia's literary renaissance at the turn of the century, S. Weir Mitchell. Deemed by his contemporaries Philadelphia's answer to Boston's Oliver Wendell Holmes, Mitchell entertained the artistic and literary elite of the city around his table and at his Saturday evenings after nine; and like Holmes writing of the Autocrat, he immortalized their conversation in his novels *Characteristics* (1891) and *Dr. North and His Friends* (1900).

The latter novel, dedicated "to Horace Howard Furness with ever pleasant memories of many years of friendship,"[52] depicts under thin disguise the cultivated conversation in Philadelphia drawing rooms and in summer houses at Mount Desert Island. Dr. North, of course, was Mitchell; his proper Philadelphia friend Mr. Vincent was Talcott Williams; the artist St. Clair was the sculptor Augustus St. Gaudens; and the scholar Clayborne was Furness. Lindenshade was converted to Holmwood, Clayborne's country estate where, like Furness, he had unexpectedly retreated from the Philadelphia society of Washington Square and Rittenhouse Square. Although such favorite Shakespearian themes as Hamlet's madness and the extent to which Shakespeare portrayed his life in his characters were discussed in the book, Clayborne devoted his life not to Shakespeare but to producing the definitive work on Mohammedan sects and was fond of quoting the poems of El-Din-Attar, friend of Omar Khayyam. The other characters in the book often attributed spurious quotations to El-Din-Attar to tease Clayborne, just as Mitchell used to bait Furness with invented quotations from Shakespeare.

During one of the interminable conversations in this loosely organized novel, Dr. North delivers his medical opinion about the jealousy of Leontes in *The Winter's Tale*. "'Evidently,' said I, 'the dramatist meant to draw a portait of insanity, the homicidal outcome of sudden jealousy. It is too abrupt in its onset. Nothing prepares the mind for his unreason.'"[53] This defense no doubt sprang from the unintended snare set for Mitchell when Furness was editing *The Winter's Tale* in 1897. As in *Othello* where Furness polled the medical faculty of the University of Pennsylvania for their opinions on Desdemona's death, Furness had again written to Mitchell about Leontes' sudden jealousy. Mitchell's reply Furness described to Nannie:

> You know the sudden outburst of insane jealousy in Leontes, in *A Winter's Tale*, has been considered monstrous, and, though allowable in fiction, really untrue to nature. Anxious to find authentic parallel cases in real life I wrote to Weir Mitchell for any within his knowledge or experience. I rehearsed the exact plot of A Wint. Tale, prefacing the account with the remark that he and I both knew well the parties. I never imagined that he would not detect at once my object, which was simply to divest the drama of all distracting elements & present the facts as though in a medical report. He replied:—'The sad case of which you write is by no means unique(!). I have known several, and

one especially is perfectly clear in all its details to my mind now. (This is because I said that he & I knew the parties.) This condition sometimes comes to women as well as men and it brings with it an element of sad regret which may or may not be emphasized by death.' I did not reply. How could I? Vox faucibus haesit. I then duplicated my note and sent it to Horatio Wood, the eminent authority on Diseases of the Mind. He answered at great length with the details of a case of simple though extreme jealousy & then asked if I would 'confidentially give him the names of my friends.' Well, well, well. And I'm in a fix. I shall be accused of laying a trap for my friends. But could not a tiny bit of mother wit come to the aid of Weir and of Wood, leading them to suspect a Shakespearean problem under my very thin disguise?[54]

With essayist Agnes Repplier, another frequent dinner and house guest at Lindenshade, Furness shared his love for cats. When Furness received a copy of *The Fireside Sphinx*, immortalizing Miss Repplier's cat Agrippina who was buried at Lindenshade, he replied,

After reading your exquisite, exquisite Preface last evening, I breathed a holy vow that Agrippina's resting-place should be incontinently marked by a headstone, diminutive but proportionate. Is the simple name carved therein sufficient? or will you send me the years of her birth and death? Had she any love of humour beyond the resources of her tail, whereby she would relish the addition of 'Requies-cat'?[55]

The antics of his two Siamese cats named Banquo and Banshee and his cat of uncertain origin named Romeo he related in letters to Repplier, and she in turn told of listening to Furness step onto his porch and call "Romeo! Romeo!" to which she could never resist adding, "Wherefore are thou, Romeo?"[56] So strong was his preference for cats that when two acquaintances referred to him for arbitration a quarrel over whether a bulldog's jaw should be undershot or overshot, he wrote in reply: "My Dear Sir: You are in error—to me a flattering error. It is my brother Frank not myself who has a knowledge of dogs. But as you have done me the honor to ask for an opinion I take the liberty of expressing my own opinion candidly, and that is a bulldog should neither be undershot nor overshot, but shot as near the heart as possible."

With such repartee among family and friends, whose laughter

and conversation surged around his deaf ears, Furness kept the memories at bay, and Lindenshade once again became the family center that it had been twenty years before. Until his death on January 30, 1896, Furness's father had lived with him at Lindenshade, and Nannie, whose husband Caspar Wister had died in 1888, lived for a while at the Furness family home at 1426 Pine Street, and then also joined her brother at Lindenshade in March 1903 for the final five years of her life. Two nearby houses on the estate accomodated other family members during the summer. On one side before her death lived Caroline and Horace and their children Kate Jayne and Horace Howard Furness Jayne; on the other, Furness's granddaughter Kate Thompson, her husband Wirt, and his two greatgrandchildren. Horrie and his wife Louise were frequent overnight guests, and Willie, between exploring expeditions to Borneo and the Far East, stayed as often at Lindenshade as he did in his rooms in town.

Without Kate at the family center, Furness worked hard to keep the family united and happy, writing weekly letters to children away at school or travelling and expecting weekly letters in return. When family vacations at Cape May had become too filled with painful memories after Kate's death, he had purchased in September 1886 a summer cottage at Point Pleasant, New Jersey, next door to his old friend L. Clarke Davis and his wife, the novelist Rebecca Harding Davis. "I try my best to give my children a happy childhood—they are full of the heyday of youth & lustihood," he had written to Gosse in July 1887. "I want them to be at home on the water and so have just built a cottage by the sea, on the Manasquan River close to the ocean. I've had a fine sail boat made for them & my little girl has cristened it 'Marina.' 'Tother day my boys were there & the old boat builder asked them what the name was for he 'disremembered it.' 'Marina,' replied they, 'That's it!' said the old fellow slapping his thigh, 'somebody asked me & I told 'em 'Flannel.' I *knew* it was some kind o' dress goods.'"[57] There on the Jersey shore amid his family and his books Furness spent part of July and August every year for the next twenty years until he sold the property in 1906.

The cries of the sea gulls and the smell of salt water, however, gradually lured Furness from his books and added another annual ritual to the family summer calendar: deep sea fishing for tarpon in Florida or the Gulf of Mexico. Setting aside proofsheets of the

Polychrome Bible in April 1896, Furness had spent two weeks with Walter fishing off Pine Island in Southern Florida. On his return he described this first fishing adventure to Wright.

> Your letter came while I was a thousand miles away in Florida, on a fishing trip—the very first vacation I had taken winter or summer, night or day, for thirteen years, my children insisted upon it. I really did have, unexpectedly, a *grand* time. The game was tarpons, a fish six feet long, weighing upwards of two hundred pounds. To catch these with a rod and reel is something of a feat—and I didn't catch any. I caught, however, lots of other fish, among them ten or fifteen sharks—horrible creatures, that turn their eyes and look at you, full of malignity, when the gaff hauls them up to the side of the boat. Ah, but the beauty of the scene, the soft, caressing air, the mangrove islands with palms and tropical foliage, the cormorants and pelicans flying hither & thither and high up in heaven the vultures sailing without a movement of the wings—it was too lovely. As I lay back in my boat, smoking my pipe, and overcome by the Southern languor, I thought over all my friends & I wondered how you would treat my intruding proofs.[58]

The proofs did intrude again on his return to Philadelphia, yet Furness had been hooked. Although he complained to his sister that "the endless rocking in a dazzling sea, watching a stupid string, cannot be made thrilling"[59], nevertheless, two years later, when he landed his first tarpon, he too was caught. "Even at Punta Garda we began to feel Tarpon in the air," he wrote to Nannie,

> and by the time we reached St. James there was nothing but Tarpon, Tarpon everywhere. The people there think and breathe nothing else. The sole standard of manhood is the catching of Tarpon, and the skill shown therein. Well, the next day, we were in our boats at eight o'clock, and an hour's rowing brought us to the fishing grounds. There we cast in our lines, laid the rods in front of us and took out our novels to read; the boat rocks soothingly, the warm breeze blows caressingly around us, and the sun looks out of a cloudless sky. The minute the reel begins to unwind, then the novel must be dropped, the rod seized, and the fishing begins, and lucky indeed is the man on whose line there is a tarpon. No such luck came to either of us. . . . So on the second day we were rowed by our boatmen about six miles away to a place where they said tarpon frequented. Scarcely had we

been fishing there an hour before, O joy! hold my sides! your brother, O Nannie! caught and actually 'landed' a tarpon! and I sat back in the boat knowing that the utmost height of my life had been attained. Perish the Variorum! Perish Shakespeare! The hands that have reeled in a tarpon need never thereafter descend to puny themes. It was a fine one, weighing a hundred and thirty-five pounds and six feet long. Verily it is the most exciting work on earth. In order to shake the hook out of his mouth the huge creature leaps out of the water, a dazzling column of pure silver, rushes hither and thither, dives down deep, comes up again with a mighty rush of water, darts off swift as lightning. After it was all over, and it sometimes lasts an hour, I quaked in every limb and I was so weak I couldn't have raised my hand to my mouth. Walter caught one very soon afterwards, and then my content was absolute. We came home in triumph. The object of our trip had been attained. Walter was in great spirits. We are now Past Masters in the gentle craft. Our skill as fishers is now beyond cavil.[60]

With the tarpon safely stuffed and hung above the fireplace in his dining room, Furness repeated his boast to Andrew Lang, Folger, Gosse, Stedman ("Compliment me on my Shakespeare, and I bow stiffly. Compliment me on my fishing, and I beam with ecstatic delight."),[61] and Wright ("Come, congratulate me. This year's fishing places me beyond criticism in the ranks of fishermen. I am now a Past Grand Master in the Art. 'Tis not given to everyone to catch a tarpon: 'non cuivis homini contingit adire Corinthum'—many a man goes thousands of miles, as I did, to catch one & returns a sadder and no wiser man.)[62] Wright called him "a very Nimrod of the sea" and, feigning relief at receiving a letter from Furness in June 1901, wrote, "At one time I was tempted to imagine that like Peter you had gone a-fishing and that instead of catching you had been caught by a big tarpon, who determined to revenge his ancestor's death at your hands some two years ago, and that after suffering a sea change he had hung you up in his dining room. But all these morbid apprehensions are set at rest."[63] When Furness later added a 312 pound sea bass and a record-breaking 246 pound tarpon (noticed by *The Athenaeum* on June 14, 1902), Wright dubbed him "the Tarpon Slayer." Andrew Lang, an inveterate fly fisherman, however, in a series of humorous letters scorned Furness's fish stories. When he heard during a visit from Nannie in 1902 of Furness's record catch, he wrote, "Let me congratulate you. But I would rather get a 70 lb. salmon, and so would you, for he is yours to eat, and rises to a fly. Mrs. Wister fled so abruptly that a copy of my Queen Mary book, packed up for her, could not reach her, and I do not know where to send it. It weighs 246 lbs."[64] Returning to the same theme in February 1905, he added: "The tarpons do not attract me, they are ugly brutes who don't rise at fly. They are big, but not gentlefolk, like trout and salmon. They are the Carnegies of the sea."[65]

As the final decade advanced, less strenuous vacations and interests replaced tarpon fishing, yet still Furness focused on his family. In 1906, with Caroline, Horace, and their two children, Willie, a doctor, and a cook, Furness travelled by private railway car west to the Grand Canyon, still a novelty during the first decade of the century. "I purpose to leave it all next week," he reported to Wright,

and travel three thousand miles to Arizona, the land of the Grand Canyon, where is, I suppose, the most stupendous scenery to be found on this planet. Imagine a cañon over two hundred mile long, with a mighty river rushing along at the bottom, a mile below, and with sides at the top a dozen miles apart, and eroded and gashed into every conceivable shape and of every conceivable colour. We shall travel leisurely homeward, stopping at many a town in this region of the oldest civilisation in the United States—Santa Fe was settled in 1605. And we shall visit the petrified Forest of about a hundred square miles in extent with trunks of trees ten and twenty feet long and two or three feet in diameter turned into marvellous variegated agate. We shall visit the Zūnis, the Apaches & the Pueblos, most interesting folk dwelling in cliffs and crannies. This region is very little known. I have certainly never met more than three or four persons who have visited it.[66]

In 1907, proofsheets of *Antony and Cleopatra* prevented one last tarpon expedition, but in 1908, with Willie and Walter, Furness enjoyed a long-awaited West Indian cruise to St. Kitts, Santa Cruz, Antigua, Dominica, Martinique, and Barbados. When Caroline's death in June 1909 interrupted plans for a similar cruise with the whole family to Buenos Aires, Furness settled down at Lindenshade, after a short European trip that August, to wait for the end amid his books.

In spite of the devotion of his children and his literary friends,

in the years following Caroline's death the isolation of deafness and
advancing age tightened its grip, and memories of the past impinged
on plans for the future. He had made new Shakespearian friends, of
course, as the decade passed, but the old camaraderie was gone, the
old network of editors and antiquarians who had argued over
emendations and exulted in the appearance of each new Variorum
volume had disintegrated in death. Robert Underwood Johnson and
Richard Watson Gilder, editors of *The Century Magazine*, still consulted him frequently on Shakespearian articles submitted to their
journal. J.J. Jusserand sent copies of his Shakespeare books and
lectures, and William Winter dedicated to Furness the second
volume of his *Shakespeare on the Stage*. Yet in a letter to Samuel
Chew in 1908, Furness revealed his loneliness: "Wherever you see
any words in reference to Shakespeare by Professor A.C. Bradley
[Professor of Poetry at Oxford University from 1901 to 1906], don't
pass them by, but read and inwardly digest. In the Shakespearean
world, at present, I hear no voice but his."[67] The old Shakespearian
world had vanished. Among those friends included on the gift list for
the Variorum *Macbeth* in 1873—names like Hudson, R.G. White,
Ingleby, Halliwell-Phillipps, Staunton, Collier, Elze, and Ulrici—only
two remained on the gift list for *Love's Labour's Lost* in 1904—Rolfe
and Wright, and Rolfe too died in 1910. Death had broken forever the
old Shakespeare cohort that had so eagerly collaborated on the
Variorum in its early years, and now Furness himself was ready to
surrender the battle to new forces. "To know that fresh, young,
enthusiastic spirits are entering the world of Shakespeare, wherein
there lies for them illimitable growth, cannot but fill with measureless content one who is finishing the journey, and to whom that
world is fast vanishing in the lengthening shadows."[68]

The sense of isolation increased as personal friends and family
passed on, and his faith in immortality grew more dim. Close upon
the deaths of Nannie and Caroline came those of his dear friends
Charles Eliot Norton and Henry Charles Lea. To Sara Norton he
wrote in September 1909,

> My sole comfort now is that my days of torture cannot be long
> protracted, they must end soon. At the most, it cannot be many years
> before I am changed and become like those who have already gone. If
> they live, I shall live. If they have ceased to live, I shall cease to live,
> and this 'Dull deep pain and constant anguish of patience' will also

cease. Until the dawn of that blest morning which is to be my last, I'll keep a brave front and try to believe that your father and I are wrong in supposing that this life ends all.[69]

Furnivall and Rolfe died in 1910, and in June 1912 Furness travelled to Harvard to serve as an honorary pallbearer for his old friend William Watson Goodwin, long-time Professor of Latin and Greek. Hardly had he returned from Cambridge when on June 27, 1912, his brother Frank died, leaving Furness the sole surviving member of his father's family. "Death is always sudden, no matter how long we have expected it," he wrote a week later to Molly Wister,

> and in contemplating Frank's I had always pictured the loss of his society as the chief grief—but I had not imagined the isolation in which I should instantly stand. This dazed me strangely, clouds and darkness enveloped me and I felt like groping my way. And I have not yet emerged, but am still standing without and all my youth, and family and loves more precious than life are locked away from me on the other side. Of course this will yield to time's strong hours. In the meantime I can work at what will fill the gap in time.[70]

And work he did—"pegging away at *Cymbeline*"—through the hot summer days of July and early August. Andrew Lang wrote on July 6, requesting permission to dedicate to Furness his last book *Shakespeare, Bacon, and the Great Unknown* (1912), but before either saw a copy, they both had passed for themselves into that great unknown. Death came quickly on the afternoon of August 13, after a sudden attack of pneumonia, and took him from his beloved Shakespeare as he worked in his library on *Cymbeline*, his favorite play, and Imogen, his favorite character. "You ask me to name my favourite character in Shakespeare," he had written several years earlier when beginning to edit *Cymbeline*.

> My chronic answer to similar requests is,—the character I have studied last. I think, however, that there is no one character which throughout ranks above all others. Possibly, if I were restricted to the study of one sole male character for the rest of my days I should choose Brutus. If female, it should be Imogen, with an imploring prayer to be allowed, now and then, a glimpse of Cleopatra (not that I so ardently admire the latter, but in the portrayal of no female

character do I bow down so low before Shakespeare's infinite genius as in this 'serpent of old Nile.') After having thus committed myself, in black and white, I must shut my eyes tight against Hermione and Portia and Rosalind, and Henry the Fifth, and Falstaff, and Lear's Fool and a dozen others. And I can't do it. 'Tis impossible. As each one creeps into the study of my imagination in all its charm and fascination I am ready to swear, by all the pretty oaths that are not dangerous, that it alone has my undivided heart. I take back, therefore, all that I have written and recur to my sole true answer that my favourite is the one that I have read the last.[71]

EPILOGUE

"Methinks 'tis prize enough to be his son."
—*3 Henry VI* 2.1.20

"Come and take choice of all my library,
And so beguile thy sorrow."
—*Titus Andronicus* 4.1.34-35

The Furness Variorum story did not end on August 13, 1912. Even as the Shakspere Society of Philadelphia, the University of Pennsylvania, the American Philosophical Society, and Harvard University made plans for a memorial meeting to honor Horace Howard Furness, his son Horace Howard Furness, Jr. was guiding *Julius Caesar* through the press and prepared to continue the Variorum as his own life's work. After graduating from Harvard in 1888, Furness, Jr. had studied graduate courses in astronomy and music at the University of Pennsylvania and, after acquiring a certificate of "Proficiency in Music" in 1891, had accepted an appointment as instructor in physics in the Episcopal Academy, a position he held until 1900. He had always followed his father's work with great interest, however, reading the Variorum volumes from preface to appendix. When a disastrous fire destroyed the entire plant of J.B. Lippincott Company on December 2, 1899, including the plates of the early Variorum *Macbeth* and *Hamlet*, Furness, Jr. resigned from his teaching position and with his father's guidance undertook a revision of *Macbeth*, adopting the First Folio as his text and updating the commentary with the additions of the previous thirty years. For the next two years father and son wrote, revised, and collaborated on the collation and commentary of *Macbeth*. "I am, very naturally, much interested in my boy's Revised ed. of 'Macbeth,' which will be out before Christmas," Furness reported to Rolfe in September 1902. "He will prove a far better editor than I am. This 'Macbeth' is his apprenticeship. Thereafter he will strike out for himself on one of the Historical Plays."[1] His apprenticeship served with the publication of *Macbeth* in 1903, Furness, Jr. went on to edit *Richard III* (1907), *Julius Caesar* (1913), *King John* (1919), and *Coriolanus* (1928), and at his death was working on *Henry V*.

For most of his contemporaries Furness, Jr. so resembled his father not only in name but also in temperament, accomplishments, and devotion to Shakespeare that the Variorum seemed to continue without interruption, an unbroken scene played without intermission. Although he deserted the family's Unitarian faith for the more fashionable Protestant Episcopal Church, and although he established his residence at 2034 Delancey Place in the heart of Philadelphia's elite Rittenhouse Square district, in other ways the son carefully understudied the father. Furness's will had contained the bequest, "To my son Horace Howard Furness Jr. I bequeath all my books relating to Shakespeare and Elizabethan and dramatic literature, together with my Shakespearian relics"[2]; and in the library of 2034 Delancy Place, Furness, Jr. established his own Shakespearian shrine. Like his father, he belonged to the Shakspere Society of Philadelphia, having been elected, along with Felix Schelling, on November 22, 1898, and he served as secretary in 1905, vice-dean in 1911, and dean from April 23, 1913 until his death in 1930. Recalling his father's enthusiasm in the 1860s and early 1870s before deafness dulled the delight, Furness, Jr. regularly attended the bi-weekly meetings, prepared the bill of fare for the annual dinner, and entertained such visiting Shakespearians as Archibald Flower and Johnston Forbes-Robertson. A memorial minute adopted by the society after his death reads in part,

> He gave to this Society the full measure of his devotion. It was rarely that he missed a meeting. This was not because it was his duty, but because it was his pleasure. He was a lover of Shakespeare by inheritance, training, and choice. He knew the plays almost by heart. Their study and elucidation had occupied the best part of his life. When at our meetings the table was cleared, and the book of the play opened, a look of intense earnestness and pleasure would spread over the face of our late Dean. Thereupon all the resources of his mind well stored with Elizabethan thought, literary history, archaeology and philology, and all lore pertaining to the play before us, would be at our disposal. It was our delight to ask and his to answer our questions, and few indeed were the subjects which he could not illuminate from the resources of his scholarship. But although a great Shakespearian scholar there was nothing in him of the pedant. It was all human and real. The fascination of the myriad-minded Shakespeare had caught hold of him. With this came the natural desire to impart the same taste and enthusiasm to others.[3]

As with his father before him, his contemporaries rewarded Furness, Jr. for his enthusiasm and devotion to Shakespeare. Like his father, he was elected a member of the American Philosophical Society, a member of the National Institute of Arts and Letters, and a Fellow of the American Academy of Arts and Sciences. In Philadelphia he was a member of the Franklin Institute, president of the English Speaking Union, and a director of The Library Company. On the three hundreth anniversary of Shakespeare's death in 1916, the University of Pennsylvania awarded him the honorary degree of Litt. D., and in April 1929 called him to serve on the Board of Trustees, where he served, like his father, as Chairman of the Library Committee.

Like his father Furness, Jr. also enjoyed his clubs. He belonged to the Art Club, the Merion Cricket Club, the Penn Club, the Racquet Club, and the Rittenhouse Club, where he served on the Board of Governors, and the Franklin Inn Club, where he was elected to finish his father's unexpired term as a director in 1913 and continued on the Board of Directors, serving as vice-president for eleven years. The literary members of The Franklin Inn Club annually celebrated

Franklin's birthday on January 6 with dramatic farces performed for
the entertainment of the club, and Furness, Jr. entered into these
activities with enthusiasm, writing at least two of these productions
and acting in others. In January 1911 the club produced his satire on
Maeterlinck, Ibsen, and Rostand, called "A Mid-Winter Day Dream,"
which contains such clever, but forgettable, scenes as Nora Helmer
explaining how Ibsen works on a new plot while he, like Macbeth's
witches, stirs a strange mixture of dirt and broken china, chanting:

> Here within this earthen pot
> First throw in a wornout plot.
>   (Picks up a toy balloon.)
> Next a reputation (breaks balloon) cracked.
> And a small, distorted fact,
> Brainstorm in degenerate mind,
> Eyes of husband—somewhat blind,
> Marriage held in light esteem,
> Thoughts to form a fever dream,
> Wifely duty—quite forsworn,
> Sins before the child is born.
> Just a little spice of fear,
> Atrabilious views of life,
> Discord betwixt man and wife,
> Infidelity condoned,
> Sensuality enthroned,—
> Loathsome thoughts regarding sex
> Meant to puzzle and perplex,
> Now the sophist's glozing speech,
> Selfishness to all and each.
> Gibble, gabble, noise and babble
> Critic, rave and fool the rabble.
> Throw the rising hopes away,
> There! we have an Ibsen play![4]

In 1920, for Franklin's birthday Furness, Jr. wrote *The Gloss of
Youth: An Imaginary Episode in the Lives of William Shakespeare
and John Fletcher*, later printed by J.B. Lippincott Company and
glossed by *The Nation* as "an eminent scholar's brief diversion."[5]
The play, set in Shakespeare's house, Blackfriars, in April 1615, no
doubt reflects Furness, Jr.'s own preferences in Shakespearian
study. Shakespeare, who quotes throughout lines from various

plays, despairs because the public likes his comedies and dislikes his histories and tragedies:

> The ignorant rabble care but for a comedy or a jig, and I care not for their praise of what any man may do as well as I. Two lovers in a forest—sugared lines—enough for the clown or the fool's zany to get abundance of laughter; or two or three wastrels in a drinking bout interrupted by a solemn ass and told to mend their ways. This is your comedy.[6]

He is cheered by three children—Nan Bellott, aged nine, daughter of Mistress Stephan Bellott; Noll, aged fourteen, (Oliver Cromwell) who prefers the histories and wants to become king; and Jack, aged ten, (John Milton) who can quote *Hamlet* by heart and plans to become a poet.

Furness, Jr.'s interest in drama was not just literary, however, and like his father he befriended actors and actresses and actively supported the theatre. He entertained Francis Wilson, Walter Hampden, Forbes-Robertson, Julia Marlowe, Edward Sothern, and Otis Skinner. In New York he belonged to The Players, and in Philadelphia he served as a director of the Edwin Forrest Home for Actors and Actresses and as manager, director, and president of the Plays and Players at 1714 Delancey Street. A year before his death he joined with Joseph Parker Norris, Jr. to organize the Philadelphia Theatre Association, founded to present in Philadelphia "famous plays produced, acted and staged by professionals, entirely independent of presentation elsewhere."[7] For a year he served as president of the association and advanced $3,000 cash to back their initial production of Aristophanes' *Lysistrata* which opened six weeks after his death.

Even though Furness, Jr. in many ways resembled his father as he devoted his life to carrying on the Variorum, neither the quantity nor the quality of his work matched that of his father. In January 1903, Furness had repeated in the preface to *Macbeth* his confidence in his son's ability and scholarship. "Surely, the instances are not many where a literary task begun by a father is taken up and carried forward by a son; still fewer are they where the father can retire within the shadow with such conviction, as is now mine, that the younger hands are the better hands, and that the work will be done more deftly in the future than in the past."[8] Talcott Williams, in *The*

Outlook predicted, "Those who have sat with the younger student in the Philadelphia Shakespeare Society know that this vast work, if not in one life, in two, will be well ended and well done"[9]; and Rolfe added in a congratulatory letter in March 1903, "I was delighted to get the new *Macbeth*, and to see how beautifully your boy has rejuvenated his father's work on the play. You have every reason to be proud of him"[10]; and he added in a second letter a few days later, "The future of the great edition is now assured, with you and him to carry it along to a brilliant conclusion."[11] Yet not all Shakespearians agreed. When reviewing *Julius Caesar* for the July 16, 1913 issue of *The Dial*, Samuel Tannenbaum pointed out numerous typographical errors, errors of fact, and errors of collation; and Lawrence Mason, Professor of English at Yale, listed others in his review of *Julius Caesar* for the *Journal of English and Germanic Philology* in 1919. The *Dictionary of American Biography* summed up his Shakespearian career as follows: "It is clear that in learning, critical judgment, originality, and mastery of detail he was not the equal of his father. It was his good fortune to be the son and pupil of the greatest of Shakespeare's editors, his misfortune that he must stand comparison with him."[12]

During the 1920s, as he spent nine years working on *Coriolanus*, Furness, Jr. realized that he would never finish the work that his father had begun. The contract for *Coriolanus* was signed with J.B. Lippincott Company in March 1926, but when the volume finally appeared in 1928, father and son had finished only half of Shakespeare's plays. In 1921, Samuel Hemingway, Professor of English at Yale University and editor of *I Henry IV* for the Yale Shakespeare series, had approached Furness, Jr., offering him textual notes that he had made and urging him to take up that play next. Furness, Jr. asked Hemingway to proceed with collation of the texts for *I Henry IV*, intending to prepare the commentary and appendix himself; but when Hemingway finished the collation, Furness, still enmeshed in *Coriolanus*, had invited him to continue with the commentary and appendix as well. In 1928, with *Coriolanus* completed and *Henry V* begun, Furness, Jr. turned for advice to Felix Schelling. Matthias Shaaber, in a report to the American Philosophical Society, tells the story.

> About a year before his death, remembering the advice his father had given him years back that if he ever got into difficulties he should

consult Professor Felix E. Schelling, Dr. Furness asked Professor Schelling to suggest two young men from the Department of English of the University of Pennsylvania who could assist him in his work. Professor Schelling named my colleague Dr. Matthew W. Black and me. Dr. Furness invited us to become co-editors with him and assigned us *Richard II* and *2 Henry IV* to work on. We were working under his supervision at the time of his sudden death in 1930. At this time, then, four plays (including *Henry V*, which Dr. Furness himself had begun) were actually in process of preparation.[13]

In 1929, with the death of his wife, the former Louise Brooks Winsor, the slow progress on the Variorum *Henry V* slowed to a stop. Alone without siblings—Caroline had died in 1909, Walter in 1914, and Willie in 1920—and without children to cheer him, Furness, Jr. sought solace in a whirl of activity. "I have thrown myself into a deal of work this winter, in fact, have had but little time to sit down and think," he wrote about a month before his death.

You know, only too well, the terrible blankness that assails one at such times. O for the touch of a vanished hand, The *sound* of a voice that is still! Last Spring I was elected President of Plays and Players, one of the foremost dramatic organisations owning its own Theatre— one of the most beautiful and completely equipped small playhouses in this city—and I have been the Director and Manager, superintending the productions of the plays and guiding the destinies of the organisation. It has been intensely interesting work and the high artistic quality of our productions is now becoming recognised; then I have been also at work on my next volume of the Variorum *Henry the Fifth*, and closely associated with the work of the University of Pennsylvania having been elected a Trustee last April. I feel like an aeroplane; as long as the engine is working at top speed the whole machine travels along, but let that engine stop for a minute and the whole thing comes crashing down. I am going abroad next June, to spend a few weeks at Vevey with Edward and Julia Sothern, friends of forty years now, and shall return about September 1st.[14]

But June never came for Furness, Jr. On April 15, 1930, just hours before a dedication service for a window placed in memory of his wife at the Church of St. Luke's and the Epiphany, Furness, Jr. died peacefully in his sleep.

When Furness Jr.'s will was filed a week later on April 22, the eve of Shakespeare's 366th birthday, the University of Pennsylvania found itself the recipient of the Furness Shakespeare collection, valued at $500,000, along with a further gift of $100,000 to maintain the collection as a working library for Shakespearian scholars. According to terms of the will, the University could either take possession of 2034 Delancey Place and operate it as a literary club for faculty, graduate students, and visiting scholars; or, using up to half of the additional bequest, the University could erect on its own land a building, patterned after the English Gothic style of his own library, named the Horace Howard Furness Memorial, and administered as an adjunct to the University Library. Having debated the two plans, the Trustees chose the latter and voted to construct an addition to the University Library in English Gothic style to house the Furness Memorial Library. By January 1932, the 12,000 volumes of the collection including the rare Shakespearian folios and quartos and the works of his contemporary Elizabethan dramatists, had been shelved, and the library was formally dedicated on April 23, 1932. During the 1930s the University Garden Club planted, tended, and expanded a Shakespeare garden, displaying many of the herbs and flowers mentioned by Shakespeare and embellished by a bronze sundial created by sculptor Beatrice Fenton. In March 1962, when the University Library moved into its new building, known as the Charles Patterson Van Pelt Library, the Horace Howard Furness Memorial Library moved with it to its present location among the special collections on the library's sixth floor. Beginning on July 1, 1933, Felix Schelling was appointed by the Trustees as Curator of the Horace Howard Furness Memorial Library, and since then has been succeeded by Matthew Black in 1945, Matthias Shaaber in 1965, Roland Mushat Frye in 1980, and Georgianna Ziegler in 1983.

During the 1930s, aided by grants from the American Philosophical Society, Matthew Black and Matthias Shaaber continued work on *Richard II* and *2 Henry IV*; but, without the leisure of independent wealth and pressed by their teaching responsibilities at the University of Pennsylvania, they could not alone guarantee the future of the Variorum. As early as 1919, scholars had called for the Modern Language Association of America to assume responsibility for the Variorum Shakespeare, and in December 1932, a committee of that body, headed by Felix Schelling, recommended sponsorship of the entire project and appointed Joseph Quincy Adams, director of the Folger Shakespeare Library, as general editor. Over the next twenty years the Shakespeare Variorum Committee of the Modern Language Association, aided by a grant from the Carnegie Corporation of New York, oversaw the publication of six new Variorum volumes: Hemingway's *I Henry IV* in 1936; Shaaber's *2 Henry IV* in 1940; the *Poems* in 1938 and the *Sonnets* in 1944, both edited by Hyder Rollins; *Troilus and Cressida*, edited by H.N. Hillebrand in 1953; and Black's *Richard II* in 1955. During the fifties and the sixties, under the general editorship of James G. McManaway, the Variorum foundered for lack of funds. Discouraged by bleak hopes of publication and the rapidly expanding quantity of Shakespearian criticism, many editors resigned or worked on other projects. In 1973, however, the Modern Language Association itself decided to become the Variorum's publisher. In 1977, a new edition of *As You Like It*, with a survey of criticism by Evelyn Joseph Mattern, was completed by Richard Knowles; and 1980 saw the publication of *Measure for Measure*, begun by Mark Eccles in 1947. In the 1980s, led by Senior Editor Robert K. Turner, Jr., the New Variorum Edition of Shakespeare, begun bravely over a century earlier by a solitary lawyer in the Philadelphia Shakspere Society, bearing a name then unknown in the halls of English and German universities, has become an institution of American scholarship, engaging and challenging the best Shakespearians of the twentieth century.

Notes
Son of New England

[1]"Honor to the Memory of Horace Howard Furness," *Old Penn*, 1 February 1913, p. 581.

[2]Hollis French, *Jacob Hurd and his Sons Nathaniel and Benjamin, Silversmiths 1702-1781* (Cambridge: The Riverside Press, 1939), p. 60n.

[3]Richard D. Pierce, ed., *The Records of the First Church in Boston 1630-1868*, Publications of the Colonial Society of Massachusetts, 3 vols. (Boston: Published by the Society, 1961), 2:477.

[4]Boston, Suffolk County Courthouse, Probate Registry, Administration 23548, 16 July 1810.

[5]Pierce, *Records of the First Church*, 2:481.

[6]Medford, Middlesex County Courthouse, Deed Book 223, p. 30.

[7]Eleanor M. Tilden, *Amiable Autocrat: a Biography of Dr. Oliver Wendell Holmes* (New York: Henry Schuman, 1947), p. 24.

[8]"William Henry Furness," *The Nation*, 6 February 1896, p. 114.

[9]Ibid.

[10]For the above information about the Furness's residences and servants I am indebted to notes provided by Elizabeth M. Geffen.

[11]For Vaughan's memberships and those of the other Unitarians listed below, see Elizabeth M. Geffen, *Philadelphia Unitarianism 1796-1861* (Philadelphia: University of Pennsylvania Press, 1961), pp. 278-93.

[12]Horace Howard Furness, *Historical Address Delivered in Connection*

with the Installation of The Reverend Charles E. St. John as Minister of The First Unitarian Church of Philadelphia 12th of January, 1908 (Philadelphia, 1908), p. 8.

[13]Charles Gordon Ames, "William Henry Furness," *The Harvard Graduates' Magazine*, 4 (June 1896): 548-49.

[14]Richard L. Hernstadt, ed., *The Letters of Amos Bronson Alcott* (Ames, Iowa: The Iowa State University Press, 1969), pp. 20-1.

[15]Franklin B. Sanborn and William T. Harris, *A. Bronson Alcott: His Life and Philosophy*, 2 vols. (Boston: Roberts Brothers, 1893; rpt. New York: Biblo and Tannen, 1965), 1:243.

[16]Odell Shepard, ed., *The Journals of Bronson Alcott* (Boston: Little, Brown and Company, 1938), p. 105.

[17]Horace Howard Furness Memorial Library, ALS, Jared Sparks, 1 September 1849, Cambridge, to W.H. Furness.

[18]Harvard University Archives, ALS, W.H. Furness, 1 August 1853, Philadelphia, to Dr. Walker.

[19]Fanny Kemble Wister, *Fanny: The American Kemble: Her Journal and Unpublished Letters* (Tallahassee: South Pass Press, 1972), p. 208.

[20]Henry Wadsworth Longfellow, *The Works of Henry Wadsworth Longfellow*, 14 vols. (Boston: Houghton Mifflin and Company, 1886), 1:285-86.

[21]"Mrs. Kemble's Shakespeare Readings," *Evening Bulletin*, 29 September 1849, p. 2.

[22]"Mrs. Frances Anne Kemble," *Evening Bulletin*, 2 October 1849, p. 2.

[23]*Evening Bulletin*, 20 October 1849, p. 2.

[24]*Evening Bulletin*, 25 October 1849, p. 2.

[25]*Evening Bulletin*, 5 November 1849, p. 2.

[26]"How did you become a Shakespeare Student?" *Shakespeariana*, 5 (October 1888): 438-39.

[27]Geffen, *Philadelphia Unitarianism*, pp. 144-45.

[28]Ibid., p. 187.

[29]Walter M. Merrill and Louis Ruchames, *The Letters of William Lloyd Garrison*, 6 vols. (Cambridge: The Belknap Press of Harvard University Press, 1971), 1:469.

[30]H.H. Furness, *Historical Address*, p. 10.

[31]Wendell Phillips Garrison and Francis Jackson Garrison, *William Lloyd Garrison 1805-1879*, 4 vols. (New York: The Century Co., 1889; rpt. New York: Arno Press, 1969), 3:45.

[32]Geffen, *Philadelphia Unitarianism*, p. 194.

[33]Furness, *Historical Address*, pp. 10-11.

[34]Garrison and Garrison, *William Lloyd Garrison*, 3:290.

[35]Ibid., p. 294.

Notes
Student of the World

[1]Wendell Phillips Garrison and Francis Jackson Garrison, *William Lloyd Garrison 1805-1879*, 4 vols. (New York: The Century Company, 1889; rptd. New York: Arno Press, 1969), 3:409.

[2]Horace Howard Furness Jayne, ed., *The Letters of Horace Howard Furness*, 2 vols. (Boston: Houghton Mifflin Company, 1922), 1:33-35. Hereafter referred to as *Letters*.

[3]Furness Family Letters, ALS, H.H. Furness, 28 May 1854, Cambridge, to W.H. Furness.

[4]Furness Family Letters, ALS, H.H. Furness, 30 January [1910], Wallingford, to F.R. Furness.

[5]*Twenty-Sixth Annual Report of the President of Harvard College to the Overseers, 1850-1851* (Cambridge: Metcalf & Co., 1852), p. 29.

[6]Horace Howard Furness Memorial Library, ALS, H.H. Furness, 13 October 1884, Wallingford, to H.H. Furness, Jr.

[7]Furness Family Letters, ALS, H.H. Furness, 11 September 1853, Cambridge, to W.H. Furness.

[8]Furness Family Letters, ALS, H.H. Furness, 18 September 1853, Cambridge, to W.H. Furness and A.P. Furness.

[9]Furness Family Letters, ALS, H.H. Furness, 2 October 1853, Cambridge, to W.H. Furness.

[10]Ibid.

[11]Furness Family Letters, ALS, H.H. Furness, 26 June 1853, Cambridge, to W.H. Furness.

[12]Furness Family Letters, ALS, H.H. Furness, 3 April 1853, Cambridge, to W.H. Furness.

[13]Furness Family Letters, ALS, H.H. Furness, 8 May 1853, Cambridge, to W.H. Furness.

[14]Furness Family Letters, ALS, H.H. Furness, 18 December 1853, Cambridge, to W.H. Furness.

[15]Lloyd McKim Garrison, *An Illustrated History of The Hasty Pudding Club Theatricals* (Cambridge: Hasty Pudding Club, 1897), p. 21.

[16]Furness Family Letters, ALS, H.H. Furness, 15 May 1853, Cambridge, to W.H. Furness.

[17]Furness Family Letters, ALS, H.H. Furness, 1 May 1853, Cambridge, to W.H. Furness.

[18]Furness Family Letters, ALS, H.H. Furness, 9 January 1853, Cambridge, to W.H. Furness.

[19]Horace Howard Furness Memorial Library, ALS, E.A. Sophocles, 28 July 1856, Cambridge, to W.H. Furness.

[20]Furness Family Letters, ALS, W.H. Furness, Jr., 19 April 1852, Boston, to W.H. Furness.

[21]Furness Family Letters, ALS, W.H. Furness, Jr., 17 March 1852, Boston, to W.H. Furness.

[22]Furness Family Letters, ALS, W.H. Furness, Jr., 30 March 1852, Boston, to W.H. Furness.

[23]Furness Family Letters, ALS, H.H. Furness, 5 December 1854, Munich, to W.H. Furness.

[24]Furness Family Letters, ALS, H.H. Furness, 2 April 1855, Munich, to W.H. Furness.

[25]Furness Family Letters, ALS, H.H. Furness, 5 December 1854, Munich, to W.H. Furness.

[26]Ibid.

[27]Furness Family Letters, ALS, H.H. Furness, 16 April 1855, Munich, to W.H. Furness.

[28]Furness Family Letters, ALS, H.H. Furness, 24 June 1855, Dresden, to W.H. Furness.

[29]Furness Family Letters, ALS, H.H. Furness, 4 June 1855, Weimar, to W.H. Furness.

[30]Furness Family Letters, ALS, H.H. Furness, 1 July 1855, Vienna, to A.L. Wister.

[31]Furness Family Letters, ALS, H.H. Furness, 8 July 1855, Regensbourg, to W.H. Furness.

[32]Furness Family Letters, ALS, H.H. Furness, 29 July 1855, Innsbruck, to W.H. Furness.

[33]Furness Family Letters, ALS, H.H. Furness, 22 November 1855, Paris, to W.H. Furness.

[34]Furness Family Letters, ALS, H.H. Furness, 8 October 1856, Paris, to W.H. Furness.

[35]Furness Family Letters, ALS, H.H. Furness, 10 July 1856, Paris, to W.H. Furness.

[36]Furness Family Letters, ALS, H.H. Furness, 8 October 1856, Paris, to W.H. Furness.

[37]Ibid.

Notes
A Philadelphia Lawyer

[1]City of Philadelphia, Department of Records, City Archives, District Court Minutes Book, 19 November 1859, p. 477.

[2]William Still, *The Underground Rail Road* (Philadelphia, 1871; rptd. Chicago: Johnson Publishing Company Inc., 1970), pp. 684-85.

[3]H.H. Furness, *Historical Address Delivered in Connection With the Installation of The Reverend Charles E. St. John as Minister of The First Unitarian Church of Philadelphia* (Philadelphia, 1908), p. 12.

[4]Edward Pierce, *Memoir and Letters of Charles Sumner*, 4 vols. (Boston: Roberts Brothers, 1894), 3: 505.

[5]Furness Family Letters, W.H. Furness, ALS, 27 November 1859, Philadelphia, to W.H. Furness, Jr.

[6]*Letters*, 1: 105.

[7]Furness, *Historical Address*, pp. 16-18.

[8]Elizabeth M. Geffen, *Philadelphia Unitarianism, 1796-1861* (Philadelphia: University of Pennsylvania Press, 1961), p. 231.

[9]Ibid., p. 232.

[10]Still, *The Underground Rail Road*, pp. 688-89.

[11]Anna Lea Merritt, *Love Locked Out: The Memoirs of Anna Lea Merritt with A Checklist of Her Works*, ed. Galina Gorokhoff (Boston: Museum of Fine Arts, n.d.), p. 186.

[12]Robert E. Lewis, *Report of the General Superintendent of the Philadelphia Branch of the U.S. Sanitary Commission to the Executive Committee, February 1st, 1864* (Philadelphia: King & Baird, Printers, 1864), p. 3.

[13]*Letters*, 1:111-12.

[14]Ibid., 1:115-17.

[15]Historical Society of Pennsylvania, ALS, H.H. Furness, 28 October 1862, New Haven, to W.L. Gage.

[16]*Letters*, 1:137.

[17]Ibid., 1:124-25.

[18]Winnifred K. MacKay, "Philadelphia During the Civil War, 1861-1865," *The Pennsylvania Magazine of History and Biography* 70(1946): 26.

[19]Maxwell Whiteman, *Gentlemen in Crisis: The First Century of The Union League of Philadelphia 1862-1962* (Philadelphia, 1975), p. 18.

[20]Charles J. Stillé', *Memorial of the Great Central Fair for the U.S. Sanitary Commission, held at Philadelphia, June, 1864* (Philadelphia, 1864), pp. 134, 150.

[21]Harvard University Library, ALS, H.H. Furness, 16 July [1908], Wallingford, to C.E. Norton.

[22]Harvard University Library, ALS, H.H. Furness, [March 1912], Wallingford, to J.J. Chapman.

[23]*Letters*, 1:143.

[24]Somerset Record Office, ALS, H.H. Furness, 30 August 1892, Wallingford, to E. Strachey.

[25]Somerset Record Office, ALS, H.H. Furness, 1 July 1892, Wallingford, to E. Strachey.

[26]"Notes of Painters and Pictures: The Late Wm. H. Furness," *The Nation*, 18 April 1867, p. 319.

[27]Horace Howard Furness Memorial Library, Untitled MS Journal, 7 April 1868.

[28]The Folger Shakespeare Library, ALS, H.H. Furness, 12 February 1884, Philadelphia, to J.H. Martin.

Notes

Montagues, Capulets, and a Shakespearian Feud

[1]*The Shakspere Society of Philadelphia* (Philadelphia: Printed for the Society by King and Baird, 607 Sansom Street, 1860), p. 5.

[2]Shakspere Society of Philadelphia, Minutes, 2:11.

[3]"How did you become a Shakespeare Student?" *Shakespeariana* 5 (October 1888): 439-40.

[4]*Letters*, 2:54-55. Here Furness alludes to Sir Benjamin Backbite's lines about "a beautiful Quarto page where a neat rivulet of Text shall murmur thro' a meadow of margin" in Sheridan's *The School for Scandal*; see *The Dramatic Works of Richard Brinsley Sheridan*, ed. Cecil Price (Oxford: The Clarendon Press, 1973), 1:367.

[5]"Shakesperian Study in Philadelphia," *American Literary Gazette and Publishers' Circular*, 15 October 1866, p. 285.

[6]The Folger Library, ALS, H.H. Furness, 6 August 1871, Philadelphia, to Clement Mansfield Ingleby.

[7]"The Cambridge Shakspeare," *The Athenaeum*, 29 January 1870, p. 161.

[8]"The Cambridge Shakspeare," *The Athenaeum*, 19 March 1870, p. 388.

[9]Edinburgh University Library, ALS, J.O. Halliwell-Phillipps, 21 March 1870, to H.H. Furness.

[10]Horace Howard Furness Memorial Library, ALS, W.A. Wright, 21 March 1870, Cambridge, to H.H. Furness.

[11]Horace Howard Furness Memorial Library, ALS, H.H. Furness, 4 April 1870, Philadelphia, to W.A. Wright.

[12]"The Cambridge Shakespeare," *The Athenaeum*, 2 April 1870, p. 452.

[13]Edinburgh University Library, ALS, H.H. Furness, 16 April 1870, Philadelphia, to J.O. Halliwell-Phillipps.

[14]Trinity College, Cambridge, ALS, H.H. Furness, 30 April 1870, Philadelphia, to W.A. Wright.

[15]Horace Howard Furness Memorial Library, ALS, W.A. Wright, 19 April 1870, Isle of Wight, to H.H. Furness.

[16]Horace Howard Furness Memorial Library, ALS, Henry Norman Hudson, 14 March 1870, Boston, to H.H. Furness.

[17]Horace Howard Furness Memorial Library, ALS, R.G. White, 16 June 1871, New York, to H.H. Furness.

[18]Horace Howard Furness Memorial Library, ALS, Samuel Timmins, 20 August 1870, Birmingham, to H.H. Furness.

[19]Edinburgh University Library, ALS, H.H. Furness, 15 September 1870, Philadelphia, to J.O. Halliwell-Phillipps.

[20]Edinburgh Univerisity Library, ALS, H.H. Furness, 14 October 1870, Philadelphia, to J.O. Halliwell-Phillipps.

[21]Edinburgh University Library, ALS, H.H. Furness, 6 December 1870, Philadelphia, to J.O. Halliwell-Phillipps.

[22]*A New Variorum Edition of Shakespeare. Romeo and Juliet.* Edited by Horace Howard Furness. (Philadelphia: J.B. Lippincott Company, 1871), xvi.

[23]Shakspere Society of Philadelphia, Minutes, Vol. 3.

[24]Horace Howard Furness Memorial Library, ALS, Furman Sheppard, 7 February 1871, Philadelphia, to H.H. Furness.

[25]Horace Howard Furness Memorial Library, ALS, H.N. Hudson, 28 February 1871, Boston, to H.H. Furness.

[26]Horace Howard Furness Memorial Library, ALS, Hiram Corson, 30 September 1872, Ithaca, to H.H. Furness.

[27]Cornell University Library, Bayard Taylor, 5 April 1871, Cedarcroft, Kennet Square, to H.H. Furness.

[28]Horace Howard Furness Memorial Library, ALS, J.O. Halliwell-Phillipps, 25 March 1871, London, to H.H. Furness.

[29]Horace Howard Furness Memorial Library, ALS, Howard Staunton, 26 February 1872, London, to H.H. Furness.

[30]Horace Howard Furness Memorial Library, ALS, John Payne Collier, 17 September 1871, Maidenhead, to H.H. Furness.

[31]"Book Notice: The New 'Variorum' Shakspeare," *Legal Intelligencer*, 3 February 1871.

[32]"Book Notices: The New Variorum Shakespeare," *American Literary Gazette and Publishers' Circular*, 1 April 1871, p. 231.

[33]"Literature of the Day," *Lippincott's Magazine of Popular Literature and Science*, May 1871, p. 559.

[34]"Literary Matters," *Boston Transcript*, 1 May 1871.

[35]Edward E. Hale, Jr., "Our Shakespearian Scholar," *The Dial*, 1 October 1895, p. 176.

[36]"Literature: *A New Variorum Edition of Shakespeare*," *The Athenaeum*, 18 March 1871, p. 329.

[37]Ibid., p. 330.

[38]"A New Variorum Shakespeare," *The Spectator*, 1 July 1871.

[39]*The Stratford-on-Avon Herald*, 24 March 1871.

[40]Samuel Timmins, "Shakespeare in America," *Birmingham Daily Post*, 11 August 1871.

[41]Richard L. Ashhurst, "The Variorum Shakespeare," *The Penn Monthly*, March 1871, p. 144.

[42]"Literature," *The Athenaeum*, 18 March 1871, p. 330.

[43]Richard Grant White, "New Publications," *The New York Times*, 18 May 1871, p. 2.

[44]*Letters*, 2:55.

[45]New York Historical Society, ALS, H.H. Furness, 21 February 1871, Philadelphia, to R.G. White.

[46]"Furness's Shakespeare," *The Nation*, 4 May 1871, p. 307.

[47]*Letters*, 2:55.

[48]The Folger Library, ALS, H.H. Furness, 7 June 1871, Philadelphia, to C.M. Ingleby.

Notes
The Early Variorums
(1871–1880)

[1]Edinburgh University Library, ALS, H.H. Furness, 10 March 1871, Philadelphia, to J.O. Halliwell-Phillipps.

[2]"Foreign Literary Intelligence," *The Book Buyer*, 15 March 1871, p. 3.

[3]Birmingham Memorial Shakespeare Library, ALS, George Dawson, 20 November 1874, Philadelphia, to Samuel Timmins.

[4]ALS, John Ward, 31 May 1769, Leominster, to David Garrick, as quoted by W.B. Redfern in *Royal and Historic Gloves and Shoes Illustrated and Described* (London: Methuen & Co., 1904), p. 29; see also "Shakespeare's Gloves," *The Century* 80 (August 1910): 507.

[5]Massachusetts Historical Society, ALS, H.H. Furness, 7 October 1874, to C.G. Dall.

[6]"Shakespeare," *The Salem Gazette*, 21 January 1879.

[7]The Folger Shakespeare Library, ALS, H.H. Furness, 5 October 1872, Lindenshade, to C.M. Ingleby.

[8]*Letters*, 1:176.

[9]The Folger Shakespeare Library, ALS, H.H. Furness, 28 April 1873, Philadelphia, to C.M. Ingleby.

[10]Cornell University Library, ALS, H.H. Furness, 21 October 1872, Philadelphia, to H. Corson.

[11]Cornell University Library, ALS, H.H. Furness, 7 September 1873, Philadelphia, to H. Corson.

[12]The Folger Shakespeare Library, ALS, H.H. Furness, 1 June 1879, Lindenshade, to C.M. Ingleby.

[13]Folger Shakespeare Library, ALS, H.H. Furness, 23 May 1886, Wallingford, to C.M. Ingleby.

[14]Edinburgh University Library, ALS, H.H. Furness, 14 January 1872, to J.O. Halliwell-Phillipps.

[15]The Folger Shakespeare Library, ALS, H.H. Furness, 2 June 1872, Philadelphia, to C.M. Ingleby.

[16]*Letters*, 1:177.

[17]Cornell University Library, ALS, H.H. Furness, 21 January 1873, Philadelphia, to H. Corson.

[18]Edinburgh University Library, ALS, H.H. Furness, 16 March 1873, Philadelphia, to J.O. Halliwell-Phillipps.

[19]Horace Howard Furness Memorial Library, H.H. Furness, Daily Memoranda, 20 March 1873.

[20]Horace Howard Furness Memorial Library, ALS, W.J. Rolfe, 26 September 1873, Cambridgeport, to H.H. Furness.

[21]The Folger Shakespeare Library, ALS, H.H. Furness, 3 March 1872, Philadelphia, to C.M. Ingleby.

[22]The Folger Shakespeare Library, ALS, H.H. Furness, 18 April 1875, Philadelphia, to C.M. Ingleby.

[23]*The New "Variorum Shakespeare,"* Privately Printed, n.d., p. 2.

[24]Horace Howard Furness Memorial Library, F.A. March, 9 July 1873, Easton, Pa., to H.H. Furness.

[25]The Folger Shakespeare Library, ALS, H.H. Furness, 3 January 1875, Philadelphia, to C.M. Ingleby.

[26]Edinburgh University Library, ALS, H.H. Furness, 23 June 1873, Philadelphia, to J.O. Halliwell-Phillipps.

[27]Cornell University Library, ALS, H.H. Furness, 10 October 1872, Philadelphia, to H. Corson.

[28]Edinburgh University Library, ALS, H.H. Furness, 16 April 1873, Philadelphia, to J.O. Halliwell-Phillipps.

[29]Edinburgh University Library, ALS, H.H. Furness, 23 June 1873, Philadelphia, to J.O. Halliwell-Phillipps.

[30]"Literary Notices," *North American and United States Gazette*, 30 May 1874.

[31]A.I. Fish, "Some Recent Helps in the Study of Shakespeare," *The Penn Monthly* 5 (December 1874): 882.

[32]The Furness Library, ALS, W.A. Wright, 28 July 1874, Trinity College, Cambridge, to H.H. Furness.

[33]Edinburgh University Library, ALS, H.K. Furness, 29 November 1874, Philadelphia, to J.O. Halliwell-Phillipps.

[34]J. Parker Norris, "Shakespearian Gossip," *The American Bibliopolist,* February 1875, p. 33.

[35]Cornell University Library, ALS, H.H. Furness, 30 April 1875, Philadelphia, to H. Corson.

[36]The Folger Shakespeare Library, ALS, H.H. Furness, 30 May 1875, Philadelphia, to C.M. Ingleby.

[37]The Folger Shakespeare Library, ALS, H.H. Furness, 25 June 1875, Philadelphia, to C.M. Ingleby.

[38]Ibid.

[39]The Folger Shakespeare Library, ALS, H.H. Furness, 13 October 1875, Philadelphia, to C.M. Ingleby.

[40]The Folger Shakespeare Library, ALS, H.H. Furness, 16 January 1876, Philadelphia, to C.M. Ingleby.

[41]The British Library, ALS, H.H. Furness, 3 June 1876, Philadelphia, to F.J. Furnivall.

[42]Ibid.

[43]The Folger Shakespeare Library, ALS, H.H. Furness, 3 September 1876, Lindenshade, to C.M. Ingleby.

[44]H.H. Furness, ed., *A New Variorum Edition of Shakespeare,* 4 vols. (Philadelphia: J.B. Lippincott & Co., 1877), vol. 3: *Hamlet,* pp. xi-xii.

[45]Horace Howard Furness Memorial Library, ALS, H. Ulrici, 30 October 1876, Halle, to H.H. Furness.

[46]Horace Howard Furness Memorial Library, ALS, August Freiherr von Loën, 30 November 1877, Weimar, to H.H. Furness.

[47]Horace Howard Furness Memorial Library, ALS, K. Elze, 27 January 1878, Halle, to H.H. Furness.

[48]Cornell University Library, ALS, H.H. Furness, 16 March 1877, Philadelphia, to H. Corson.

[49]The Folger Shakespeare Library, ALS, H.H. Furness 1 April 1877, Philadelphia, to C.M. Ingleby.

[50]The Folger Shakespeare Library, ALS, H.H. Furness, 12 December 1875, Philadelphia, to C.M. Ingleby.

[51]*Letters,* 1:191.

[52]*A New Variorum Edition of Shakespeare,* 3: ix.

[53]*Letters,* 1:340-41.

[54]Horace Howard Furness Memorial Library, ALS, C.W. Eliot, 18 July 1877, Cambridge, to H.H. Furness.

[55]*Letters,* 1:191-92.

[56]The Folger Shakespeare Library, ALS, H.H. Furness, 6 January 1878, Philadelphia, to C.M. Ingleby.

[57]The Folger Shakespeare Library, ALS, H.H. Furness, 1 April 1878, Philadelphia, to C.M. Ingleby.

[58]Martin Luther University of Halle-Wittenberg Archives, Faculty Minutes, Circular 12, 17 June 1877 (translation).

[59]Horace Howard Furness Memorial Library, ALS, K. Elze, 2 August 1878, Halle, to H.H. Furness.

[60]The Folger Shakespeare Library, ALS, H.H. Furness, 1 October 1878, Lindenshade, to J.P. Norris. Norris printed the citation in "Shakespearian Gossip," *The Epitome of Literature*, October 1878, p. 156.

[61]Martin Luther University of Halle-Wittenberg Archives, ALS, H.H. Furness, 21 September 1878, Philadelphia, to A.F. Pott.

[62]The Folger Shakespeare Library, ALS, H.H. Furness, 23 September 1878, Lindenshade, to C.M. Ingleby.

[63]James T. Fields and Edwin P. Whipple, eds., *The Family Library of British Poetry from Chaucer to the Present Time (1350-1878)*, (Boston: Houghton Osgood, and Company, 1878), p. iii.

[64]The Folger Shakespeare Library, ALS, H.H. Furness, 23 February 1879, Philadelphia, to C.M. Ingleby.

[65]The Folger Shakespeare Library, ALS, H.H. Furness, 10 December 1876, Philadelphia, to J.P. Norris.

[66]Horace Howard Furness Memorial Library, ALS, W.J. Rolfe, 17 March 1878, Cambridge, to H.H. Furness.

[67]Horace Howard Furness Memorial Library, ALS, W.J. Rolfe, 24 March 1878, Cambridge, to H.H. Furness.

[68]Horace Howard Furness Memorial Library, ALS, W.J. Rolfe, 23 June 1878, Cambridge, to H.H. Furness.

[69]New York Historical Society, ALI, H.H. Furness, 19 April 1880, Philadelphia, to R.G. White.

[70]Horace Howard Furness Memorial Library, ALS, J.P. Norris, 29 January 1880, Philadelphia, to H.H. Furness.

[71]The Folger Shakespeare Library, ALS, H.H. Furness, 21 December 1879, Philadelphia, to C.M. Ingleby.

[72]The Folger Shakespeare Library, ALI, H.H. Furness [August 1879], Lindenshade, to C.M. Ingleby.

[73]*A New Variorum Edition of Shakespeare*, 5:223.

[74]The Folger Shakespeare Library, ALS, H.H. Furness, 8 June 1880, Wallingford, to F.A. Kemble.

[75]The Folger Shakespeare Library, ALS, H.H. Furness, 12 February 1879, Philadelphia, to F.G. Fleay.

[76]Horace Howard Furness Memorial Library, ALS, F.J. Furnivall, 26 March 1880, London, to H.H. Furness.

[77]The Folger Shakespeare Library, ALS, H.H. Furness, 23 February 1879, Philadelphia, to C.M. Ingleby.

[78]New York Historical Society, ALI, H.H. Furness, 19 April 1880, Philadelphia, to R.G. White.

[79]Walter Hampden-Edwin Booth Memorial Theatre Library, ALS, H.H. Furness, 30 December 1878, to E. Booth.

[80]The Folger Shakespeare Library, ALS, H.H. Furness, 23 February 1879, Philadelphia, to C.M. Ingleby.

[81]*A New Variorum Edition of Shakespeare*, 5:v-vi.

[82]Horace Howard Furness Memorial Library, ALS, A. Carlyle, 10 April 1880, Chelsea, to H.H. Furness.

Notes
Man about Town

[1]The Folger Shakespeare Library, ALS, H.H. Furness, 12 December 1873, Philadelphia, to C.M. Ingleby.

[2]Horace Howard Furness Memorial Library, H.H. Furness, Journal, 4 May 1879.

[3]*Charter and By-Laws with List of Members of The Penn Club* (Privately Printed, 1 March 1890), p. 3.

[4]Charles J. Cohen, *History of the Penn Club* (Philadelphia, 1924), p. 105.

[5]American Philosophical Society, Minutes of the Fortnightly Club, p. 4.

[6]Hampton L. Carson, *The Centenary of the Wistar Party: An Historical Address* (Philadelphia: Printed for the Wistar Association, 1918), p. 26.

[7]Cornell University Library, ALS, H.H. Furness, 6 March 1878, Philadelphia, to B. Taylor.

[8]Horace Howard Furness Memorial Library, H.H. Furness, "History of 'The Triplets,'" unpublished typescript, pp. 1-2.

[9]Col. John W. Forney (1817-1881) founded both the Philadelphia *Press* and the Philadelphia weekly magazine *Progress* that often puffed and printed Walt Whitman.

[10]Horace Howard Furness Memorial Library, H.H. Furness, Journal, 16 March 1879.

[11]Somerset Record Office, ALS, H.H. Furness, 2 October 1892, Wallingford, to E. Strachey.

[12]Walt Whitman Collection (#3829-i), Clifton Waller Barrett Library, University of Virginia Library, ALS, H.H. Furness, 29 March 1892, to E. Gosse.

[13]Somerset Record Office, ALS, H.H. Furness, 1 July 1892, Wallingford, to E. Strachey.

[14]*Walt Whitman: The Correspondence*, ed. Edwin Haviland Miller, 6 vols. (New York: New York University Press, 1961-1969), 3 (1964): 150.

[15]Ibid., 5 (1969): 35.

[16]Horace Traubel, *With Walt Whitman in Camden*, 3 (New York: Rowman and Littlefield, Inc., 1961): 520.

[17]The Folger Shakespeare Library, ALS, H.H. Furness, 21 September 1885, Wallingford, to T. Donaldson.

[18]Pierpont Morgan Library, ALS, H.H. Furness, 24 November 1889, Wallingford, to S.W. Mitchell.

[19]William R. Thayer, "Personal Recollections of Walt Whitman," *Scribner's Magazine* 65 (1919): 685.

[20]University of Leeds Library, ALS, H.H. Furness, 20 July 1899, Wallingford, to E. Gosse.

[21]The Folger Shakespeare Library, ALS, H.H. Furness, 30 January 1875, Philadelphia, to C.M. Ingleby.

[22]Cornell University Library, ALS, H.H. Furness, 27 February 1876, Philadelphia, to B. Taylor; and Bayard Taylor, 1 March 1876, New York, to H.H. Furness.

[23] The Folger Shakespeare Library, ALS, H.H. Furness, 1 March 1877, Philadelphia, to J.P. Norris.

[24]Horace Howard Furness Memorial Library, H.H. Furness, Journal, 3 March 1878.

[25]The Folger Shakespere Library, ALS, H.H. Furness, 12 December 1873, Philadelphia, to C.M. Ingleby.

[26]Horace Howard Furness Memorial Library, H.H. Furness, Journal, 3 November 1878.

[27]The Folger Shakespeare Library, ALS, H.H. Furness, 28 February 1875,to C.M. Ingleby.

[28]Horace Howard Furness Memorial Library, H.H. Furness, Journal, 18 August 1875.

[29]Horace Howard Furness Memorial Library, Journal, 12 May 1878.

[30]Horace Howard Furness Memorial Library, Journal, 15 October 1876.

[31]New York Historical Society, ALS, H.H. Furness, [1880], Philadelphia, to R.G. White.

[32]Horace Howard Furness Memorial Library, H.H. Furness, Journal, 1 July 1876.

[33]The Folger Shakespeare Library, ALS, H.H. Furness, February 1880, Philadelphia, to C.M. Ingleby.

[34]The Folger Shakespeare Library, ALS, H.H. Furness, 19 April 1880, Philadelphia, to C.M. Ingleby.

[35]Calvin B. Knerr was the son-in-law and associate of Constantine Hering, founder in 1867 of the Hahnemann Medical College in Philadelphia, named after the founder of homeopathy, Samuel Hahnemann. Furness believed so firmly in homeopathic medicine that he wrote the article on the subject for the *Supplement to the Encyclopaedia Britannica*, 9th edition, in 1886.

[36]The Folger Shakespeare Library, ALS, H.H. Furness, 8 June 1880, Wallingford, to F. Kemble.

[37]Horace Howard Furness Memorial Library, ALS, J.O. Halliwell-Phillipps, 25 March 1880, Brighton, to H.H. Furness.

[38]The Folger Shakespeare Library, ALS, H.H. Furness, 19 April 1880, Philadelphia, to C.M. Ingleby.

[39]Edinburgh University Library, ALS, H.H. Furness, 30 May 1880, Philadelphia, to J.O. Halliwell-Phillipps.

[40]New York Historical Society, ALS, H.H. Furness, 15 June 1880, to R.G. White.

[41]The Folger Shakespeare Library, ALS, H.H. Furness, 31 July 1880, Fenton's Hotel, London, to C.M. Ingleby.

[42]The Folger Shakespeare Library, ALS, H.H. Furness, 24 January 1881, Philadelphia, to C.M. Ingleby.

[43]Trinity College, Cambridge, ALS, H.H. Furness, 24 January 1881, Philadelphia, to F.J. Furnivall.

Notes
The Penn Years

[1]The Folger Shakespeare Library, ALS, H.H. Furness, 30 April 1881, Philadelphia, to J.P. Collier.

[2]*Letters*, 1:194.

[3]The Folger Shakespeare Library, ALS, H.H. Furness, 8 August 1881, Wallingford, to J.P. Norris.

[4]The Folger Shakespeare Library, ALS, H.H. Furness, 12 September 1881, Wallingford, to C.M. Ingleby.

[5]Cornell University Library, ALS, H.H. Furness, 28 November 1881, Wallingford, to H. Corson.

[6]Edinburgh University Library, ALS, H.H. Furness, 30 December 1881, Philadelphia, to J.O. Halliwell-Phillipps.

[7]Horace Howard Furness Memorial Library, ALS, H.N. Hudson, 14 May 1881, Cambridgeport, to H.H. Furness.

[8]The Folger Shakespeare Library, ALS, H.H. Furness, 8 November 1882, to C.M. Ingleby.

[9]The Folger Shakespeare Library, ALS, H.H. Furness, 2 September 1883, Philadelphia, to C.M. Ingleby.

[10]Horace Howard Furness Memorial Library, ALS, W.A. Wright, 16 December 1883, Trinity College, Cambridge, to H.H. Furness.

[11]"Miscellany," *Shakespeariana* 1(December 1883): 64.

[12]Furness Family Letters, ALS, H.H. Furness, 24 July 1884 and 28 July 1884, Cape May, to W.R. Furness.

[13]Horace Howard Furness Memorial Library, ALS, H.H. Furness, 30 October 1884, Philadelphia, to H.H. Furness, Jr. and W.H. Furness, III.

[14]Robert Browning, "Prospice," in *The Works of Robert Browning*, The Centenary Edition (London: Smith Elder & Co., 1912), 4: 306.

[15]University of Leeds Library, ALS, H.H. Furness, 24 May 1885, Philadelphia, to E. Gosse.

[16]Colorado College Library, ALS, H.H. Furness, 19 May 1884, Philadelphia, to Dr. Caldwell.

[17]Colorado College Library, ALS, H.H. Furness, 28 November 1884, Philadelphia, to Dr. Caldwell.

[18]Tulane University Library, ALS, H.H. Furness, [3 April 1884], Philadelphia, to W.J. Rolfe.

[19]Cornell University Library , ALS, H.H. Furness, 4 February 1885, Philadelphia, to H. Corson.

[20]Massachusetts Historical Society, ALS, H.H. Furness, 5 March 1885, Philadelphia, to J.C. Bancroft.

[21]Cornell University Library, ALS, H.H. Furness, 1 October 1884, Wallingford, to H. Corson.

[22]Horace Howard Furness Memorial Library, ALS, H.H. Furness, [26 October 1884], Philadelphia, to H.H. Furness, Jr. and W.H. Furness, III.

[23]Cornell University Library, ALS, H.H. Furness, 29 December 1884, to H. Corson.

[24]*Preliminary Report of the Seybert Commission for Investigating Modern Spiritualism* (Philadelphia: J.B. Lippincott Company, 1887), p. 150.

[25]*Letters*, 1:250.

[26]Horace Howard Furness Memorial Library, ALS, H.H. Furness, 9 November 1884, Philadelphia, to H.H. Furness, Jr., and W.H. Furness, III.

[27]Horace Howard Furness Memorial Library, ALS, H.H. Furness, 30 November 1884, Philadelphia, to H.H. Furness, Jr. and W.H. Furness, III.

[28]*Preliminary Report*, p. 27.

[29]Ibid., p. 146.

[30]Ibid., p. 155.

[31]A.B. Richmond, *What I Saw at Cassadaga Lake: a Review of the Seybert Commissioners' Report*, 2nd edition (Boston: Colby & Rich, Publishers, 1888), p. 31.

[32]*Letters*, 1:347.

[33]University of Pennsylvania Archives, Library Committee Report, H.H. Furness, [December 1883], to University of Pennsylvania Trustees.

[34]University of Pennsylvania Archives, Library Committee Report, H.H. Furness, 2 November 1886, to University of Pennsylvania Trustees.

[35]University of Pennsylvania Archives, Library Committee Report, H.H. Furness, 6 December 1886, to University of Pennsylvania Trustees.

[36]"The Laying of the Corner-Stone of the Library Building," *The Pennsylvanian*, 17 October 1888, p. 105.

[37]"University of Pennsylvania," *The Keystone*, 3 November 1888.

[38]The Folger Shakespeare Library, ALS, H.H. Furness, [February 1899], Wallingford, to M. Conway.

[39]"English in the High School," *Modern Language Notes* 1(November 1886): 109.

[40]Ibid.

[41]University of Pennsylvania Archives, ALS, H.H. Furness, 21 December [1890], Philadelphia, to W. Pepper.

[42]University of Pennsylvania Archives, ALS, H.H. Furness, 10 February 1891, Philadelphia, to W. Pepper.

[43]Horace Howard Furness Memorial Library, ALS, H.H. Furness, 7 November 1890, Wallingford, to F. Schelling.

[44]"Dr. Furness' Readings," *The Pennsylvanian*, 14 March 1893, p. 1.

[45]"Notes and News," *Poet-Lore* 1(June 1899): 249-50.

[46]*Letters*, 1:285.

[47]University of Leeds, ALS, H.H. Furness, 22 March 1885, Philadelphia, to E. Gosse.

[48]Horace Howard Furness Memorial Library, ALS, H.N. Hudson, 29 April 1885, Cambridgeport, to H.H. Furness.

[49]Horace Howard Furness Memorial Library, ALS, H.H. Furness, 15 June 1885, Wallingford, to H.H. Furness, Jr. and W.H. Furness, III.

[50]The Folger Shakespeare Library, ALS, H.H. Furness, 17 October 1885, Wallingford, to M. Handy.

[51]Horace Howard Furness Memorial Library, ALS, H.H. Furness, 18 October 1885, Wallingford, to W. Wright.

[52]University of Leeds, ALS, H.H. Furness, [March 1886], Philadelphia, to E. Gosse.

Notes
The Variorum Resumes
(1886–1901)

[1]*Letters*, 2:49.

[2]Folger Shakespeare Library, ALS, H.H. Furness, 24 November 1889, Wallingford, to F.A. Leo.

[3]*Letters*, 2:242-43.

[4]Horace Howard Furness Memorial Library, ALS, H.H. Furness, 25 August 1895, Wallingford, to W.A. Wright.

[5]Harvard University Library, ALS, H.H. Furness, 5 March 1898, Wallingford, to C.E. Norton.

[6]Cornell University Library, ALS, H.H. Furness, 18 October 1901, Wallingford, to H. Corson.

[7]University of Leeds Library, ALS, H.H. Furness, 2 April [1905], Wallingford, to E. Gosse.

[8]The Folger Shakespeare Library, ALS, H.H. Furness, 24 November 1889, Wallingford, to F.G. Fleay.

[9]*Letters*, 1:342-43.

[10]Horace Howard Furness Memorial Library, ALS, M. Cowden Clarke, 13 May 1895, Genoa, to H.H. Furness.

[11]Samuel Johnson, *Proposals* (1756), 3, as quoted by F.P. Wilson, *Shakespeare and the New Bibliography,* Revised and edited by Helen Gardner (Oxford: The Clarendon Press, 1970), p. 11

[12]Wilson, *op. cit.*, pp. 97-98.

[13]J.O. Halliwell-Phillipps, *Outlines of the Life of Shakespeare*, 7th ed., (1887), 1:289-92, 295.

[14]New York Historical Society, ALS, H.H. Furness, 15 June 1880, Wallingford, to R.G. White.

[15]*A New Variorum Edition of Shakespeare. Othello*, edited by Horace Howard Furness (Philadelphia: J.B. Lippincott Company, 1886), pp. v-vi.

[16]"A New Edition of Shakespeare," *The Saturday Review*, 15 June 1895, pp. 794-95.

[17]Joseph Knight, "Drama," *The Athenaeum*, 21 August 1886, p. 250.

[18]George Lyman Kittredge, "The Variorum Midsummer Night's Dream," *The Nation*, 1 August 1895, p. 84.

[19]Horace Howard Furness Memorial Library, ALS, W.J. Rolfe, 14 April 1886, Cambridgeport, to H.H. Furness.

[20]*Letters*, 2:14-15.

[21]*A New Variorum Edition of Shakespeare. A Midsommer Nights Dreame*, edited by Horace Howard Furness (Philadelphia: J.B. Lippincott Company, 1895), pp. xxi-xxii.

[22]W.W. Greg, *The Library*, 4th ser., 4 (1924): 217.

[23]*A New Variorum Edition of Shakespeare. The Tempest*, edited by Horace Howard Furness (Philadelphia: J.B. Lippincott Company, 1892), p. viii.

[24]"Furness's Twelfth Night," *The Nation*, 30 January 1902, p. 95.

[25]*A New Variorum Edition of Shakespeare. The Winter's Tale*, edited by Horace Howard Furness (Philadelphia: J.B. Lippincott Company, 1898), p. 86.

[26]Ibid., p. 141.

[27]*A New Variorum Edition of Shakespeare. Othello*, p. 462.

[28]Cornell University Library, ALS, H.H. Furness, 2 October 1885, Wallingford, to H. Corson.

[29]*Letters*, 1:339.

[30]Horace Howard Furness Memorial Library, ALS, E. Gosse, 1 May 1895, London, to H.H. Furness.

[31]Horace Howard Furness Memorial Library, ALS, J.F. Kirk, 21 March [1892], Germantown, to H.H. Furness.

[32]Horace Howard Furness Memorial Library, ALS, F.J. Furnivall, 28 March 1892, London, to H.H. Furness.

[33]"Notes on Books," *Notes and Queries*, 30 July 1892, p. 99.

[34]"The Shakespeare Year," *Birmingham Daily Post and Journal*, 23 April 1890.

[35]Henry Austin Clapp, "Dr. Furness's Variorum Edition of Shakespeare," *The Atlantic Monthly*, July 1900, p. 127.

[36]*A New Variorum Edition of Shakespeare. The Merchant of Venice*, edited by Horace Howard Furness (Philadelphia: J.B. Lippincott Company, 1888), p. 73.

[37]*Letters*, 2:100-01.

[38]New York Public Library, ALS, H.H. Furness, 7 April 1910, Wallingford, to R.U. Johnson.

[39]Library of Congress, ALS, H.H. Furness, 11 October 1899, Wallingford, to O. Wister.

[40]The Folger Shakespeare Library, ALS, H.H. Furness, [May 1877], Philadelphia, to F.G. Fleay.

[41]H.H. Furness, "Review of *Outlines of the Life of Shakespeare*," *The Nation*, 7 December 1882, p. 491.

[42]*A New Variorum Edition of Shakespeare. As You Like It*, edited by Horace Howard Furness (Philadelphia: J.B. Lippincott Company, 1890), p. viii.

[43]*A New Variorum Edition of Shakespeare. A Midsommer Nights Dreame*, pp. xx-xxi.

[44]Edward E. Hale, "Our Shakespearian Scholar," *The Dial*, 1 October 1895, p. 177.

[45]Horace Howard Furness Memorial Library, ALS, F.J. Furnivall, 25 April 1895, London, to H.H. Furness.

[46]"A New Edition of Shakespeare," *The Saturday Review*, 15 June 1895, p. 795.

[47]*A New Variorum Edition of Shakespeare. Much Adoe About Nothing*, edited by Horace Howard Furness (Philadelphia: J.B. Lippincott Company, 1899), pp. xxviii-xxix.

[48]William Allan Neilson, "The Variorum Twelfth Night," *The Atlantic Monthly*, May 1902, pp. 715-16.

[49]Horace Howard Furness Memorial Library, ALS, W.J. Rolfe, 16 October 1901, Cambridgeport, to H.H. Furness.

[50]Horace Howard Furness Memorial Library, ALS, F.J. Furnivall, 31 October 1901, London, to H.H. Furness.

[51]Somerset Record Office, ALS, H.H. Furness, 26 April 1895, Wallingford, to E. Strachey.

[52]New York Historical Society, ALS, H.H. Furness, 5 December 1885, Philadelphia, to Mrs. R.G. White.

[53]Horace Howard Furness Memorial Library, ALS, W.J. Rolfe, 14 April 1886, Cambridgeport, to H.H. Furness.

[54]The Folger Shakespeare Library, ALS, H.H. Furness, 11 June 1887, Wallingford, to J.O. Halliwell-Phillipps.

[55]Horace Howard Furness Memorial Library, ALS, J.O. Halliwell-Phillipps, 23 July 1888, Brighton, to H.H. Furness.

[56]Cornell University Library, ALS, H.H. Furness, 31 March 1889, Philadelphia, to H. Corson.

[57]The Folger Shakespeare Library, ALS, H.H. Furness, 28 April, 1889, Philadelphia, to F.A. Leo.

[58]*Letters*, 2:55-56.

[59]The Folger Shakespeare Library, ALS, H.H. Furness, 25 July 1894, Wallingford, to E. Folger.

[60]The Folger Shakespeare Library, ALS, H.H. Furness, 12 June 1896, Wallingford, to E. Folger.

[61]Edwina Booth Grossmann, ed. *Edwin Booth: Recollections by His Daughter Edwina Booth Grossmann and Letters to Her and to Her Friends* (New York: The Century Company, 1894), pp. 54-55.

[62]Horace Howard Furness Memorial Library, ALS, H.H. Furness, 19 April 1885, Philadelphia, to H.H. Furness, Jr. and W.H. Furness, III.

[63]Grossmann, *Edwin Booth*, p. 55.

[64]Ibid., pp. 256-57.

[65]Ibid., pp. 268-69.

[66]Charlotte Porter, "Reviews: A New Variorum Edition of Shakespeare," *Shakespeariana* 5(July 1888): 320.

[67]Horace Howard Furness Memorial Library, ALS, L. Barrett, 14 June 1888, New York, to H.H. Furness.

[68]*Letters*, 1:338-39.

[69]Horace Howard Furness Memorial Library, ALS, H.H. Furness, 15 February 1885, Philadelphia, to H.H. Furness, Jr. and W.H. Furness, III.

[70]Horace Howard Furness Memorial Library, ALS, H.H. Furness, 18 January 1885, Philadelphia, to H.H. Furness, Jr., and W.H. Furness, III.

[71]Ellen Terry, *The Story of My Life: Recollections and Reflections* (New York: The McClure Company, 1908), p. 323.

[72]Horace Howard Furness Memorial Library, ALS, E. Terry, 7 March 1901, Boston, to H.H. Furness.

[73]The Folger Shakespeare Library, ALS, H.H. Furness, 22 June 1884, Wallingford, to A. Daly.

[74]The Folger Shakespeare Library, ALS, H.H. Furness, 23 January 1890, Philadelphia, to A. Daly.

[75]Horace Howard Furness Memorial Library, ALS, A. Daly, 22 March 1892, New York, to H.H. Furness.

[76]The Folger Shakespeare Library, ALS, H.H. Furness, 27 January 1893, Philadelphia, to A. Daly.

[77]The Folger Shakespeare Library, ALS, H.H. Furness, 29 January 1894, Philadelphia, to A. Daly.

[78]The Folger Shakespeare Library, ALS, H.H. Furness, 12 April 1896, Pine Island, Florida, to A. Daly.

[79]University of Pennsylvania Library, copy of letter from H.H. Furness, 11 October 1896, Wallingford, to A. Rehan, in the hand of the latter.

[80]The Folger Shakespeare Library, ALS, H.H. Furness, 6 October 1898, Wallingford, to A. Daly.

[81]*Letters*, 1:351.

[82]*Letters*, 2:94.

[83]"New Theater Gives Dr. Furness a Medal," *The North American*, 13 April 1910.

[84]"Commencement," *The Harvard Graduates' Magazine* 3(September 1894): 55.

[85]*The Record of the Celebration of the Two Hundreth Anniversary of the Founding of Yale College, Held at Yale University, in New Haven, Connecticut, October the Twentieth to October the Twenty-Third, A.D. Nineteen Hundred and One* (New Haven: Published by the University, 1902), p. 401.

[86]The Folger Shakespeare Library, ALS, H.H. Furness, 18 June 1899, London, to H.C. Folger.

[87]The Historical Society of Pennsylvania, ALS, H.H. Furness, 24 July 1899, Wallingford, to S.B. Wister.

Notes
The Public Years

[1]University of Pennsylvania Library, ALS, H.H. Furness, 22 December [1892] to H.C. Lea.

[2]The Folger Shakespeare Library, ALS, H.H. Furness, 6 February 1893, Philadelphia, to A. Daly.

[3]Francis Newton Thorpe, ed., "Letters of Horace Howard Furness," *Lippincott's Magazine*, April 1914, p. 449.

[4]Johns Hopkins University Library, ALS, H.H. Furness, 16 October 1893, Wallingford, to Dr. Gilman.

[5]American Antiquarian Society, ALS, H.H. Furness, 10 February 1889, Philadelphia, to D.C. Heath & Co.

[6]*Letters*, 1:310.

[7]Ibid., pp. 315-16.

[8]*Public Ledger*, 30 March 1898.

[9]*Letters*, 2:64-65.

[10]Ibid., 1:343.

[11]Agnes Repplier, *Agnes Irwin: A Biography* (Garden City, New York: Doubleday, Doran & Co., 1934), pp. 46-47.

[12]Ibid., pp. 38-39.

[13]Anna Robeson Burr, *Weir Mitchell: His Life and Letters* (New York: Duffield and Company, 1929), p. 354.

[14]Silas Weir Mitchell, *The Complete Poems* (New York, 1914), pp. 362-63. For a comparison of the three versions of this poem, see my article "S. Weir Mitchell and the Germination of a Poem," *The Library Chronicle* 41 (Winter 1977):180-85.

[15]William Croswell Doane, "'Αριστον μὲν ὕδωρ (To Dr. Furness, After hearing Him Read a Play of Shakespeare)" *The Critic*, 3 October 1896, p. 195.

[16]Horace Howard Furness Memorial Library, ALS, H.H. Furness, 30 December 1900, to W.A. Wright.

[17]Bryn Mawr College Library, ALS, H.H. Furness, 14 January [1905] to H.E. Allen.

[18]*Letters*, 2:130-31.

[19]Horace Howard Furness Memorial Library, ALS, H.H. Furness, 31 October 1894, Wallingford, to W.A. Wright.

[20]Trinity College (Hartford) Library, ALS, H.H. Furness, 7 July 1895, Wallingford, to D. Macdonald.

[21]Trinity College (Hartford) Library, ALS, H.H. Furness, 18 July 1895, Wallingford, to D. Macdonald.

[22]Trinity College (Hartford) Library, ALS, H.H. Furness, 28 July 1895, Wallingford, to D. Macdonald.

[23]Ibid.

[24]Trinity College (Hartford) Library, ALS, H.H. Furness, 18 July 1895, Wallingford, to D. Macdonald.

[25]Trinity College (Hartford) Library, ALS, H.H. Furness, 8 September 1895, to D. Macdonald.

[26]*The Book of Psalms: A New English Translation* (New York: Dodd, Mead, and Company, 1898), pp. 78-79.

[27]Horace Howard Furness Memorial Library, ALS, W.A. Wright, 9 April 1896, Beccles, Suffolk, to H.H.F.

[28]*Letters*, 1:308.

[29]Ibid., p. 313.

[30]Horace Howard Furness Memorial Library, ALS, H.H. Furness, 12 May 1897, Wallingford, to W.A. Wright.

[31]Horace Howard Furness Memorial Library, ALS, H.H. Furness, 18 January 1898, Wallingford, to W.A. Wright.

[32]Horace Howard Furness Memorial Library, ALS, H.H. Furness, 18 December 1898, Wallingford, to W.A. Wright.

[33]Horace Howard Furness Memorial Library, ALS, W.A. Wright, 31 March 1899, Beccles, Suffolk, to H.H. Furness.

[34]*Letters*, 2:63-64.

[35]Ibid., p. 15.

[36]*University of Pennsylvania Commencement, 7 June 1894. Address by Horace Howard Furness. Delivered at the Request of His Co-Trustees, in*

Accordance with a Resolution Passed At a Trustees' Meeting When the Provost's Resignation Was Accepted. (Philadelphia, 1894), p. 4.

[37]*Letters,* 2:24-25.

[38]"The Philadelphia Philological Congress," *The Critic,* 11 January 1895, p. 23.

[39]Harvard University Library, ALS, H.H. Furness, [8 June 1908], Wallingford, to C.E. Norton.

[40]*University of Pennsylvania: Proceedings of "University Day" February 22, 1902* (Philadelphia: Published by the University, 1902), p. 5.

[41]Ibid., p. 7.

[42]*The Philadelphia Press,* 22 February 1903.

[43]"Dr. Furness' Oration," *The Alumni Register* 7 (July 1903): 453-67.

[44]Harvard University Library, ALS, H.H. Furness, 29 January 1908, Wallingford to C.E. Norton.

[45]"On Shakespeare, 'Or, What You Will,'" *The Harvard Graduates' Magazine,* September 1908, pp. 1-25.

[46]*Letters,* 2:173.

[47]Horace Howard Furness Memorial Library, untitled autograph speech presented at the Pennsylvania Academy of Fine Arts, 23 February 1905.

[48]*Letters,* 2:124.

[49]Ibid., pp. 127-29.

[50]Swarthmore College Library, ALS, H.H. Furness, 8 September 1911, Wallingford, to I.H. Clothier.

Notes
The Final Variorums
(1904–1912)

[1]*Letters*, 2:67-68.

[2]Horace Howard Furness Memorial Library, ALS, H.H. Furness, 16 January 1902, Wallingford, to W.A. Wright.

[3]*Letters*, 2:91-92.

[4]Ibid., p. 101.

[5]Ibid., p. 107.

[6]Horace Howard Furness Memorial Library, ALS, H.H. Furness, 13 July [1905] Paris, to W.A. Wright.

[7]The Historical Society of Pennsylvania, ALS, H.H. Furness, 8 August [1905], Wallingford to S.B. Wister.

[8]Horace Howard Furness Memorial Library, ALS, H.H. Furness [28 March 1906], Wallingford, to W. Wright.

[9]Horace Howard Furness Memorial Library, ALS, H.H. Furness, 29 June [1907] Wallingford, to W. Wright.

[10]Harvard University Library, ALS, H.H. Furness, Friday [19 June 1908], Wallingford, to C.E. Norton.

[11]Harvard University Library, ALS, H.H. Furness, Monday [6 July 1908], Wallingford to C.E. Norton.

[12]Harvard University Library, ALS, H.H. Furness, 16 October [1908], Wallingford, to C.E. Norton.

[13]University of Leeds, ALS, H.H. Furness, 2 November [1908], Wallingford, to E. Gosse.

[14]Horace Howard Furness Memorial Library, ALS, H.H. Furness, 15 November [1908], Wallingford, to W. Wright.

[15]Horace Howard Furness Memorial Library, ALS, W. Wright, 9 July 1909, Trinity College, Cambridge, to H.H. Furness.

[16]Cornell University Library, ALS, H.H. Furness, 6 January [1903], Wallingford, to H. Corson.

[17]Furness Family Letters, ALS, H.H. Furness, 30 January [1910], Wallingford, to W.R. Furness.

[18]*Letters*, 2:253.

[19]*Letters*, 2:277-78.

[20]*A New Variorum Edition of Shakespeare: The Tragedie of Anthonie, and Cleopatra*. Edited by Horace Howard Furness (Philadelphia: J.B. Lippincott Company, 1907), p. 78.

[21]Harvard University Library, ALS, H.H. Furness, 7 January [1908], Wallingford, to C.E. Norton.

[22]Montgomery Schuyler, "Furness's Latest 'Variorum' Volume," *The New York Times Saturday Review of Books*, 1 February 1908, p. 59.

[23]"Writers and Books," *Boston Evening Transcript*, 16 October 1907.

[24]William Allan Neilson, "The Variorum Antony and Cleopatra," *The Atlantic Monthly*, March 1908, p. 424.

[25]Samuel A. Tannenbaum, "The Variorum 'Cymbeline'" *The Dial*, March 1, 1914, p. 184.

[26]Joseph Quincy Adams, "A New Variorum Edition of Shakespeare. The Tragedie of Cymbeline." *Journal of English and Germanic Philology* 14 (1915): 308.

[27]"Drama," *The Nation*, 17 October 1907, p. 356.

[28]Library of Congress, ALS, H.H. Furness, 1 April 1910, Wallingford, to O. Wister.

[29]*A New Variorum Edition of Shakespeare: The Tragedie of Cymbeline*. Edited by Horace Howard Furness (Philadelphia: J.B. Lippincott Company, 1913), p. vii.

[30]*Letters*, 1:245-46.

[31]*The New Variorum Edition of Shakespeare: The Tragedie of Anthonie, and Cleopatra*. Edited by Horace Howard Furness (Philadelphia: J.B. Lippincott Company, 1907), pp. xi-xii.

[32]Ibid., pp. xiii-xiv.

[33]William Allan Neilson, "The Variorum Antony and Cleopatra," *The Atlantic Monthly*, March 1908, p. 427.

[34]*Daily Post & Mercury*, 2 October 1907.

[35]"Writers and Books," *Boston Evening Transcript*, 16 October 1907.

[36]"Shakespeare To-Day," *The Outlook*, 19 October 1907, pp. 329-30.

[37]"Dr. Furness Eulogized," *Public Ledger*, 20 November 1909.

[38]*Year Book of the Pennsylvania Society* 11 (1910): 29.

[39]Brander Matthews, "The American Academy of Arts and Letters," *The Outlook*, 27 November 1909, p. 690.

[40]"Gaynor Receives Savants," *Public Ledger*, 9 December 1910.

[41]"The American Academy," *Public Ledger*, 11 December 1910, sec. 1, p. 10.

[42]Columbia University Library, ALS, H.H. Furness, 12 January [1905], Wallingford, to E.C. Stedman.

[43]*Book of the Franklin Inn Club* (Philadelphia, 1914), p. 3.

[44]*Letters*, 2:230.

[45]Graham Price, "An Hour at Lindenshade with Dr. Horace Howard Furness," *Sine Nomine*, 15 June 1912, p. 13.

[46]*Letters*, 1:336.

[47]Columbia University Library, ALS, H.H. Furness, 14 October [1900], Wallingford, to E. Stedman.

[48]The Furness Collection of Horace, now numbering 565 editions and 235 critical works, is located in the Wahlert Memorial Library at Loras College in Dubuque, Iowa.

[49]*Letters*, 1:322-24.

[50]Horace Howard Furness Memorial Library, unpublished typescript, Harrison Morris, "Horace Howard Furness: A Half-Length Portrait," 19 May 1917.

[51]Owen Wister, "Horace Howard Furness," *Harvard Graduates' Magazine*, December 1912, p. 206.

[52]S. Weir Mitchell, *Dr. North and His Friends* (New York: Century Co., 1900).

[53]Ibid., p. 364.

[54]*Letters*, 1:312-13.

[55]George Stewart Stokes, *Agnes Repplier: Lady of Letters* (Philadelphia: University of Pennsylvania Press, 1949), p. 135.

[56]Ibid., p. 136.

[57]University of Leeds, ALS, H.H. Furness, 10 July 1887, Wallingford, to E. Gosse.

[58]Horace Howard Furness Memorial Library, ALS, H.H. Furness, 3 May 1896, Wallingford, to W. Wright.

[59]*Letters*, 2:3.

[60]Ibid., pp. 6-7.

[61]Columbia University Library, ALI, H.H. Furness, 1 February [1902], to E. Stedman.

[62]Horace Howard Furness Memorial Library, ALS, H.H. Furness, 29 June 1898, Wallingford, to W. Wright.

[63]Horace Howard Furness Memorial Library, TLS, W. Wright, Trinity College, Cambridge, 25 June 1901, to H. Furness.

[64]Horace Howard Furness Memorial Library, ALS, A. Lang, 8 June 1902, St. Andrews, to H. Furness.

[65]Horace Howard Furness Memorial Library, ALS, A. Lang, 16 February 1905, St. Andrews, to H. Furness.

[66]Horace Howard Furness Memorial Library, ALS, H.H. Furness, [9 July 1906], Wallingford, to W. Wright.

[67]*Letters*, 2:191.

[68]Samuel C. Chew, "To the Editor of the Nation," *The Nation*, 29 August 1912, p. 189.

[69]*Letters*, 2:206-07.

[70]Library of Congress, ALS, H.H.F., July [1912] Wallingford, to W. Wister.

[71]Notre Dame University Library, ALS, H.H. Furness, 5 April, Wallingford, to Mrs. Immen.

Notes
Epilogue

[1]*Letters*, 2:102.

[2]Philadelphia City Hall, Register of Wills, Will 1912, no. 1889, p. 8.

[3]Shakspere Society of Philadelphia, Minutes, V, 23 May 1930.

[4]"Franklin Birthday at Franklin Inn," *The Public Ledger*, 18 January 1911.

[5]"The Changing Drama," *The Nation*, 3 July 1920, p. 18.

[6]H.H. Furness, Jr., *The Gloss of Youth: An Imaginary Episode in the Lives of William Shakespeare and John Fletcher* (Philadelphia: J.B. Lippincott Company, 1920).

[7]"Dr. H.H. Furness Pneumonia Victim," *The Public Ledger*, 16 April 1930, p. 8.

[8]*The New Variorum Edition of Shakespeare: The Tragedie of Macbeth*. revised edtion by H.H. Furness, Jr. (Philadelphia: J.B. Lippincott Company, 1903), p. xiii.

[9]Talcott Williams, "Horace Howard Furness," *The Outlook*, 6 December 1902, p. 811.

[10]Horace Howard Furness Memorial Library, ALS, W.J. Rolfe, 9 March 1903, Cambridgeport, to H.H. Furness.

[11]Horace Howard Furness Memorial Library, ALS, W.J. Rolfe, 31 March 1903, Cambridgeport, to H.H. Furness.

[12]*Dictionary of American Biography*, 1st ed., s.v. "Furness, Horace Howard."

[13]M.A. Shaaber, "The Furness Variorum Shakespeare," *Proceedings of the American Philosophical Society*, 75(1935): 283.

[14]Boston University Library, ALS, H.H. Furness, Jr., 17 February [1930], Philadelphia, to Bessie.

Index

301

Fortnightly Club, 112, 115. *See also* Wistar Association.
Fraley, Frederick, 139
Franklin, Benjamin, 149, 222–23, 260
Franklin Inn Club, 203, 240–41, 259–61
Franklin Institute, 259
Frye, Roland Mushat, 264
Fullerton, George, 139
Furnace. *See* Furness.
Furnass. *See* Furness.
Furness, Ann Hurd, 3–4
Furness, Annis Lee, 6, 11, 31, 55, 122, 125, 141, 144, 164, 170, 173, 188, 199, 201–04, 212–13, 215, 221, 226–31, 245–48, 250–54
Furness, Annis Pulling, 5–6, 53, 121, 125, 159
Furness, Caroline Augusta, 92, 121, 125, 128–30, 135, 140–41, 208, 222, 231, 244–46, 250, 253–54, 263
Furness, Elizabeth Milliken, 3
Furness, Fairman Rogers, 24
Furness, Fanny Fassitt, 55
Furness, Frank, 4, 6, 31, 47, 52, 55, 111, 116, 118, 122–23, 125, 141, 146, 221, 249, 255
Furness, Hannah, 55
Furness, Helen Bullitt, 208
Furness, Helen Kate, 41, 50, 53–54, 56, 78, 81, 91–93, 96, 120, 125, 127–39, 144–45, 162–63, 173, 185, 197, 208, 227, 230, 250; *Concordance to Shakespeare's Poems,* 91–93, 137; death of, 134–36; Helen Kate Furness Prize, 136–37
Furness, Horace Howard
deafness, 47, 126–27, 247; education, 11–12, 21–31; editorial method, 164–74, 232–34; honorary degrees, 101–04, 159, 196; law career, 41–56, 126, 238–39; New Variorum Edition of Shakespeare. *See* individual plays; public speaking, 147–48, 214–224; reader of Shakespeare, 156–58, 198–207, 227, 240; tarpon fishing, 250–53
Furness, Horace Howard, Jr., 120–23, 125, 128–30, 133, 135, 138, 150, 186, 189, 195, 208, 235, 242, 244–46, 250, 257–63
Furness, James Thwing, 4, 6, 43, 52, 102, 122

Furness, John, 3–4
Furness, John Mason, 3
Furness, Jonathan, 3
Furness, Louise Brooks Winsor, 208, 246, 250, 263
Furness, Mary Ann, 6
Furness, Nathaniel Hurd, 4
Furness, Rebecca Thwing, 4–5
Furness, Sara Jenks, 5
Furness, Walter Rogers, 54, 99, 106, 120–23, 125, 128–30, 135, 138, 208, 231, 245–46, 251–53, 263
Furness, William, 4, 5
Furness, William Henry, 4, 7–8, 10, 12, 15–20, 31, 41–46, 53–55, 82–83, 95, 97, 111, 118, 121, 125, 141, 157, 159, 221–22, 230
Furness, William Henry, Jr., 4, 6, 9–10, 31–33, 36, 43, 55, 58, 241
Furness, William Henry, III, 54–55, 102, 120–23, 125, 128–30, 133, 135, 138, 186, 189, 195, 231, 241, 245–46, 250, 253, 263
Furnivall, Frederick James, 89–91, 96, 108, 110, 129–30, 159, 174, 176, 179, 181, 183, 227, 254

Garrick, David, 81–82, 193, 242
Garrison, William Lloyd, 16–19, 53–54
Gilder, Richard Watson, 118, 223, 240, 254
Gillespie, Elizabeth Duane, 218
Gladstone, William, 110
Gloves, Shakespeare's, 81–82, 88
Goodwin, William Watson, 122, 254
Gosse, Edmund, 114–15, 117, 119, 136, 158–60, 163, 173, 184, 227, 243, 250, 252
Grace Auchester, 245–46
Greet, Ben, 195
Greg, W. W., 166, 171
Greville, Madame Henri, 114

Hale, Edward, 179
Halliwell-Phillipps, James Orchard, 62–67, 79, 82–83, 85, 87–89, 92–93, 99, 101, 110, 113, 128, 132, 134, 159, 167, 177, 182–83, 219, 254
Hamlet, 2, 13, 15, 59–60, 80–82, 108,

AMS Studies in the Renaissance: No. 23

ISSN: 0195-8011